Dewii

1982

CORNISH

FEASTS AND FOLK-LORE.

CORNISH

FEASTS AND FOLK-LORE.

BY

MISS M. A. COURTNEY,

AUTHOR OF "GLOSSARY OF WORDS USED IN WEST CORNWALL."

REVISED AND REPRINTED FROM THE FOLK-LORE
SOCIETY JOURNALS, 1886-87.

With a new Foreword by
A. E. GREEN
Institute of Dialect and Folk Life Studies,
University of Leeds

1973
ROWMAN AND LITTLEFIELD
Totowa, New Jersey

Published for the first time in the United States
1973 by Rowman and Littlefield, Totowa, New Jersey

Reprinted from the 1890 edition published
by Beare and Son, Penzance

Copyright © in reprint 1973 EP Publishing Limited

Copyright © in new foreword 1973 A. E. Green

ISBN 0-87471-020-0

Printed in Great Britain by
The Scolar Press Limited, Menston, Yorkshire

FOREWORD

Margaret Ann Courtney was born in Penzance on April 16th, 1834 and died there on May 12th, 1920. Her mother, Sarah (née Mortimer; 1810-1859) was a Scillonian, and her father John Sampson Courtney (1803-1881), a North Devon man, had come to Penzance, via Bristol and Falmouth, in 1825.

Margaret Ann was the second child and eldest daughter of a large and gifted family. After his arrival in Penzance, for thirteen years her father kept the books for a linen draper called Molyneaux, before joining the staff of Bolitho's bank in 1838. He stayed with Bolitho's for the rest of his career, and when he retired only four years before his death, he had reached the position of principal manager. This steady and conventional career presumably provided some outlet for the mathematical talent and financial acumen which were to show themselves more dramatically in two of his sons; and in addition it provided him and his family with security and prosperity — enough, at any rate, to cover the lease on Alverton House, a substantial seventeenth century dwelling standing in its own grounds. But John Sampson was more than a prudent and skilful accountant and banker; he was also, according to his eldest son's testimony, a cultivated man with a love of music, literature and history, whose leisure hours were "occupied with books and the education of his children."[1] In addition, he published a number of poems, a volume of reminiscences entitled *Half a Century at Penzance*[2] edited by his youngest daughter Louise, and

1. G. P. Gooch, *Life of Lord Courtney*, London (Macmillan), 1920, pp 4/5. My information on Margaret Courtney and her family derives largely from this source, and from Mr. M. Salvadori, Mr. P. A. S. Pool, and Mr. Ralph Steele, all of Penzance; from Mr. H. L. Douch, Curator of the Royal Institution of Cornwall and Mr. R. D. Hale, the County Librarian, both of Truro; and last but not least from Captain Ivan Agar Courtney, great-nephew of Margaret Ann, and apparently the only surviving relative. To all of whom my thanks.

2. Louise d'Este Courtney, *Half a Century at Penzance* (1825-1875): *From Notes by J. S. Courtney*, Penzance (Beare and Son), 1878.

FOREWORD

A Guide to Penzance and its Neighbourhood[3] (regarded by at least one authority as still the best work on the locality), as well as a series of papers devoted to the statistical description of Cornwall.[4]

All this intellectual activity was not lost on his eight children, most of whom took up at least one of his interests, three of whom achieved national and even international fame, and only one of whom failed, at the very least, to publish something.

The eldest son, Leonard Henry, later Lord Courtney of Penwith, was educated at St. John's College, Cambridge, where he was Second Wrangler in 1855, and equal as Smith's prizeman in the same year. In 1856 he became a Fellow of his College, but left Cambridge late in 1857 to study law. He was called to the bar in 1858 and took chambers at Lincoln's Inn. Fourteen years as a barrister (during most of which he was also a leader-writer with The Times) came to an end with his appointment to the Chair of Political Economy at University College, London, a position he held for only three years before entering the House of Commons as Liberal member for the Borough of Liskeard. By 1882 he had risen to the position of Financial Secretary to the Treasury in Gladstone's second administration, and seemed destined for a ministry until in 1884 he resigned over the government's unwillingness to include proportional representation in its Redistribution Bill. His entry in the *Dictionary of National Biography* describes him as "perhaps the greatest British statesman since Cobden, of those who have never held Cabinet office." In 1906 he was created first Baron Courtney of Penwith, a title which died with him in 1918. Lord Courtney's numerous publications (not including his journalism) range widely over politics, economics, English literature, Christianity, and the history and antiquities of Cornwall.

Less varied, perhaps, but scarcely less distinguished, was the career of the second brother, John Mortimer (1838-1920), later Sir John, who emigrated to Canada where he too went into politics. At the age of forty he reached the position of Deputy

---

3. John Sampson Courtney, *A Guide to Penzance and its Neighbourhood, including the Islands of Scilly, with an Appendix, containing the Natural History of Western Cornwall*, Penzance (E. Rowe) and London (Longman), 1845.

4. See the *Report of the Royal Cornwall Polytechnic Society*, 1838/42.

FOREWORD

Minister of Finance and Receiver-General and Secretary of the Treasury Board of Canada, which he held until 1906.

Of the other Courtney children, special mention need only be made of William Prideaux. His professional career, like his father's, was unremarkable. Born in 1845, he was educated at the City of London School from 1859 to 1864, and on leaving, entered the office of the Ecclesiastical Commission where he remained throughout his working life. His literary activity, however, was far from unremarkable. His output, some of it under the pseudonym P. W. Trepolpen, matches in breadth and scope that of his eldest brother, and it was as a bibliographer that he excelled. His first published bibliography, the immensely useful *Bibliotheca Cornubiensis*[5] (would that every county were similarly equipped) began to appear in 1874, and reflected the focus of his interests up to that date. Thereafter appeared between 1905 and 1912 *A Register of National Bibliography* [6]; in 1908 *The Secrets of our National Literature*[7]; and, two years after his death in 1913, the work for which he is best known nationally, his bibliography of Johnson.[8]

It is reasonable to suppose that William Prideaux's bibliographical investigations assisted Margaret Ann in the compilation of *Cornish Feasts and Folk-lore*, and likewise that her extensive reading contributed entries to the *Bibliotheca*.

A talented family, then, with a good record of contributions to scholarship and to public life; and it cannot be claimed that Margaret Courtney made the greatest. Rather, she participated in the interests of her family, and, appropriately enough for one who lived out her life (holidays and visits aside) in the place of her birth, selected from among them the local topics of Cornish dialect and folk-lore as her special field.

5. William Prideaux Courtney and George Clement Boase, *Bibliotheca Cornubiensis. A Catalogue of the writings, both manuscript and printed, of Cornishmen and of works relating to the county of Cornwall*, 3 vols, London (Longmans), 1874, 1878, 1882.

6. *A Register of National Bibliography, with a selection of the chief bibliographical books and articles printed in other countries*, 3 vols, London (Constable), 1905/1912.

7. *The Secrets of our National Literature; chapters in the history of the anonymous and pseudonymous writings of our countrymen*, London (Constable), 1908.

8. "A Bibliography of Samuel Johnson", revised by David Nicol Smith, *Oxford Historical and Literary Studies*, vol 4, Oxford (The Clarendon Press), 1915.

FOREWORD

Why she never left home and, indeed, why she never married is not clear. The second problem, of course, is always likely to be obscure, and as for the first it might seem explicable simply by the fact that she was a woman and born in the first half of the nineteenth century. But this would almost certainly be wrong; for the youngest of the three Courtney sisters, Louise d'Este, born when Margaret was sixteen, was sent to London to be educated at Bedford College, and there is no reason to suppose that John and Sarah Courtney shared the contemporary prejudice against the education of women.

It may be that the explanation of Margaret's domesticity lies in her mother's early death. Sarah Courtney had not been well for some years.[9] Between 1832 and 1850 she had borne nine children, of whom eight survived to adulthood; at her death, Margaret, the eldest girl, was twenty-five, and there were three children under fifteen. It seems a reasonable conjecture that she took her mother's place in the household, and it is at least possible, in view of Mrs. Courtney's poor health, that Margaret's presence at home had been necessary or at least desirable for some time before 1859.

These conjectures perhaps derive a little support from the fact that she appears never to have worked for a living, and from her record of publication. Her debut in print came at the age of forty-six — rather late in the day for a Courtney — with her collaborative volume on Cornish dialect.[10] There followed in 1886 and 1887 her articles for the Folk-lore Society, and three years later their re-issue as the book *Cornish Feasts and Folk-lore*.[11] Finally in 1892 appeared her *Poems of Cornwall*. While there is nothing conclusive here, it is possibly significant that her first publication appeared some nine years after the youngest child, Louise, could reasonably be regarded as no longer her responsibility; and the other works followed hard upon Louise's marriage in 1885, by which time their father too had died and Margaret's other brothers and sisters had left home.

9. Gooch, op. cit., p.41.

10. M. A. Courtney and Thomas Quiller Couch, *Glossary of Words in Use in Cornwall*, English Dialect Society Publication No. 27, London (Truber), 1880.

11. See below for bibliographical details and a discussion the folkoristic works.

FOREWORD

In the end it must be said that little is known of Margaret Ann Courtney. Of force or out of choice, she lived quietly where she was born, and her writings were on local topics. Nothing that she did created enough interest to entitle her to an obituary in a national periodical; and surprisingly perhaps, even the local papers seem to have denied her that. The importance of her small but valuable contribution to the study of popular traditions seems to have been recognised only by the companion of her last years, her niece, Sarah Courtney Julyan, who thought it worthwhile to present some of her aunt's papers to the Penzance Library.[12]

It is, then, chiefly through her publications that Margaret Ann Courtney's memory lives, and it is to the most important of these that we must now turn.

Cornish Feasts and Folk-lore was first published as a series of five articles printed in the Folk-lore Society's journal in 1886 and 1887.[13] Three years later a local printer issued as a book, for the benefit of the general public — or at least the Cornish part of it, for the edition seems to have been a small one — a 'revised' version of the work. The revisions, in fact, were very slender. In the interval between the publication of the final article in the series and that of the book, Margaret Courtney had made a bound copy of the original articles (excluding, for some reason, the third part of "Cornish Folk-lore"), cut up and mounted on paper, with room for additions and corrections.[14] To this copy she added a few brief manuscript annotations, most of which found their way into the book. Although this volume was not the copy-text for the published book, it is fair to assume that it formed the basis of it, for very little material appears in the book that is not included in the working copy: the only significant additions being the passage on *kinning stones* quoted on pp 144/5, and the observations on snakes and snake-charms given on pp155/6. It would seem that

---

12. These are described below. Unfortunately they contain no autobiographical material.

13. "Cornish Feasts and Feasten Customs", Pt I, *Folk-lore Journal*, Vol IV, 1886, pp 109/132; Pt II, ibid., pp 221/249. "Cornish Folk-lore", Pt I, *Folk-lore Journal*, Vol V, 1887, pp 14/61; Pt II, ibid., pp 85/112; Pt III, ibid., pp 177/220.

14. This volume is now in the possession of Mr. S. E. Schofield, of Breage, Helston, to whom I am indebted for access to it.

FOREWORD

between 1887 and 1890 Miss Courtney had found little new to say and even less to correct.

The 'revisions' come down to this: the two-part article of 1886 becomes Chapter I of *Cornish Feasts and Folk-lore*, under the same title; the first part of the 1887 article is split up, half of it going into chapter 2 of *Cornish Feasts*, as "Legends of Parishes etc." and the other half receiving separate treatment as chapter 6, "Cornish Games"; the remainder of chapter 2 is provided by the second part of the 1887 article (now rather arbitrarily preceding what formerly it followed); and the third and final part of the 1887 article is divided into three chapters on "Fairies", "Superstitions: Miners', Sailors', Farmers'" and "Charms etc." All these chapters are practically word for word from the articles; there are, as stated, one or two small additions, and the occasional sentence is rewritten in the interests of fluency or clarity; but for the most part it is a matter of shifting material about, and dividing up the highly generalised articles into chapters under more specific headings. With the addition of a new chapter giving a handful of songs and riddles (notable mainly for a dockers' work-song, "The Long Hundred", reprinted from *Notes and Queries*), a preface and an index, the book is complete. The revision does not present, as might be supposed, the intellectual crystallisation or expansion of a series of exploratory articles; it is journalistic, not scholarly. The truth of this, if further evidence is needed, and the extent to which the work — in both its published forms — is a miscellany, may be assessed by close comparison of the articles to the chapter divisions of the book. The classic example is the break between the chapters on "Superstitions" and "Charms", which occurs in mid-paragraph, without any rewriting.

Until the present reprinting, that, as far as the reading public was concerned, was the end of *Cornish Feasts and Folk-lore*. Miss Courtney, however, seems to have had other ideas. For she continued until very late in her life to annotate yet another cut and mounted copy of the original articles, which, together with an index compiled by Miss Julyan, is now in the Penzance Library.[15]

15. I am grateful to the Committee of the Penzance Library, and particularly to the Hon. Librarian, Mr. Ralph Steele, for lending me this unique volume.

FOREWORD

This copy has very extensive manuscript additions, almost all of them taken from published sources ranging from local newspapers such as the *Western Morning News* to the standard Cornish collections of Bottrell and Hunt,[16] and presumably Miss Courtney planned a new edition.

Under the circumstances, the reader might reasonably enquire why, in justice to the author, this intention has not been carried out; and, aside from the practical considerations of book-productions, there is a good reason. The adidtions are numerous, but intellectually they are insignificant; they add quite substantially to the bulk of the work, without modifying its character in the least, that is, without adding one jot of analysis or argument. In its final form, the work remains the miscellany that it was from the start.[17]

What, then, is the significance of the book, and what is the justification for its re-issue? Works of this kind — and scarcely a county or shire is without at least one of them — are valuable in three ways. First, they have an obvious appeal to everyone interested in the history and traditions of their own region; of that nothing more need be said — it is a universal and honourable interest, and one, by and large, which is responsible for their existence. Second, they are useful, within limits, as source books for an historical ethnography of the people of the British Isles. Third, they are an interesting chapter in the history of ideas, not only for the information they contain — which is already covered under the previous heading — but also, paradoxically, for their omissions and half-truths, for the reasons why they are as they are, and for their relationship to other aspects of thought in the society in which their authors were, or are living.[18]

16. William Bottrell, *Traditions and Hearthside Stories of West Cornwall*, 3 series, Penzance, 1870, 1873, 1880. Robert Hunt, *Popular Romances of the West of England*, 2 series, London, 1865.

17. Those wishing to consult Miss Courtney's final version should apply to the Honorary Librarian, The Penzance Library, Morrab Gardens, Penzance, Cornwall; or to the Archivist, The Institute of Dialect and Folk Life Studies, University of Leeds, where, by courtesy of the Committee of the Penzance Library, a photocopy is now housed.

18. It is quite surprising, in some ways, to find that such works are still being written. See, for instance, Jacqueline Simpson's *The Folklore of Sussex*, London, 1973. one of an ongoing series published by Batsford. It is no accident that both Miss Simpson and the general editor of the series, Mrs. Venetia Newall, are members of the Folklore Society. One of the less creditable achievements of that society is to have ensured the perpetuation of some social and intellectual equations of the second half of the nineteenth century into the second half of the twentieth.

FOREWORD

These second and third points demand a little closer consideration, specifically with reference to *Cornish Feasts and Folk-lore*, and they are best dealt with together.

The division between Margaret Courtney and the people about whom she was writing is summed up in a little episode which must have impressed her, for she used it not only in *Cornish Feasts*[19] but also in her preface to the *Glossary* as follows —

"Once I asked an old Lands End guide what made all those earth-heaps in a field through which we were passing? His reply was 'What you rich people never have in your house, a want' (a mole)"

No doubt the jibe was genially enough meant; it must have been nice for the old man to get the chance of taking a rise out of a banker's daughter, and the banker's daughter, in fairness, obviously took it well; but the situation is none the less clear: the informant is relatively poor, the collector relatively prosperous; the informant a manual worker with comparatively little formal education, speaking the dialect of the region which, perhaps, he has never left, the collector a member of the educated middle class, with wider contacts and experience, writing it down and glossing it for the benefit of her peers. And so far so good; any social scientist, certainly any social anthropologist, is doing much the same.

But there is more to it. For there is little doubt that, in general, the folklorists of the late nineteenth century regarded themselves not merely as socially different from their informants — which was realistic enough, if not very constructive — but as different in a more fundamental sense. Few of them, perhaps, went so far as to wonder whether savages could actually feel pain like civilized people,[20] but the prevailing attitude was well expressed by one of the most prolific and, in his day, influential of them, Andrew Lang —

"About twenty years ago, the widow of an Irish farmer, in Derry, killed her deceased husband's horse. When remonstrated with by her landlord, she said, 'Would you have my man go

19. p. 139.

20. See Alfred Ernest Crawley, *The Mystic Rose*, London (Macmillan), 1902.

FOREWORD

about on foot in the next world?' She was quite in the savage intellectual state."[21]

Once scholarship has decided that there is not merely a social hierarchy, but even a hierarchy of states of mind, the divorce between student and informant is complete. Lang, like Sir James Frazer, did little or no field-work. Nor indeed did those contemporaries of Lang's who formed with him the intellectual core of the Folk-lore Society in its heyday — those nominated by Professor Dorson, presumably ironically (since their ideas and attitudes came very close to killing the study of popular traditions in England stone dead) as the "Great Team of English Folklorists".[22] It is quite clear why. It was not that they considered field-work unimportant: quite the contrary, they needed field-reports as vultures need carcasses, and these people like Margaret Courtney would provide them with. What they did not need was the experience of ritual, or story-telling, or magic, as human behaviour. What they did not need was a sense of the relationship between every individual and his or her culture, of the way in which people live in their culture just as certainly as they live in their physical environment, and modify the former as surely as they modify the latter. What, finally, they did not need was an awareness that every living tradition, no matter how ancient it might be (not, as it happens, something that is often easy to prove) is also contemporary, and that this is not the tautology it might seem; that is, that no matter how strange or been absurd or reprehensible it may look to an outsider, every tradition has in it something which gives its exponents a reason far deeper than mechanical force of habit for practising it. They did not need these insights because any of them might have thrown into doubt not only their glib generalizations, but their view of themselves.

Margaret Courtney, however, was a field-worker. Her book is not simply a field-report, for it contains many references to published sources; but in among them are accounts of customs and games which she personally witnessed or even participated in,

---

21. Andrew Lang, *Custom and Myth*, 3rd edition, London (Longmans, Green, & Co.), 1901, pp 11/12.

22. Richard M. Dorson, "The Great Team of English Folklorists", *Journal of American Folklore*, Vol. 64, No. 251, 1951, pp 1/10. See also his useful reference work, *The British Folklorists*, London, 1968.

FOREWORD

and of stories which she herself has heard. Granted that she had the living experience of the customs she was describing, why is her book still — like all the other regional folklore collections — merely a compendium of unassimilated cultural facts recorded virtually at random?

First, the failure to produce something more creative cannot be attributed solely to the bad influences of Lang and the other London-based intellectuals. Miss Courtney was working solidly within a tradition of regional scholarship which had existed before the Folk-lore Society was formed in 1878 — a tradition which went back to 1850 at least, with the publication of Thomas Sternberg's *Dialect and Folklore of Northamptonshire*, and had taken in, for example, Hunt's *Popular Romances*, William Henderson's *Notes on the Folk-lore of the Northern Counties of England and the Borders* (1866), John Harland and T. T. Wilkinson's *Lancashire Folk-lore* (1867) and *Lancashire Legends, Traditions, Pageants, Sports* (1873) and Bottrell's *Traditions and Hearthside Stories* (not by any means a complete list) before it reached Miss Courtney.[23] Thus, working procedures were already laid down for the kind of book Margaret Courtney was planning long before she sat down to write it; and these procedures she, along with the others, evidently thought satisfactory.

Again, why? Margaret Courtney's interests lay chiefly in her native West Cornwall, but she was no narrow-minded provincial. She visited her brothers Leonard and William in London and through the former met the philosopher and sociologist Herbert Spencer. She travelled in France and had some knowledge of the language; she seems to have been well-versed in English literature; and it is particularly noteworthy that, unless his biographer gives a wrong impression, when Leonard wanted to write to his family about politics, and especially about his own sometimes shaky position within the Party, it was usually to Margaret that he wrote.[24] None of this argues an unsophisticated mind closed to all but local interests and unaware of wider human and intellectual

23. Of these works, all but Hunt and Bottrell have been reprinted by S. R. Publishers Ltd. or EP Publishing Ltd.; Bottrell's first series has been re-issued by Frank Graham.

24. See Gooch, op. cit., passim.

FOREWORD

issues.

The truth lies probably in the fact that for Margaret Courtney, as for the other regional miscellanists, the recording and study of popular traditions was, however passionately pursued, a hobby. There was no central forum in which the regional collectors could discuss theoretical issues in order to take new ideas back with them. The "Great Team" at the centre of English folklore scholarship was only too happy for the collectors to keep the raw material pouring in so that they themselves could turn it into grand global theories and vivid conjectures. There existed, in short, nothing to turn the collectors into field-workers, nothing to stimulate the antiquarian dabblers into analytical activity. The Folklore Society's official guide for collectors with its astonishing insistence that the field-worker should work "independently of theory", merely reinforced existing practice.[25]

But in spite of all this, there is something there. In a close study of the jumble of facts, questions begin to obtrude themselves.

Evidence of rowdyism and violence associated with traditional festivals appears again and again; sometimes it is so bad (or thought by respectable people to be so bad) that, as in the case of the Penzance Goose-Dancers (pp 10/11), the custom has to be put down by law — and even then it continues. Sometimes, even, it seems to be getting worse, and an element of class conflict is apparently involved —

> "Formerly all the respectable people at Padstow kept this anniversary (May Day) decorated with the choicest flowers; but some unlucky day a number of rough characters from a distance joined in it, and committed some sad assaults upon old and young, spoiling all their nice summer clothes, and covering their faces and persons with smut. From that time [c.1815] the procession is formed of the lowest." (p.31)

Of course, we all know that the Padstow hobby-horse ceremonial has been going for thousands of years, and that it used to be a great deal rougher than it is now — something to do with fertility

---

25. Charlotte S. Burne, *The Handbook of Folklore*, London (The Folklore Society), 1914, p 5. (Miss Burne's *Handbook* was an extensively revised and greatly expanded version of a volume published in 1890 by G. L. Gomme.)

FOREWORD

and life forces, no doubt. At least, to listen to the pronouncements of journalists, broadcasters, and other popularisers, you would think so. But it is at best a half-truth; the custom may have been rougher in 1850 than in 1950, but apparently it only became rough early in the nineteenth century. A bit late, surely, for life-forces and fertility rites.

Then again, at Hayle in 1883, the fire-balls (bundles of rags soaked in petroleum) which are kicked about the streets are described as a "new and dangerous plaything" — another violent innovation. There is not the evidence in this work alone, to prove that, in England at least, violence in traditional custom is a late innovation; but reference to the many similar books might. It would at least be worth investigating the hypothesis that Miss Courtney and her fellow miscellanists were describing not the vestigial rituals of a "traditional" society in stasis or decline but the only too lively festivities of a society in upheaval.

Provocative, too, are the hints that what demands presentation, according to Miss Courtney's inherited format, as a homogenous traditional culture of Cornwall, is really something else. The sense of social conflict, referred to above, leads us towards this conclusion, and we are taken a little further along that road by the descriptions of festive foods. On Christmas Eve, for example, a "plentiful Supper was always provided", involving egg-nog and a sweet giblet pie; but a footnote (p.8) informs us that "a very general [supper] for poor people in some parts of the county on Christmas-eve was pilchards and unpeeled potatoes boiled together in one 'crock' " — which cannot have been very different from their fare during the rest of the year. As Christmas, so Shrove Tuesday, if a little more complicated. —

"The dinner on Shrove Tuesday in many Cornish houses consists of fried eggs and bacon, or salt pork, followed by the universal pancake, which is eaten by all classes. It is made the full size of the pan, and currants are put into the batter.
In Penzance large quantities of limpets and periwinkles are gathered in the afternoon by poor people, to be cooked for their supper." (pp.21/22)

FOREWORD

Thus at least two groups within Cornwall are implicitly distinguished by their festive foods. How many more groups might have been defined by a more detailed description and a finer analysis of social distinctions in culture; and nationally how many such groups — whether socially, geographically economically, or occupationally based — could be determined by the close comparative study of source-books such as this?

It would be easy to amass further examples of the kind of question that arises from this rich, if sometimes annoyingly incomplete collection of data. But the book is here, and there is no point in paraphrasing it; I am concerned only to suggest how it might constructively be approached. If the present reprinting helps to raise, at however late a date, the kind of question which its author never asked and which those whose responsibility it properly was never stimulated her to consider, it will have done its job.

A. E. Green,
Institute of Dialect and
Folk Life Studies
Leeds 1973

PREFACE.

Few Cornish people are probably aware how wide-spread still with us is the belief in charms and charmers, ghosts, and all other superstitions; nor that there are witches in our county, shunned and dreaded by some who fear their supposed power to ill-wish those who offend them, and sought out by others who want by their aid to avert the evil eye, or by their incantations to remove the spells already cast on them and their cattle by an ill-wisher who has "overlooked" them.

Folk-lore is an almost inexhaustible subject. There must be many charms in use here that have not come under my notice; a few are too coarse to record, as are some of the tales.

A book on folk-lore cannot in this century contain original matter; it must be compiled from various sources. I have when quoting from other writers given my authority, and to communications from friends generally appended their names. To "One and All" I beg leave to tender my sincere thanks.

M. A. COURTNEY.

INDEX.

Index.

CORNISH FEASTS AND "FEASTEN" CUSTOMS.

ORNWALL has always been a county largely given to hospitality, and, as "all Cornish gentlemen are cousins," they have from time immemorial made it a practice to meet at each other's houses to celebrate their feasts and saints' days.

Since "there are more saints in Cornwall than there are in heaven," these friendly gatherings must necessarily be very numerous. Each parish has its own particular saint to which its church is dedicated. The feasts held in their honour, probably dating from the foundation of the churches, are kept on the nearest Sunday and Monday to dedication day, called by the people "feasten" Sunday and Monday.

Every family, however poor, tries to have a better dinner than usual on feasten Sunday; generally a joint of meat with a "figgy-pudden" (a baked or boiled suet-pudding with raisins in it).

On the preceding Saturdays large quantities of "plum cake" are baked; light currant cakes raised with barm (yeast), and coloured bright yellow with saffron (as dear as "saffern" is a very common simile in Cornwall). This "saffern cake" at tea is often supplemented with "heavy cake" (a delicacy peculiar to the county), a rich currant paste, about an inch thick, made with clotted cream, and eaten hot.

The Western hounds meet in all the villages situated at a convenient distance from their kennel, at ten o'clock on feasten Mondays, and, after a breakfast given by the squire of the parish to the huntsmen, start for their run from somewhere near the parish church (the "church town"). Three or four houses clustered together, and even sometimes a single house, is called in Cornwall "a town," a farmyard is "a town place," and London is often spoken of as " Lunnon church town."

The first of the West Penwith feasts is that of Paul, a parish close to Penzance, which has not the Apostle Paul but St. Pol-de-Lion for its patron saint. It falls on the nearest Sunday to 10th of October. An old proverb says, " Rain for Paul, rain for all," therefore, should the day be wet, it is of course looked upon by the young people as a bad sign for their future merry-makings. An annual bowling-match was formerly held on feasten Monday, between Paul and Mousehole men (Mousehole is a fishing village in the same parish); the last of them took place sixty years ago. Up to that time the bowling-green, an artificially raised piece of ground, was kept in order by the parishioners. No one in the neighbourhood now knows the game; the church schools are built on a part of the site, and the remainder is the village playground. If there were ever any other peculiar customs celebrated at Paul feast they are quite forgotten, and the Monday night's carousal at the public-houses has here, as elsewhere, given place to church and chapel teas, followed by concerts in the school-rooms, although there are still a few "standings" (stalls) in the streets, for the sale of gingerbread nuts and sweetmeats, and one or two swings and merry-go-rounds, largely patronised by children.

October 12th. A fair, called Roast Goose Fair, is held at Redruth.

On the nearest Saturday to Hallowe'en, October 31st, the fruiterers of Penzance display in their windows very large apples, known locally as "Allan" apples. These were formerly bought by the inhabitants and all the country people from the neighbourhood (for whom Penzance is the market-town), and one was given to each member of the family to be eaten for luck. The elder girls put theirs, before they ate them, under their pillows, to dream of their sweethearts. A few of the apples are still sold; but the custom, which, I have lately been told, was also observed at St. Ives, is practically dying out. On "Allantide," at Newlyn West, two strips of wood are joined crosswise by a nail in the centre; at each of the four ends a lighted candle is stuck, with apples hung between them. This is fastened to a beam, or the ceiling of the kitchen, and made to revolve rapidly. The players, who try to catch the apples in their mouths, often get instead a taste of the candle.

In Cornwall, as in other parts of England, many charms were tried on Hallowe'en to discover with whom you were to spend your future life, or if you were to remain unmarried, such as pouring melted lead through the handle of the front door key. The fantastic shapes it assumed foretold your husband's profession or trade.

Rolling three names, each written on a separate piece of paper, tightly in the centre of three balls of earth. These were afterwards put into a deep basin of water, and anxiously watched until one of them opened, as the name on the first slip which came to the surface would be that of the person you were to marry.

Tying the front door key tightly with your left leg garter between the leaves of a Bible at one particular chapter in the Song of Solomon. It was then held on the forefinger, and when the sweetheart's name was mentioned it turned round.

Slipping a wedding-ring on to a piece of cotton, held between the forefinger and thumb, saying, " If my husband's name is to be ―― let this ring swing ! " Of course, when the name of the person preferred was spoken, the holder unconsciously made the ring oscillate. I have, when a school-girl, assisted at these rites, and I expect the young people still practise them.

In St. Cubert's parish, East Cornwall, is a celebrated Holy well, so named, the inhabitants say, from its virtues having been discovered on All Hallows-day. It is covered at high spring tides.

St. Just feast (which, when the mines in that district were prosperous, was kept up with more revelry than almost any other) is always held on the nearest Sunday to All Saints'-day. Formerly, on the Monday, many games were played, viz.—"Kook, a trial of casting quoits farthest and nearest to the goal, now all but forgotten" (Bottrell), wrestling, and kailles, or keels (ninepins), &c. Much beer and "moonshine" (spirit that had not paid the duty) were drunk, and, as the St. Just men are proverbially pugnacious, the sports often ended with a free fight. A paragraph in a local paper for November, 1882, described a St. Just feast in those days as " A hobble, a squabble, and a 'hubbadullion' altogether." Rich and poor still at this season keep open house, and all the young people from St. Just who are in service for many miles around, if they can possibly be spared, go home on the Saturday and stay until the Tuesday morning. A small fair is held in the streets on Monday evening, when the young men are expected to treat their sweethearts liberally, and a great deal of "foolish money" that can be ill afforded is often spent.

In many Cornish parishes the bells are rung on November 4th, " Ringing night."

The celebration of Gunpowder Plot has quite died out in West Cornwall, but in Launceston, and in other towns in the eastern part of the county, it is still observed. As regularly as the 5th of November comes around, fireworks are let off, and bonfires lit, to lively music played by the local bands.

" This year, 1884, ' Young Stratton' celebrated the Fifth with much more than his customary enthusiasm. A good sum was raised by public subscription by the energy of Mr. C. A. Saunders. The Bude fife and drum band headed a grotesque procession, formed at Howl's Bridge, and second in order came a number of equestrian torch-bearers in all kinds of costumes, furnished by wardrobes of Her Majesty's navy, the Royal Marines, the Yeomanry, and numerous other sources. 'Guido Faux' followed in his car, honoured by a postilion and a band of Christy Minstrels; then came foot torch-bearers, and a crowd of enthusiastic citizens, who ' hurraed' to their hearts' content. Noticeable were the banners, 'Success to Young Stratton,' the Cornish arms, and 'God save the Queen.' The display of fireworks took place from a field overlooking the town, and the inhabitants grouped together at points of vantage to witness the display. The bonfire was lit on Stamford Hill, where the carnival ended. Good order and good humour prevailed."—(*Western Morning News.*)

When I was a girl, I was taught the following doggerel rhymes, which were on this day then commonly chanted:—

> " Please to remember the fifth of November !
> A stick or a stake, for King George's sake.
> A faggot or rope, to hang the Pope.
> For Gunpowder Plot, shall never be forgot,
> Whilst Castle Ryan stands upon a rock. "

This was in Victoria's reign; where Castle Ryan stands I have never been able to learn.

The old custom formerly practised in Camborne, of taking a marrow-bone from the butchers on the Saturday before the feast, which is held on the nearest Sunday to Martinmas, was, in 1884, revived in its original form. "A number of gentlemen, known as the 'Homage Committee,' went round the market with hampers, which were soon filled with marrow-bones, and they afterwards visited the public-houses as 'tasters.' "—(*Cornishman.*)

One night in November is known in Padstow as "Skip-skop night," when the boys of the place go about with a stone in a sling; with this they strike the doors, and afterwards slily throw in winkle-shells, dirt, &c. Mr. T. Q. Couch says: "They strike violently against the doors of the houses and ask for money to make a feast."

At St. Ives, on the Saturday before Advent Sunday, "Fair-mo" (pig fair) is held. This town is much celebrated locally for macaroons; a great many are then bought as "fairings." The St. Ives fishing (pilchard) season generally ends in November, consequently at this time there is often no lack of money.

The feast of St. Maddern, or Madron feast, which is also that of Penzance (Penzance being until recently in that parish), is on Advent Sunday.

The last bull-baiting held here was on the "feasten" Monday of 1813, and took place in the field on which the Union is now built. The bull was supplied by a squire from Kimyel, in the neighbouring parish of Paul. A ship's anchor, which must have been carried up hill from Penzance quay, a distance of nearly three miles, was firmly fixed in the centre of the field, and to it the bull was tied. Bull-baiting was soon after discontinued in Cornwall. The following account of the last I had from a gentleman who was well known in the county. He said, "This I think took place in a field adjoining Ponsandane bridge, in Gulval parish, at the east of Penzance, in the summer of 1814. I remember the black bull being led by four men. The crowd was dispersed early in the evening by a severe thunder-storm, which much alarmed the people, who thought it (I was led to believe) a judgment from heaven."—(T.S.B.)

The second Thursday before Christmas is in East Cornwall kept by the "tinners" (miners) as a holiday in honour of one of the reputed discoverers of tin. It is known as Picrous-day. Chewidden Thursday (White Thursday), another "tinners'" holiday, falls always on the last clear Thursday before Christmas-day. Tradition says it is the anniversary of the day on which "white tin" (smelted tin) was first made or sold in Cornwall.

On Christmas-eve, in East as well as West Cornwall, poor women, sometimes as many as twenty in a party, call on their richer neighbours asking alms. This is "going a gooding."

At Falmouth the lower classes formerly expected from all the shop-keepers, of whom they bought any of their Christmas groceries, a slice of cake and a small glass of gin. Some of the oldest established tradespeople still observe this custom; but it will soon be a thing of the past.

In some parts of the county it is customary for each household to make a batch of currant cakes on Christmas-eve. These cakes are made in the ordinary manner, coloured with saffron, as is the custom in these parts. On this occasion the peculiarity of the cakes is, that a small portion of the dough in the centre of each top is pulled up and made into a form which resembles a very small cake on the top of a large one, and this centre-piece is usually called "the Christmas." Each person in a house has his or her especial cake, and every person ought to taste a small piece of every other person's cake. Similar cakes are also bestowed on the hangers-on of the establishment, such as laundresses, sempstresses, charwomen, &c.;

and even some people who are in the receipt of weekly charity call, as a matter of course, for their Christmas cakes. The cakes must not be cut until Christmas-day, it being probably "unlucky to eat them sooner."—(Geo. C. Boase, *Notes and Queries*, 5th series, Dec. 21st, 1878.)

The materials to make these and nearly all the cakes at this season were at one time given by the grocers to their principal customers.

In Cornwall, as in other English counties, houses are at Christmas "dressed up" with evergreens, sold in small bunches, called "Penn'orths of Chris'mas"; and two hoops fastened one in the other by nails at the centres are gaily decorated with evergreens, apples, oranges, &c., and suspended from the middle beam in the ceiling of the best kitchen. This is the "bush," or "kissing bush." At night a lighted candle is put in it, stuck on the bottom nail; but once or twice lately I have seen a Chinese lantern hanging from the top one.

In a few remote districts on Christmas-eve children may be, after nightfall, occasionally (but rarely) found dancing around painted lighted candles placed in a box of sand. This custom was very general fifty years ago. The church towers, too, are sometimes illuminated. This of course, on the coast can only be done in very calm weather. The tower of Zennor church (Zennor is a village on the north coast of Cornwall, between St. Ives and St. Just) was lit up in 1883, for the first time since 1866.

When open chimneys were universal in farmhouses the Christmas stock, mock, or block (the log), on which a rude figure of a man had been chalked, was kindled with great ceremony; in some parts with a piece of charred wood that had been saved from the last year's "block." A log in Cornwall is almost always called a "block." "Throw a block on the fire."

Candles painted by some member of the family were often lighted at the same time.

The choir from the parish church and dissenting chapels go from house to house singing "curls" (carols), for which they are given money or feasted; but the quaint old carols, "The first good joy that Mary had," "I saw three ships come sailing in," common forty years ago, are now never heard. The natives of Cornwall have been always famous for their carols; some of their tunes are very old. Even the Knockers, Sprig-gans, and all the underground spirits that may be always heard working where there is tin (and who are said to be the ghosts of the Jews who crucified Jesus), in olden times held mass and sang carols on Christmas-eve.

In the beginning of this century at the ruined baptistery of St. Levan, in West Cornwall (Par-chapel Well), all the carol-singers in that district, after visiting the neighbouring villages, met and sang together many carols. Mr. Bottrell says, "One was never forgotten, in which according to our West Country version, Holy Mary says to her dear Child :—

> 'Go the wayst out, Child Jesus,
> Go the wayst out to play ;
> Down by God's Holy Well
> I see three pretty children,
> As ever tongue can tell.'

"This for its sweet simplicity is still a favourite in the west."
An old carol or ballad,

> "Come and I will sing you," etc.,

known to many old people in all parts of the county, has been thought by some to be peculiar to Cornwall; but this is an error, as it has been heard elsewhere.

At the plentiful supper always provided on this night,* egg-hot, or eggy-hot, was the principal drink. It was made with eggs, hot beer, sugar, and rum, and was poured from one jug into another until it became quite white and covered with froth. A sweet giblet pie was one of the standing dishes at a Christmas dinner—a kind of mince-pie, into which the giblets of a goose, boiled and finely chopped, were put instead of beef. Cornwall is noted for its pies, that are eaten on all occasions; some of them are curious mixtures, such as squab-pie, which is made with layers of well-seasoned fat mutton and apples, with onions and raisins. Mackerel pie : the ingredients of this are mackerel and parsley stewed in milk, then covered with a paste and baked. When brought to table a hole is cut in the paste,

---

* A very general one for poor people in some parts of the county on Christmas-eve was pilchards and unpeeled potatoes boiled together in one " crock."

and a basin of clotted cream thrown in it. Muggetty pie, made from sheep's entrails (muggets), parsley, and cream. "The devil is afraid to come into Cornwall for fear of being baked in a pie." There is a curious Christmas superstition connected with the Fogo, Vug, or Vow (local names for a cove) at Pendeen, in North St. Just.

"At dawn on Christmas-day the spirit of the 'Vow' has frequently been seen just within the entrance near the cove, in the form of a beautiful lady dressed in white, with a red rose in her mouth There were persons living a few years since who had seen the fair but not less fearful vision ; for disaster was sure to visit those who intruded on the spirit's morning airing."—(Bottrell, *Traditions, &c., West Cornwall,* 2nd series.)

The following is an account by an anonymous writer of a Christmas custom in East Cornwall :—

" In some places the parishioners walk in procession, visiting the principal orchards in the parish. In each orchard one tree is selected, as the representative of the rest; this is saluted with a certain form of words, which have in them the form of an incantation. They then sprinkle the tree with cider, or dash a bowl of cider against it, to ensure its bearing plentifully the ensuing year. In other places the farmers and their servants only assemble on the occasion, and after immersing apples in cider hang them on the apple-trees They then sprinkle the trees with cider; and after uttering a formal incantation, they dance round it (or rather round them), and return to the farmhouse to conclude these solemn rites with copious draughts of cider.

" In Warleggan, on Christmas-eve, it was customary for some of the household to put in the fire (bank it up), and the rest to take a jar of cider, a bottle, and a gun to the orchard, and put a small bough into the bottle. Then they said :—

> " Here's to thee, old apple-tree !
> Hats full, packs full, great bushel-bags full !
> Hurrah ! and fire off the gun."

—(Old Farmer, Mid Cornwall, through T. Q. Couch, Sept. 1883, *W. Antiquary.*)

C

The words chanted in East Cornwall were :—

> " Health to thee, good apple-tree,
> Pocket-fulls, hat-fulls, peck-fulls, bushel-bag fulls."

An old proverb about these trees runs as follows :—

> " Blossom in March, for fruit you may search,
> Blossom in April, eat you will,
> Blossom in May, eat night and day."

"At one time small sugared cakes were laid on the branches. This curious custom has been supposed to be a propitiation of some spirit."—(Mrs. Damant, Cowes, through Folk-Lore Society.)

From Christmas to Twelfth-tide parties of mummers known as 'Goose or Geese-dancers' paraded the streets in all sorts of disguises, with masks on. They often behaved in such an unruly manner that women and children were afraid to venture out. If the doors of the houses were not locked they would enter uninvited and stay, playing all kinds of antics, until money was given them to go away. "A well-known character amongst them, about fifty years ago (1862), was the hobby-horse, represented by a man carrying a piece of wood in the form of a horse's head and neck, with some contrivance for opening and shutting the mouth with a loud snapping noise, the performer being so covered with a horse-cloth or hide of a horse as to resemble the animal, whose curvetings, biting and other motions he imitated. Some of these 'guise-dancers' occasionally masked themselves with the skins of the head of bullocks having the horns on."—(*The Land's End District*, by R. Edmonds.)

Sometimes they were more ambitious and acted a version of the old play, "St. George and the Dragon," which differed but little from that current in other countries.

Bottrell, in his *Traditions in W. Cornwall* (2nd series), gives large extracts from another Christmas-play, "Duffy and the Devil." It turns upon the legend, common in all countries, of a woman who had sold herself to a devil, who was to do her knitting or spinning for her. He was to claim his bargain at the end of three years if she could not find out his name before the time expired. Of course, she gets it by stratagem ; her husband, who knows nothing of the compact, first meets the devil, whilst out hunting, the day before the time is up, and makes him half-drunk. An old woman in Duffy's pay (Witch Bet) completes the work, and in that state the devil sings the following words, ending with his name, which Bet remembers and tells her mistress :—

> " I've knit and spun for her
> Three years to the day ;
> To-morrow she shall ride with me
> Over land and over sea.
> Far away ! far away !
> For she can never know
> That my name is ' Tarraway.' "

Bet and some other witches then sing in chorus :—

> " By night and by day
> We will dance and play
> With our noble captain,
> Tarraway ! Tarraway ! "

Mr. Robert Hunt in his *Romances and Drolls of Old Cornwall* has a variation of this play, in which the devil sings—

> " Duffy my lady, you'll never know—what ?
> That my name is Ferry-top, Ferry-top—top."

These " goose-dancers " became such a terror to the respectable inhabitants of Penzance that the Corporation put them down about ten years since, and every Christmas-eve a notice is posted in conspicuous places forbidding their appearance in the streets, but they still perambulate the streets of St. Ives. Guise-dancing wit must have very much deteriorated since the beginning of the present century, as writers before that time speak of the mirth it afforded ; and the saying, " as good as a Christmas-play," is commonly used to describe a very witty or funny thing.

It was the custom in Scilly eighty years ago for girls to go to church on Christmas morning dressed all in white, verifying the old proverb—" pride is never a-cold."

" On Porthminster Beach on Christmas-day, as seen from the Malakoff, St. Ives, at nine o'clock in the morning the boys began to assemble on the beach with their bats and balls. As soon as twelve youths arrived a game commenced, called 'Rounders.' The first thing to be done was to right up the 'bickens.' This accomplished, the sides were chosen in the following manner:—Two of the best players, whom we will call Matthew and Phillip, went aside and selected two objects—the new and old pier. The old pier was Matthew and the new pier was Phillip. After this was arranged the 'mopper' selected the old pier, which meant he would rather have Matthew his side than Phillip. Then Phillip selected some one for his side; and so it went on until the whole twelve were elected one side or the other. Then they tossed up for the first innings. Phillip's side won the toss, and it was their luck to go in first. While they are taking off their jackets and getting ready to go in I will briefly describe the game.

"The bickens, four in number, were piles of sand thrown up; each one being about ten yards from one another, and arranged so as to form a square. In the centre of the square the bowler was placed with ball in hand. Behind the batsman stands the 'tip,' while the other four were off a long way waiting for the long hits. The coats off, in went the first batsman. The ball was thrown towards him and he tipped it. The tip instantly took the ball and threw it at the batsman, and hit him before he arrived at the first bicken, and he was consequently out. The second batsman had better luck; for on the ball being thrown to him he sent it out to sea, and by that means he ran a rounder, or in other words he ran around the four bickens without being hit by the ball. The next batsman went in. The ball was thrown to him, when, lo! it went whizzing into the bowler's hands and was caught. This unlucky hit and lucky catch got the whole side out, before three of them had a chance to show their skill. The other side then went in, laughing at the discomfiture of their opponents. The tables, however, were very soon turned; for the very first hit was caught, and this produced a row, and the game was broken up!

"I then went to the next lot: They were playing 'catchers.' There is only one bicken required in this game, and at this stood a lad called Watty, with bat and ball in hand. At last he hit the ball, and

up it went flying in the air, descended, and passed through the hands
of a boy named Peters. Peters took the ball from the sand and asked
Watty, ' How many ? ' Watty replied—

> '' Two a good scat,*
> Try for the bat.'

" Peters threw the ball to the bicken, but it stopped about three
lengths short. Watty took the ball up and again sent it a great way.
The question was again asked, and Watty gave the same answer.
Again the ball was thrown to the bicken, but this time with better
success ; for it stopped at the distance of the length of the bat and
so was within the distance named. Williams then went in. He was
a strong lusty fellow, and the ball was sent spinning along the sand.
It was picked up by Curnow, who asked, ' How many ? '

> ' Three a good scat,
> Try for the bat.'

" The ball was thrown home and rolled about three bats from the
bicken. This point, however, was the breaking-up of the game, for
Williams said it was more than three bats off, whilst Curnow main-
tained that it was not three bats off, and there being no chance of a
compromise being arrived at the game was broken up.

" The next party was one of young men. They were playing
rounders with a wooden ball, instead of an india-rubber one, as is
generally used. They were twelve each side, and the bickens were
about 20 yards distant. By this time the tide was out a great way,
so that there was no fear of the ball being knocked to sea, as was
the case with the other boys. When I got there they had been playing for about an hour, and the side that was in had been in about
half of that time. The first hit I saw was 'a beauty!' The ball
was sent about 75 yards, and the result was a rounder. Two or three
other persons went in and did the same thing, and so the game went
on for about an hour longer, when one of the fellows knocked up a
catcher and was caught. This side had stayed in for about one
hour and a half. The other side went in at about a quarter to three,
and after playing about another hour they went home to tea.

* Scat, a blow, a slap.

"I went to tea also, but was soon up in the Malakoff again. It was so dark that the play was stopped for the time. At about seven o'clock the older part of the town began to congregate, and about a quarter-past seven they began to play 'Thursa.' This game is too well known to need description, and I need only say that it was played about one hour, when they began to form a ring with the intention, I supposed, of playing that best of all games, 'Kiss-in-the-Ring.'"—(*Cornishman, 1881.*)

On St. Stephen's-day, 26th December, before the days of gun-licences, every man or boy who could by any means get a gun went out shooting, and it was dangerous to walk the lanes. The custom is said to have had its origin in the legend of one of St. Stephen's guards being awakened by a bird just as his prisoner was going to escape. A similar practice prevailed in the neighbourhood of Penzance on "feasten Monday," the day after Advent Sunday; but on that day I have never heard of any religious idea connected with it.

In the week after Christmas-day a fair is held at Launceston (and also at Okehampton in Devonshire), called "giglet fair" (a "giglet or giglot" is a giddy young woman). It is principally attended by young people. "At this 'giglet market,' or wife-market, the rustic swain was privileged with self-introduction to any of the nymphs around him, so that he had a good opportunity of choosing a suitable partner if tired of a single life."—(Britton and Brayley's *Devon and Cornwall.*)

It is unlucky to begin a voyage on Childermas (Innocents'-day), also to wash clothes, or to do any but necessary household work.

On New Year's-eve in the villages of East Cornwall, soon after dusk, parties of men, from four to six in a party, carrying a small bowl in their hands, went from house to house begging money to make a feast. They opened the doors without knocking, called out Warsail, and sang,—

> "These poor jolly Warsail boys
> Come travelling through the mire."

This custom was common fifty years since, and may still be observed in remote rural districts. There is one saint whose name is familiar to all in Cornwall, but whose sex is unknown. This saint has much to answer for ; promises made, but never intended to be kept, are all to be fulfilled on next St. Tibbs's-eve, a day that some folks say "falls between the old and new year ; " others describe it as one that comes " neither before nor after Christmas."

Parties are general in Cornwall on New Year's-eve to watch in the New Year and wish friends health and happiness ; but I know of no peculiar customs, except that before retiring to rest the old women opened their Bibles at hap-hazard to find out their luck for the coming year. The text on which the fore-finger of the right hand rested was supposed to foretell the future. And money, generally a piece of silver, was placed on the threshold, to be brought in the first thing on the following day, that there might be no lack of it for the year. Nothing was ever lent on New Year's-day, as little as possible taken out, but all that could be brought into the house. " I have even known the dust of the floor swept inwards."—(T. Q. Couch, *W. Antiquary*, September, 1883.)

Door-steps on New Year's-day were formerly sanded for good luck, because I suppose people coming into the house were sure to bring some of it in with them sticking to their feet.

Many elderly people at the beginning of the present century still kept to the " old style," and held their Christmas-day on Epiphany. On the eve of that day they said " the cattle in the fields and stalls never lay down, but at midnight turned their faces to the east and fell on their knees."

Twelfth-day (old Christmas-day) was a time of general feasting and merriment Into the Twelfth-day cake were put a wedding-ring, a sixpence, and a thimble. It was cut into as many portions as there were guests ; the person who found the wedding-ring in his (or her) portion would be married before the year was out ; the holder of the thimble would never be married, and the one who got the sixpence would die rich. After candlelight many games were played around the open fires. I will describe one :—" Robin's alight." A piece of stick was set on fire, and whirled rapidly in the hands of the first player, who repeated the words—

" Robin's alight, and if he go out I'll saddle your back."

It was then passed on, and the person who let the spark die had to
pay a forfeit.—(West Cornwall.)

This game in East Cornwall was known as "Jack's alive."

> "Jack's alive and likely to live,
> If he die in my hand a pawn I'll give."

In this county forfeits are always called "pawns"; they are cried
by the holder of them, saying,—

> "Here's a pawn and a very pretty pawn!
> And what shall the owner of this pawn do?"

After the midnight supper, at which in one village in the extreme
West a pie of four-and-twenty blackbirds always appeared, many
spells to forecast the future were practised. The following account
of them was given to me by a friend. He says—"I engaged in them
once at Sennen (the village at the Land's End) with a lot of girls,
but as my object was only to spoil sport and make the girls laugh or
speak, it was not quite satisfactory. I suppose the time to which I
refer is over forty years ago. After making up a large turf fire, for
hot 'umers' (embers) and pure water are absolutely necessary in these
divinations, the young people silently left the house in single file, to
pull the rushes and gather the ivy-leaves by means of which they were
to learn whether they were to be married, and to whom; and if any,
or how many, of their friends were to die before the end of the year.
On leaving and on returning each of these Twelfth-night diviners
touched the 'cravel' with the forehead and 'wished.' The cravel is
the tree that preceded lintels in chimney corners, and its name from
this custom may have been derived from the verb 'to crave.' Had
either of the party inadvertently broken the silence before the rushes
and ivy-leaves had been procured they would all have been obliged to
retrace their steps to the house and again touch the cravel; but this
time all went well. When we came back those who wished to know
their fate named the rushes in pairs, and placed them in the hot
embers: one or two of the engaged couples being too shy to do this
for themselves, their friends, amidst much laughing, did it for them.
The manner in which the rushes burned showed if the young people

were to be married to the person chosen or not: some, of course, burnt well, others parted, and one or two went out altogether. The couples that burnt smoothly were to be wedded, and the one named after the rush that lasted longest outlived the other. This settled, one ivy-leaf was thrown on the fire; the number of cracks it made was the number of years before the wedding would take place. Then two were placed on the hot ashes; the cracks they gave this time showed how many children the two would have. We then drew ivy-leaves named after present or absent friends through a wedding ring, and put them into a basin of water which we left until the next morning. Those persons whose leaves had shrivelled or turned black in the night were to die before the next Twelfth-tide, and those who were so unfortunate as to find their leaves spotted with red, by some violent death, unless a 'pellar' (wise man) could by his skill and incantations grant protection. These prophecies through superstition sometimes unluckily fulfilled themselves."

During the twelve days of Christmas card-playing was a very favourite amusement with all classes. Whilst the old people enjoyed their game of whist with 'swabbers,' the young ones had their round games. I will append the rules of two or three for those who would like to try them.

Whist (or whisk, as I have heard an old lady call it and maintain that that was its proper name) with "swabbers."

This game, which was played as recently as 1880, nightly, by four maiden ladies at Falmouth, is like ordinary whist; but each player before beginning to play puts into the pool a fixed sum for "swabs." The "swab-cards" are—ace and deuce of trumps, ace of hearts and knave of clubs. The four cards are of equal value; but should hearts be trumps the ace would count double.

"Board-'em," a round game that can be played by any number of players, from two to eight; it is played for fish, and there must never be less than six fish in the pool. Six cards are dealt to each person; and the thirteenth, if two are playing, the nineteenth if three, and so on, is turned up for trumps. The fore-hand plays; the next player, if he has one, must follow suit, if not, he may play another suit, or trump. The highest card of the original suit, if not

D

trumped, takes the trick and one or more fish, according to the number staked. If you have neither card in your hand that you think will make a trick you may decline to play, in which case you only lose your stake ; but should you play and fail to take a trick you pay for the whole company, and are said to " be boarded."

" Ranter-go-round " was formerly played in four divisions marked with chalk upon a tea-tray ; or even, in some cases, on a bellows— it is now played on a table, and is called " Miss Joan." Any number of players may join in it. The first player throws down any card of any suit, and says :—

> " Here's a ——— as you may see.
> *2nd Player*—Here's another as good as he.
> *3rd Player*—And here's the best of all the three.
> *4th Player*—And here's Miss Joan, come tickle me."

The holder of the fourth card wins the trick. He sometimes added the words wee-wee ; but these are now generally omitted. If the person sitting next to the fore-hand has neither one of the cards demanded (one of the same value as the first played, in another suit), he pays one to the pool, as must all in turn who fail to produce the right cards. The player of the third may have the fourth in his hand, in which case all the others pay. The holder of the most tricks wins the game and takes the pool.

I once, about thirty years since, at this season of the year, joined some children at Camborne who were playing a very primitive game called by them " pinny-ninny." A basin turned upside down was placed in the centre of a not very large round table. The players were supplied with small piles of pins—not the well-made ones sold in papers, but clumsy things with wire heads—" pound-pins." A large bottle full of them might, then, always be seen in the general shop window of every little country village. Each in turn dropped a pin over the side of the basin, and he whose pin fell and formed a cross on the top of the heap was entitled to add them to his own pile. This went on until one player had beggared all the others. Poor children before Christmas often begged pins to play this game, and their request was always granted by the gift of two.

A wishing-well, near St. Austell, was sometimes called Pennameny Well, from the custom of dropping pins into it. Pedna-a-mean is the old Cornish for " heads-and-tails."—(See *Divination at St. Roche and Madron Well.*)

All Christmas-cakes must be eaten by the night of Twelfth-tide, as it is unlucky to have any left, and all decorations must be taken down on the next day, because for every forgotten leaf of evergreen a ghost will be seen in the house in the course of the ensuing year. This latter superstition does not prevail, however, in all parts of Cornwall, as in some districts a small branch is kept to scare away evil spirits.

January 24th, St. Paul's-eve, is a holiday with the miners, and is called by them ' Paul pitcher-day,' from a custom they have of setting up a water-pitcher, which they pelt with stones until it is broken in pieces. A new one is afterwards bought and carried to a beer-shop to be filled with beer.

"There is a curious custom prevalent in some parts of Cornwall of throwing broken pitchers and other earthen vessels against the doors of dwelling-houses on the eve of the conversion of St. Paul, thence locally called ' Paul pitcher-night.' On that evening parties of young people perambulate the parishes in which the custom is retained, exclaiming as they throw the sherds, ' St. Paul's-eve and here's a heave.' According to the received notions the first heave cannot be objected to ; but, upon its being repeated, the inhabitants of the house whose door is thus attacked may, if they can, seize the offenders and inflict summary justice upon them."—(F.M., *Notes and Queries*, March, 1874.)

I have heard of this practice from a native of East Cornwall, who told me the pitchers were filled with broken sherds, filth, &c.

The weather on St. Paul's-day still, with the old people, foretells the weather for the ensuing year, and the rhyme common to all England is repeated by them :—

" If St. Paul's-day be fine and clear," &c.

St. Blazey, a village in East Cornwall, is so named in honour of St. Blaize, who is said to have landed at Par, a small neighbouring seaport, when he came on a visit to England. His feast, which is held on 3rd February, would not be worth mentioning were it not for the fact that—"This saint is invoked in the county for toothache, while applying to the tooth the candle that burned on the altar of the church dedicated to him. The same candles are good for sore-throats and curing diseases in cattle."—(Mrs. Damant, Cowes.)

On the Monday after St. Ives feast, which falls on Quinquagesima Sunday, an annual hurling-match is held on the sands. Most writers on Cornwall have described the old game. The following account is taken from *The Land's End District*, 1862, by R. Edmonds:—

"A ball about the size of a cricket-ball, formed of cork, or light wood, and covered with silver, was hurled into the air, midway between the goals. Both parties immediately rushed towards it, each striving to seize and carry it to its own goal. In this contest, when any individual having possession of the ball found himself overpowered or outrun by his opponents, he hurled it to one of his own side, if near enough, or, if not, into some pool, ditch, furze, brake, garden, house, or other place of concealment, to prevent his adversaries getting hold of it before his own company could arrive."

The hurlers, quaintly says Carew (*Survey of Cornwall*, p. 74), "Take their next way ouer hills, dales, hedges, ditches—yea, and thorou bushes, briers, mires, plashes, and rivers whatsoever—so as you shall sometimes see twenty or thirty lie tugging together in the water, scrambling and scratching for the ball. A play verily both rude and rough."

Hurling between two or more parishes, and between one parish and another, has long ceased in Cornwall: but hurling by one part of a parish against another is still played at St. Ives, as well as other places in Cornwall. At St. Ives all the Toms, Wills, and Johns are on one side, while those having other Christian names range them-selves on the opposite. At St. Columb (East Cornwall) the towns-people contend with the countrymen; at Truro, the married men with the unmarried; at Helston, two streets with all the other streets; on the 2nd of May, when their town-bounds are renewed.

"Fair-play is good play," is the hurlers' motto. This is some-times engraven on their balls in the old Cornish language. Private

families possess some of these balls won by their ancestors early in
the last century that are religiously handed down as heirlooms.
A Druidic circle at St. Cleer, in East Cornwall, is known as the
Hurlers, from a tradition that a party of men hurling on a Sunday
were there for their wickedness turned into stone.

' Peasen or Paisen Monday' is the Monday before Shrove Tuesday;
it is so called in East Cornwall from a custom of eating pea-soup
there on this day. This practice was once so universal in some
parishes that an old farmer of Lower St. Columb, who had a special
aversion to pea-soup, left his home in the morning, telling his wife
that he should not come back to dinner, but spend the day with a
friend. He returned two or three hours after in great disgust, as at
every house in the village he had been asked to stay and taste their
delicious pea-soup.

"This day also in East Cornwall bears the name of 'Hall
Monday,' why, I know not. And at dusk on the evening of the
same day it is the custom for boys, and in some cases for those
above the age of boys, to prowl about the streets with short clubs,
and to knock loudly at every door, running off to escape detection
on the slightest sign of a motion within. If, however, no attention
be excited, and especially if any article be discovered, negligently
exposed or carelessly guarded, then the things are carried away, and
on the following morning are seen displayed in some conspicuous
place, to disclose the disgraceful want of vigilance supposed to
characterise the owner. The time when this is practised is called
' Nicky Nan' night, and the individuals concerned are supposed to
represent some imps of darkness, that seize on and expose un-
guarded moments."—(*Polperro*, p. 151, by T. Q. Couch.)

A custom nearly similar to this was practised in Scilly in the last
century.

The dinner on Shrove Tuesday in many Cornish houses consists
of fried eggs and bacon, or salt pork, followed by the universal
pancake, which is eaten by all classes. It is made the full size of
the pan, and currants are put into the batter.

In Penzance large quantities of limpets and periwinkles are
gathered in the afternoon by poor people, to be cooked for their

supper. This they call "going a-trigging." Any kind of shell-fish picked up at low water in this district is known as "trig-meat."

Many other customs were formerly observed in Penzance on Shrove Tuesday, peculiar, I believe, to this town.

Women and boys stood at the corners of the streets, with well-greased, sooty hands, which they rubbed over people's faces. I remember, not more than thirty years ago, seeing a little boy run into a house in a great hurry, and ask for what was he wanted. He had met a woman who had put her hands affectionately on each side of his face, and said, "Your father has been looking for you, my dear." She had left the marks of her dirty fingers.

The butchers' market was always thoroughly cleaned in the afternoon, to see if the town hose were in perfect repair, and great merriment was often excited by the firemen turning the full force of the water on some unwary passer-by.

People, too, were occasionally deluged by having buckets of water thrown over them. Every Shrove Tuesday after dusk men and boys went about and threw handfuls of shells, bottles of filth, etc., in at the doors, It was usual then for drapers to keep their shops open until a very late hour; and I have been told that boys were occasionally bribed by the assistants to throw something particularly disagreeable in on the floors, that the masters might be frightened, and order the shops to be shut. Still later in the evening signs were taken down, knockers wrenched off, gates unhung and carried to some distance. This last was done even as far down as 1881. Pulling boats up and putting them in a mill-pool (now built over) was a common practice at Mousehole in the beginning of the century.

"In Landewednack, on Shrove Tuesday, children from the ages of six to twelve perambulate the parish begging for 'Col-perra' (probably an old Cornish word); but, whatever be its meaning, they expect to receive eatables or half-pence. As few refuse to give, they collect during the day a tolerable booty, in the shape of money, eggs, buns, apples, etc. The custom has existed from time immemorial, but none of the inhabitants are acquainted with its origin."
—(*A Week in the Lizard*, by Rev. C. A. Johns, B.B., F.L.S.)

I have been favoured by the Rev. S. Rundle, Godolphin, with the formula repeated by the children on this occasion (now almost forgotten): " Hen-cock, han-cock, give me a 'tabban' (morsel), or else 'Col-perra' shall come to your door."

Boys at St. Ives, Scilly, and other places, went about with stones tied to strings, with which they struck the doors, saying :—

> "Give me a pancake, now ! now ! now !
> Or I'll knock in your door with a row, tow, tow ! "

This custom has only lately (if it has yet) quite died out. The rhyme at Polperro ran thus :—

> " Nicky, Nicky, Nan,
> Give me some pancake, and then I'll be gone,
> But if you give me none
> I'll throw a great stone,
> And down your door shall come."
> T. Q. COUCH.

Cock-fighting at Shrovetide was once a very favourite amusement in Cornwall, and in some of the most remote western villages has until recently been continued. "The Cock-pit" at Penzance, a small part of which still remains as a yard at the Union Hotel, belonged to and was kept up by the Corporation until (I think) the beginning of the present century.

" Sir Rose Price, when young, was a great patron of the pit between the years 1780-1790. His father disapproved, and in consideration of his son giving up cock-fighting bought him a pack of hounds, the first foxhounds west of Truro."—(T.S.B.)

" At St. Columb, about sixty years ago, on Shrove Tuesday, each child in a dame's school was expected by the mistress to bring an egg, and at twelve o'clock the children had an egg-battle. Two children stood facing each other, each held an egg, and struck the end of it against that of the opponent lengthwise, the result being that one or both were broken.

" An unbroken egg was used again and again to fight the rest, and so the battle raged until all, or all but one, of the eggs were broken. The child who at the end of the fight held a sound egg was considered to be the conqueror, and was glorified accordingly.

To save the contents of the eggs, which were the perquisite of the mistress, she held a plate beneath; and at the end of the battle the children were dismissed. And the old lady having picked out all the broken shells, proceeded to prepare her pancakes, of which she made her dinner."—(Fred. W. P. Jago, M.B., Plymouth, *W. Antiquary*, March, 1884.)

"It must be now about thirty years ago that I was a day-scholar at the National School of St. Columb, and it was the custom then for each boy and girl to bring an egg. One of the senior boys stood at a table and wrote the name of the donor upon each. At about eleven o'clock the schoolmaster would produce a large punchbowl, and as he took up each egg he read the name, and broke the egg into the bowl. Eggs at that time were sold at three for a penny."— (W. B., Bodmin, *W. Antiquary*, March, 1884.)

In the eastern part of the county at the beginning of Lent a straw figure dressed in cast-off clothes, and called "Jack-o'-lent," was not long since paraded through the streets and afterwards hung. Something of this kind is common on the Continent.

The figure is supposed to represent Judas Iscariot. A slovenly ragged person is sometimes described as a "Jack-o'-lent."

1st March.—In Mid-Cornwall, people arise before the sun is up, and sweep before the door to sweep away fleas.—(T. Q. Couch, *W. Antiquary*, September, 1883.)

5th March.—St. Piran's day is a miners' holiday. St. Piran is the patron saint of "tinners," and is popularly supposed to have died drunk. "As drunk as a Piraner" is a Cornish proverb."

The first Friday in March is another miners' holiday, "Friday in Lide." It is marked by a serio-comic custom of sending a young man on the highest "bound," or hillock, of the "works," and allowing him to sleep there as long as he can, the length of his siesta being the measure of the afternoon nap of the "tinners" throughout the ensuing twelve months.—(T. Q. Couch.) Lide is an obsolete term for the month of March still preserved in old proverbs, such as "Ducks won't lay 'till they've drunk Lide water."

Of a custom observed at Little Colan, in East Cornwall, on Palm Sunday, Carew says: "Little Colan is not worth observation, unlesse you will deride or pity their simplicity, who sought at our Lady Nant's well there to foreknowe what fortune should betide them, which was in this manner. Upon Palm Sunday these idle-headed seekers resorted thither with a Palme cross in one hand and an offring in the other. The offring fell to the Priest's share, the crosse they threwe into the well; which if it swamme the party should out-liue the yeere; if it sunk a short ensuing death was boded; and perhaps not altogether vntimely, while a foolish conceite of this 'halsening' myght the sooner helpe it onwards."

Holy Thursday.—On that Thursday, and the two following Thurs-days, girls in the neighbourhood of Roche, in East Cornwall, repair to his holy or wishing well before sunrise. They throw in crooked pins or pebbles, and, by the bubbles that rise to the surface, seek to ascertain whether their sweethearts will be true or false. There was once a chapel near this well, which was then held in great repute for the cure of all kinds of diseases, and a granite figure of St. Roche stood on the arch of the building that still covers it.

" Goody Friday " (Good Friday) was formerly kept more as a feast than a fast in Cornwall. Every vehicle was engaged days before-hand to take parties to some favourite place of resort in the neigh-bourhood, and labourers in inland parishes walked to the nearest seaport to gather " wrinkles " (winkles), &c.

On the morning of Good Friday at St. Constantine, in West Cornwall, an old custom is still observed of going to Helford river to gather shell-fish (limpets, cockles, &c.); this river was once fa-mous for oysters, and many were then bought and eaten on this day.

" Near Padstow, in East Cornwall, is the tower of an old church dedicated to St. Constantine. In its vicinity the feast of St. Con-stantine used to be annually celebrated, and has only been discon-tinued of late years. Its celebration consisted in the destruction of limpet-pies, and service in the church, followed by a hurling match." —(Murray's *Cornwall.*) Another writer says: "The festival of St. Constantine" (March 9th) "was until very lately kept at St. Merran" (Constantine and Merran are now one parish) "by an annual hurling match, on which occasion the owner of Harlyn" (a house in the neighbourhood) had from time immemorial supplied

E

the silver ball. We are informed, on good authority, that a Shepherd's family, of the name of Edwards, held one of the cottages in Constantine for many generations under the owners of Harlyn, by the annual render of a Cornish pie, made of limpets, raisins, and sweet herbs, on the feast of St. Constantine."—(Lysons' *Magna Britannia*.)

At St. Day a fair was formerly held on Good Friday, now changed to Easter Monday.

"On Good Friday, 1878, I saw a brisk fair going on in the little village of Perran Porth, Cornwall, not far from the curious oratory of St. Piran, known as Perranzabuloe."—(W. A. B. C., *Notes and Queries*, April 23rd, 1881.)

But, although many still make this day a holiday, the churches are now much better attended. Good Friday cross-buns of many kinds are sold by the Cornish confectioners; some, highly spiced, are eaten hot with butter and sugar; a commoner bun is simply washed over the top with saffron, and has a few currants stuck on it. There is one peculiar, I believe, to Penzance: it is made of a rich currant paste highly covered with saffron; it is about an eighth of an inch thick, and four inches in diameter, and is marked with a large cross that divides it into four equal portions.

"In some of our farmhouses the Good Friday bun may be seen hanging to a string from the bacon-rack, slowly diminishing until the return of the season replaces it by a fresh one. It is of sovereign good in all manners of diseases afflicting the family or cattle. I have more than once seen a little of this cake grated into a warm mash for a sick cow."—(T. Q. Couch, Polperro.) There is a superstition that bread made on this day never gets mouldy.

Many amateur gardeners sow their seeds on Good Friday; superstition says then they will all grow. "There is a widely known belief in West Cornwall, that young ravens are always hatched on Good Friday."—(T. Cornish, *W. Antiquary*, October, 1887.)

On Easter Monday, at Penzance, it was the custom within the last twenty years to bring out in the lower part of the town, before the doors, tables, on which were placed thick gingerbread cakes with raisins in them, cups and saucers, etc., to be raffled for with cups and dice, called here "Lilly-bangers." Fifty years since a man, nick-named Harry Martillo, with his wife, the "lovelee," always kept one of these "lilly-banger stalls" at Penzance on market day. He would call attention to his gaming-table by shouting—

> "I've been in Europe, Ayshee, Afrikee, and Amerikee,
> And come back and married the lovelee."

I have heard that both used tobacco in three ways, and indulged freely in rum, also "tom-trot" (hardbake), strongly flavoured with peppermint. Of course a lively market would influence the dose, and as for "lovelee," it must have been in Harry's partial eyes.— (H.R.C.)

"Upon little Easter Sunday, the freeholders of the towne and mannour of Lostwithiel, by themselves or their deputies, did there assemble, amongst whom one (as it fell to his lot by turne), bravely apparelled, gallantly mounted, with a crowne on his head, a scepter in his hand, a sword borne before him, and dutifully attended by all the rest also on horseback, ride thorow the principal streete to the Church; there the Curate in his best '*beseene*' solemne receiud him at the Church-yard stile, and conducted him to heare diuine seruice; after which he repaired with the same pompe to a house fore-prouided for that purpose, made a feast to his attendants, kept the table's end himselfe, and was serued with kneeling, assay, and all other rites due to the estate of a Prince; with which dinner the ceremony ended, and every man returned home again."—(Carew.)

The ancient custom of choosing a mock mayor was observed at Lostwithiel, on 10th October, 1884, by torchlight, in the presence of nearly a thousand people. The origin of both these customs is now quite forgotten. "A custom still existing at St. John's, Helston, and also at Buryan. The last mayor of the Quay, Penzance, was Mr. Robinson, a noted authority on sea fishing, etc. He died about ten years ago."—(H.R.C.)

April 1st. The universal attempts at fooling on this day are carried on in Cornwall as elsewhere, and children are sent by their schoolfellows for penn'orths of pigeon's milk, memory powder, strap-oil, etc., or with a note telling the receiver "to send the fool farther." When one boy succeeds in taking in another, he shouts after him, Fool! fool! the "guckaw" (cuckoo).

Towednack's (a village near St. Ives) "Cuckoo" or "Crowder" feast is on the nearest Sunday to the 28th April. Tradition accounts for the first name by the story of a man who there gave a feast on an inclement day in the end of April. To warm his guests he threw some faggots on the fire (or some furze-bushes), when a cuckoo flew out of them, calling "Cuckoo! cuckoo!" It was caught and kept, and he resolved every year to invite his friends to celebrate the event. This, too, is said to be the origin of the feast.

"Crowder" in Cornwall means a fiddler, and the fiddle is called a "crowd." In former days the parishioners of Towednack were met at the church door on "feasten" day by a "crowder," who, playing on his "crowd," headed a procession through the village street, hence its second name.

The only May-pole now erected in Cornwall is put up on April 30th, at Hugh Town, St. Mary's, Scilly. Girls dance round it on May-day with garlands of flowers on their heads, or large wreaths of flowers from shoulder to waist. Dr. Stephen Clogg, of Looe, says that "May-poles are still to be seen on May-day, at Pelynt, Dulver, and East and West Looe."—(*W. Antiquary*, August, 1884.) In the beginning of this century, boys and girls in Cornwall sat up until twelve o'clock on the eve of May-day, and then marched around the towns and villages with Musical Instruments, collecting their friends to go a-maying. May-day is ushered in at Penzance by the discordant blowing of large tin horns. At daybreak, and even earlier, parties of boys, five or six in number, assemble at the street corners, from whence they perambulate the town blowing their horns and conchshells. They enter the gardens of detached houses, stop and bray under the bedroom windows, and beg for money. With what they collect they go into the country, and at one of the farmhouses they breakfast on bread and clotted cream, junket, &c. An additional ring of tin (a penn'orth) is added to his horn every year that a boy uses it.

Formerly, on May-morn, if the boys succeeded in fixing a " May bough " over a farmer's door before he was up, he was considered bound to give them their breakfasts; and in some parts of the county, should the first comer bring with him a piece of well-opened hawthorn, he was entitled to a basin of cream.

" In West Cornwall it is the custom to hang a piece of furze to a door early in the morning of May-day. At breakfast-time the one who does this appears and demands a piece of bread and cream with a basin of 'raw-milk' (milk that has not been scalded and the cream taken off).

" In Landrake, East Cornwall, it was the custom to give the person who plucked a fern as much cream as would cover it. It was also a practice there to chastise with stinging nettles any one found in bed after six on May-morning."—(Rev. S. Rundle, Vicar, Godolphin.)

Young shoots of sycamore, as well as white thorn, are known as May in Cornwall, and from green twigs of the former and from green stalks of wheaten corn the children of this county make a rude whistle, which they call a " feeper."

Until very lately parties of young men and women rose betimes on May-day and went into the country to breakfast; going a "a junket-ing" in the evening has not yet been discontinued.

At Hayle, on May-day (1883), as usual, groups of children, deco-rated with flowers and gay with fantastic paper-clothes, went singing through the streets. In the evening bonfires were lit in various parts of the town, houses were illuminated with candles, torches and fire-balls burnt until a late hour. The last is a new and dangerous plaything: a ball of tow or rags is saturated with petroleum, set fire to, and then kicked from one place to another; it leaves a small track of burning oil wherever it goes.

" On May-morning, in Polperro, the children and even adults go out into the country and fetch home branches of the narrow-leaved elm, or flowering boughs of white thorn, both of which are called 'May.' At a later hour all the boys sally forth with bucket, can, or other vessel, and avail themselves of a license which the season confers—to 'dip' or wellnigh drown, without regard to person or circumstance, the passenger who has not the protection of a piece of 'May' conspicuously stuck in his dress; at the same time they sing, 'The first of May is Dipping-day.' This manner of keeping

May-day is, I have heard, common in Cornwall. We are now favoured with a call from the boy with his pretty garland, gay with bright flowers and gaudily-painted birds'-eggs, who expects some little gratuity for the sight."—(T. Q. Couch.)

"At East and West Looe the boys dress their hats with flowers, furnish themselves with bullocks' horns, in which sticks of two feet long are fixed, and with these filled with water they parade the streets and dip all persons who have not the sprig of May in their hats."—(Bond.)

"First of May you must take down all the horse-shoes (that are nailed over doors to keep out witches, &c.) and turn them, not letting them touch the ground."—(Old farmer, Mid-Cornwall, through T. Q. Couch, *W. Antiquary*, September, 1883.)

May-day at Padstow is Hobby-horse day. A hobby-horse is carried through the streets to a pool known as Traitor's-pool, a quarter of a mile out of the town. Here it is supposed to drink: the head is dipped into the water, which is freely sprinkled over the spectators. The procession returns home, singing a song to commemorate the tradition that the French, having landed in the bay, mistook a party of mummers in red cloaks for soldiers, hastily fled to their boats and rowed away.

"The May-pole on the first of May at Padstow has only been discontinued within the last six or eight years (1883). It was erected in connection with the 'Hobby-horse' festival by the young men of the town, who on the last eve of April month would go into the country, cut a quantity of blooming yellow furze, and gather the flowers then in season, make garlands of the same; borrow the largest spar they could get from the shipwright's yard, dress it up with the said furze and garlands, with a flag or two on the top, and hoist the pole in a conspicuous part of the town, when the 'Mayers,' male and female, would dance around it on that festival-day, singing—

> ' And strew all your flowers, for summer is come in to-day.
> It is but a while ago since we have strewed ours
> In the merry morning of May,' &c.

"The May-pole was allowed to remain up from a week to a

fortnight, when it was taken down, stripped, and the pole returned."—
(Henry Harding, Padstow, *W. Antiquary*, August, 1883.)

"Formerly all the respectable people at Padstow kept this anniversary, decorated with the choicest flowers; but some unlucky day
a number of rough characters from a distance joined in it, and committed some sad assaults upon old and young, spoiling all their nice
summer clothes, and covering their faces and persons with smut.
From that time—fifty years since—(1865) the procession is formed
of the lowest.

"The May-pole was once decorated with the best flowers, now
with only some elm-branches and furze in blossom. The horse is
formed as follows: The dress is made of sackcloth painted black—
a fierce mask—eyes red, horse's head, horse-hair mane and tail;
distended by a hoop—some would call it frightful. Carried by a
powerful man, he could inflict much mischief with the snappers, &c.
No doubt it is a remnant of the ancient plays, and it represents the
devil, or the power of darkness. They commence singing at sunrise.

'THE MORNING-SONG.

'Unite and unite, and let us all unite,
For summer is comen to-day;
For whither we are going we all will unite,
In the merry morning of May.

'Arise up, Mr. ———, and joy you betide,
For summer is comen to-day;
And bright is your bride that lays by your side,
In the merry morning of May.

'Arise, up Mrs. ———, and gold be your ring,
For summer is comen to-day;
And give us a cup of ale, the merrier we shall sing
In the merry morning of May.

'Arise up, Miss ———, all in your smock of silk,
For summer is comen to-day;
And all your body under as white as any milk,
In the merry morning of May.

'The young men of Padstow might if they would,
For summer is comen to-day;
They might have built a ship and gilded her with gold,
In the merry morning of May.

'Now fare you well, and we bid you good cheer,
  For summer is comen to-day ;
He will come no more unto your house before another year,
  In the merry morning of May.'"

(George Rawlings, September 1st, 1865, through R. Hunt, F.R.S., *Droles, &c., Old Cornwall.*)

Mr. Rawlings all through his song has written " For summer has come unto day," but this is clearly a mistake. He also gives another which he calls the " May-Song," but it is not as well worth transcribing : it bears in some parts a slight resemblance to that sung at the Helston Hal-an-tow.

Mr. George C. Boase, in an article on " The Padstow May-Songs," has many additional verses in " The Morning-Song." He also gives "The Day-Song," sung in honour of St. George, of which I will quote the first verse, and the last paragraph of his paper.

" Awake, St. George, our English knight O !
  For summer is a-come and winter is a-go,
  And every day God give us His grace,
  By day and by night O !
  Where is St. George, where is he O !
  He is out in his long boat, all on the salt sea O !
  And in every land O ! the land that ere we go.

Chorus—And for to fetch the summer home, the summer and the May O !
  For the summer is a-come and the winter is a-go, etc."

The only account of " The Hobby-horse " found in the Cornish histories is in Hitchins and Drew's *Cornwall* (vol. i., p. 720 ; vol. ii., pp. 525, 529), where it is stated that there is a tradition of St. George on horseback having visited the neighbourhood of Padstow, where the indentation of his horse's hoofs caused a spring of water to arise. The spot is still known as St. George's well, and water is said to be found there even in the hottest summer.—(*W. Antiquary.*)

In East Cornwall they have a custom of bathing in the sea on the three first Sunday mornings in May. And in West Cornwall children were taken before sunrise on those days to the holy wells, notably to that of St. Maddern (Madron), near Penzance, to be there dipped into the running water, that they might be cured of the rickets and other childish disorders. After being stripped naked they were plunged three times into the water, the parents facing the sun, and passed round the well nine times from east to west. They were then dressed, and laid by the side of the well, or on an artificial mound re-made every year, called St. Maddern's bed, which faced it, to sleep in the sun : should they do so and the water bubble it was considered a good sign. Not a word was to be spoken the whole time for fear of breaking the spell.

A small piece torn (not cut) from the child's clothes was hung for luck (if possible out of sight) on a thorn which grew out of the chapel wall. Some of these bits of rag may still sometimes be found fluttering on the neighbouring bushes. I knew two well-educated people who in 1840, having a son who could not walk at the age of two, carried him and dipped nim in Madron well (a distance of three miles from their home,) on the first two Sundays in May; but on the third the father refused to go. Some authorities say this well should be visited on the first three Wednesdays in May; as was for the same purpose another holy well at Chapel Euny (or St. Uny) near Sancred.

The Wesleyans hold an open-air service on the first three Sunday afternoons in May, at a ruined chapel near Madron well, in the south wall of which a hole may be seen, through which the water from the well runs into a small baptistry in the south-west corner.

Parties of young girls to this day walk there in May to try for sweethearts. Crooked pins, or small heavy things, are dropped into the well in couples ; if they keep together the pair will be married ; the number of bubbles they make in falling shows the time that will elapse before the event. Sometimes two pieces of straw formed into a cross, fastened in the centre by a pin, were used in these divinations. An old woman who lived in a cottage at a little distance formerly frequented the well and instructed visitors how to work the charms; she was never paid in money, but small presents were placed where she could find them. Pilgrims from all parts of England centuries ago resorted to St. Maddern's well : that was famed, as was also her grave, for many miraculous cures. The late Rev. R. S. Hawker, Vicar of Morwenstow, in East Cornwall,

published a poem, called "The Doom Well of St. Madron," on one
of the ancient legends connected with it.

"A respectable tradesman's wife in Launceston tells me that the
townspeople here say that a swelling in the neck may be cured by
the patients going before sunrise on the first of May to the grave of
the last young man (if the patient be a woman), to that of the last
young woman (if a man) who had been buried in the churchyard,
and applying the dew, gathered by passing the hand three times
from the head to the foot of the grave, to the part affected by the
ailment. I may as well add that the common notion of improving
the complexion by washing the face with the early dew in the fields
on the first of May prevails in these parts (East Cornwall), and they
say that a child who is weak in the back may be cured by drawing
him over the grass wet with the morning dew. The experiment
must be thrice performed, that is, on the mornings of the 1st, 2nd,
and 3rd of May."—(H. G. T., *Notes and Queries*, 14th December,
1850.)

The 8th of May is at Helston given up to pleasure, and is known
as Flora-day, Flurry-day, Furry-day, and Faddy. To "fade" meant
in old English to dance from country to town. A legend says this
day was set apart to commemorate a fight between the devil and
St. Michael, in which the first was defeated. The name Helston
has been fancifully derived from a large block of granite which until
1783 was to be seen in the yard of the Angel hotel, the principal
inn of the place. This was the stone that sealed Hell's mouth, and
the devil was carrying it when met by St. Michael. Why he should
have burdened himself with such a "large pebble" (as Cornish
miners call all stones) is quite unknown. The fight and overthrow
are figured on the town-seal.

The week before Flora-day is in Helston devoted to the "spring-
clean," and every house is made "as bright as a new pin," and the
gardens stripped of their flowers to adorn them.

The revelry begins at day-break, when the men and maidservants
with their friends go into the country to breakfast; these are the
"Hal-an-tow." They return about eight, laden with green boughs,

preceded by a drum and singing an old song, the first verses of
which ran thus : —

> " Robin Hood and Little John
> They both are gone to fair, O !
> And we will to the merry greenwood
> To see what they do there, O !
> And for to chase—O !
> To chase the buck and doe.
>
> *Refrain*—With Hal-an-tow ! Rumbelow !
> For we are up as soon as any O !
> And for to fetch the summer home,
> The summer and the May O !
> For summer is a-come O !
> And winter is a-gone O !

The whole of this song may be found with the music in the Rev.
Baring Gould's "Songs of the West," and the first verse set to
another tune in *Specimens of Cornish Provincial Dialect*, by Uncle
Jan Trenoodle. (Sandys.)

The Hal-an-tow are privileged to levy contributions on strangers
coming into the town.

Early in the morning merry peals are rung on the church-bells,
and at nine a prescriptive holiday is demanded by the boys at the
grammar-school.   At noon the principal inhabitants and visitors
dance through the town.   The dancers start from the market-house,
and go through the streets ; in at the front doors of the houses that
have been left open for them, ringing every bell and knocking at
every knocker, and out at the back, but if more convenient they
dance around the garden, or even around a room, and return
through the door by which they entered.   Sometimes the procession
files in at one shop-door, dances through that department and out
through another, and in one place descends into a cellar.   All the
main streets are thus traversed, aud a circuit is made of the bowling-green, which at one end is the extreme limit of the town.   Two
beadles, their wands wreathed with flowers, and a band with a gaily-
decorated drum, head the procession.   The dance ends with
"hands across" at the assembly room of the Angel hotel, where
there is always a ball in the evening.   Non-dancers are admitted to

this room by a small payment (which must be a silver coin), paid as they go up the stairs either to the landlord or a gentleman,—one stands on each side of the door. The gentlemen dancers on entering pay for their partners, and by established custom, should they be going to attend the evening ball, they are bound to give them their tickets, gloves, and the first dance. The tradespeople have their dance at a later hour, and their ball at another hotel.

The figure of the Furry dance, performed to a very lively measure, is extremely simple. To the first half of the tune the couples dance along hand-in-hand; at the second the first gentleman turns the second lady and the second gentleman the first. This change is made all down the set. Repeat.

I have appended the tune, to which children have adopted the following doggerel:—

" John the bone (beau) was walking home,
When he met with Sally Dover,
He kissed her once, he kissed her twice,
And he kissed her three times over."

Some writers have made the mistake of imagining that the tune sung to the Hal-an-tow and the Furry dance are the same.

Formerly, should any person in Helston be found at work on Flora-day, he was set astride on a pole, then carried away on men's shoulders to a wide part of the Cober (a stream which empties itself into Loe-pool close by), and sentenced to leap over it. As it was almost impossible to do this without jumping into the water, the punishment was remitted by the payment of a small fine towards the day's amusement. Others say the offender was first made to jump the Cober and then set astride on a pole to dry.

In many of the villages around Helston the children, on Flora-day, deck themselves with large wreaths, which they wear over one shoulder and under the other arm ; and at Porthleven I observed, in 1884, in addition to these wreaths, several children with large white handkerchiefs arranged as wimples, kept on their heads with garlands of flowers.

One of the first objects on entering the village of St. Germans (East Cornwall) is the large walnut-tree, at the foot of what is called Nut-tree Hill. Many a gay May-fair has been witnessed by the old tree. In the morning of the 28th of the month splendid fat cattle from some of the largest and best farms in the county quietly chewed the cud around its trunk ; in the afternoon the basket-swing dangled from its branches filled with merry, laughing boys and girls from every part of the parish. On the following day the mock mayor, who had been chosen with many formalities, remarkable only for their rude and rough nature, starting from some " bush-house " where he had been supping too freely of the fair-ale, was mounted on wain or cart, and drawn around it, to claim his pretended jurisdiction over the ancient borough, until his successor was chosen at the following fair. Leaving the nut-tree, which is a real ornament to the town, we pass by a spring of water running into a large trough, in which many a country lad has been drenched for daring to enter the town on the 29th of May without the leaf or branch of oak in his hat.—(R. Hunt, F.R.S., *Drolls, &c., Old Cornwall.*)

The wrestlers of Cornwall and their wrestling-matches are still famous, and in the May of 1868 4,000 assembled one day on Marazion Green, and 3,000 the next, to see one. The wrestlers of this county have a peculiar grip, called by them "the Cornish-hug."

Any odd, foolish game is in West Cornwall called a May-game (pronounced May-gum), also a person who acts foolishly ; and you frequently hear the expression—" He's a reg'lar May-gum!" There is a proverb that says—" Don't make mock of a May-gum, you may be struck comical yourself one day."

Whit-Sunday.—It was formerly considered very unlucky in Corn-wall to go out on this day without putting on some new thing.

Children were told that should they do so "the birds would foul them as they walked along." A new ribbon, or even a shoe-lace, would be sufficient to protect them. Whit-Monday is generally kept as a holiday, and is often made an excuse for another country excursion, which, if taken in the afternoon, ends at some farm-house with a tea of Cornish "heavy-cream cake," followed (in the evening) by a junket with clotted-cream.

Carew speaks of a feast kept in his time on Whit-Monday at the "Church-house" of the different parishes called a "Church-ale." It was a sort of large picnic, for which money had been previously collected by two young men—"wardens," who had been previously appointed the preceding year by their last "foregoers." This custom has long ceased to exist.

The Wesleyans (Methodists) in Cornwall hold an open-air service on Whit-Monday at Gwennap-pit. The pit is an old earth-round, excavated in the hill-side of Carn Marth, about three miles from the small village of Gwennap, and one from Redruth. This amphitheatre, which is then usually filled, is capable of holding from four to five thousand people, and is in shape like a funnel. It is encircled from the bottom to the top with eighteen turf-covered banks, made by cutting the earth into steps. It is admirably adapted for sound, and the voice of the preacher, who stands on one side, about half way up, is distinctly heard by the whole congregation. Wesley, when on a visit to Cornwall, preached in Gwennap-pit to the miners of that district, and this was the origin of the custom. Many excursion-trains run to Redruth on Whit-Monday, and a continuous string of vehicles of every description, as well as pedestrians, may be seen wending their way from the station to the pit, which is almost surrounded by "downs," and in a road close by rows of "standings" (stalls) are erected for the sale of "fairings." An annual pleasure-fair goes on at the same time at Redruth, and many avail themselves of the excursion-trains who have not the least intention of attending the religious service.

"In Mid-Cornwall, in the second week of June, at St. Roche and in one or two adjacent parishes, a curious dance is performed at their annual 'feasts.' It enjoys the rather undignified name of

'Snails' creep,' but would be more properly called 'The Serpent's Coil.'

"The following is scarcely a perfect description of it:—The young people being all assembled in a large meadow, the village band strikes up a simple but lively air, and marches forward, followed by the whole assemblage, leading hand-in-hand (or more closely linked in case of engaged couples), the whole keeping time to the tune with a lively step. The band or head of the serpent keeps marching in an ever-narrowing circle, whilst its train of dancing followers becomes coiled around it in circle after circle. It is now that the most interesting part of the dance commences, for the band, taking a sharp turn about, begins to retrace the circle, still followed as before, and a number of young men with long, leafy branches in their hands as standards, direct this counter-movement with almost military precision."—(W. C. Wade, *W. Antiquary*, April, 1881.)

A game similar to the above dance is often played by Sunday-school children in West Cornwall, at their out-of-door summer-treats, called by them "roll-tobacco." They join hands in one long line, the taller children at the head. The first child stands still, whilst the others in ever-narrowing circles dance around singing, until they are coiled into a tight mass. The outer coil then wheels sharply in a contrary direction, followed by the remainder, retracing their steps.

23rd of June. In the afternoon of Midsummer-eve little girls may be still occasionally met in the streets of Penzance with garlands of flowers on their heads, or wreaths over one shoulder.

This custom was, within the last fifty years, generally observed in West Cornwall. And in all the streets of our towns and villages groups of graceful girls, rich as well as poor, all dressed in white, their frocks decorated with rows of laurel-leaves ("often spangled with gold-leaf"—Bottrell), might in the afternoon have been seen standing at the doors, or in the evening dancing along with their brothers or lovers.

In Penzance, and in nearly all the parishes of West Penwith, immediately after nightfall on the eves of St. John and St. Peter, the 23rd and 28th of June, lines of tar-barrels, occasionally broken by bonfires, were simultaneously lighted in all the streets, whilst, at the same time, bonfires were kindled on all the cairns and hills around Mount's Bay, throwing the outlines in bold relief against the sky. "Then the villagers, linked in circles hand-in-hand, danced round them to preserve themselves against witchcraft, and, when they burnt low, one person here and there detached himself from the rest and leaped through the flames to insure himself from some special evil. The old people counted these fires and drew a presage from them."—(Bottrell.)

Regularly at dusk the mayor of Penzance sent the town-crier through the streets to give notice that no fireworks were allowed to be let off in the town; but this was done simply that he should not be held responsible if any accident happened, for he and all in Penzance knew quite well that the law would be set at defiance. Large numbers of men, women, and boys came up soon after from the quay and lower parts of the town swinging immense torches around their heads; these torches (locally known as "to'ches") were made of pieces of canvas about two feet square, fastened in the middle either to a long pole or a strong chain, dipped until completely saturated in tar. Of course they required to be swung with great dexterity or the holder would have been burnt. The heat they gave out was something dreadful, and the smoke suffocating. Most of the inhabitants dressed in their oldest clothes congregated in groups in the street, and a great part of the fun of the evening consisted in slyly throwing squibs amongst them, or in dispersing them by chasing them with hand-rockets. The greatest good humour always prevailed, and although the revellers were thickest in a small square surrounded by houses, some of them thatched, very few accidents have ever happened. A band stationed here played at intervals. No set-pieces were ever put off, but there were a few Roman-candles. Between ten and eleven a popular mayor might often have been seen standing in the middle of this square (the Green Market), encircled by about a dozen young men, each holding a lighted hand-rocket over the mayor's head. The sparks which fell around him on all sides made him look as if he stood in the centre of a fountain of fire. The proceedings finished by the boys and girls from the quay, whose torches had by this time expired, dancing in a long line hand in hand through the streets, in and out and sometimes over the now low burning tar-barrels, crying out, " An eye, an eye." At this shout the top couple held up their arms, and, beginning with the last, the others ran under them, thus reversing their position. A year or two ago, owing to the increasing traffic at Penzance, the practice of letting off squibs and crackers in the streets was formally abolished by order of the mayor and corporation. Efforts are still made and money collected for the purpose of reviving it, with some little success ; but the Green Market is no longer the scene of the fun. A few boys still after dusk swing their torches, and here and there some of the old inhabitants keep up the custom of lighting tar-barrels or bonfires before their doors. A rite called the Bonfire Test was formerly celebrated on this night. Mr. R. Hunt, F.R.S., has described it in his *Drolls, &c. Old Cornwall :*—" A bonfire is formed of faggots of furze, ferns, and the like. Men and maidens, by locking hands, form a circle, and commence a dance to some wild native song. At length, as the dancers become excited, they pull each other from side to side across the fire. If they succeed in treading out the fire without breaking the chain, none of the party will die during the year. If, however, the ring is broken before the fire is extinguished, ' bad luck to the weak hands,' as my informant said (1865). All the witches in West Cornwall used to meet at midnight on Midsummer-eve at Trewa (pronounced Troway), in the parish of Zennor, and around the dying fires renewed their vows to their master, the Devil. Zennor boasts of some of the finest coast scenery in Cornwall, and many remarkable rocks were scattered about in this neighbourhood ; several of them (as does the cromlech) still remain, but others have been quarried and carted away, amongst them one known as Witches' Rock, which if touched nine times at midnight kept away ill-luck, and prevented people from being ' over-looked ' (ill-wished)."

On Midsummer-day (June 24th) two pleasure fairs are held in Cornwall: one at Pelynt, in the eastern part of the county, where in the evening, from time immemorial, a large bonfire has been always lighted in an adjoining field by the boys of the neighbourhood

G

(some writers fix on the summer solstice as the date of Pelynt fair, but this, I believe, is an error); and the second on the old quay at Penzance. It is called "Quay Fair," to distinguish it from Corpus Christi fair, another and much larger one held at the other extremity of the town, and which lasts from the eve of Corpus Christi until the following Saturday. Quay fair was formerly crowded by people from the neighbouring inland towns and villages; their principal amusement was to go out for a short row, a great number in one boat, the boatmen charging a penny a head. This was taking a "Pen'nord of Say." When not paid for, a short row is a "Troil." (Troil is Old-Cornish for a feast).

Although this fair has not yet been discontinued, the number of those attending it grows less and less every year, and not enough money is taken to encourage travelling showmen to set up their booths. The old charter allowed the public-houses at the quay to keep open all night on the 24th of June, but such is no longer the case. Quay fair was sometimes known as Strawberry fair, and thirty years ago many strawberries were sold at it for twopence a quart. They were not brought to market in pottles, but in large baskets containing some gallons, and were measured out to the customers in a tin pint or quart measure. They were eaten from cabbage-leaves. Before the end of the day, unless there were a brisk sale, the fruit naturally got much bruised. They are still sold in the same way, but are not nearly as plentiful. Many of the strawberry fields, through which the public footpaths often went, have been turned up, and are now used for growing early potatoes. On St. John's-day Cornish miners place a green bough on the shears of the engine-houses in commemoration of his preaching in the wilderness.

This day is with Cornish as with other maidens a favourite one for trying old love-charms. Some of them rise betimes, and go into the country to search for an even "leafed" ash, or an even "leafed" clover. When found, the rhymes they repeat are common to all England.

An old lady, a native of Scilly, once gave me a most graphic description of her mother and aunt laying a table, just before midnight on St. John's-day, with a clean white cloth, knives and forks, and bread and cheese, to see if they should marry the men to whom they were engaged. They sat down to it, keeping strict silence—

> " For, if a word had been spoken,
> The spell would have been broken."

As the clock struck twelve, the door (which had purposely been left unbarred) opened, and their two lovers walked in, having, as they said, met outside, both compelled by irresistible curiosity to go and see if there were anything the matter with their sweethearts.

It never entered the old lady's head that the men probably had an inkling of what was going on, and to have hinted that such was the case would, I am quite sure, have given dire offence.

The following charm is from the *W. Antiquary :*—Pluck a rose at midnight on St. John's-day, wear it to church, and your intended will take it out of your button-hole.—(Old Farmer, Mid-Cornwall, through T. Q. Couch.)

" It was believed that if a young maiden gathered a rose on Mid-summer-day, and folding it in white paper, forbore to look at it or mention what she had done until the following Christmas-day, she would *then* find the flower fresh and bright; and further if she placed it in her bosom and wore it at church, the person most worthy of her hand would be sure to draw near her in the porch, and beseech her to give him the rose."—Neota—Launcells. Charlotte Hawkey.

In connection with Midsummer bonfires, I mentioned those on St. Peter's-eve ; although they are no longer lighted at Penzance, the custom (never confined to West Cornwall) is in other places still observed. Many of the churches in the small fishing villages on the coast are dedicated to this saint, the patron of fishermen, and on his tide the towers of these churches were formerly occasionally illuminated.

On St. Peter's-eve, at Newlyn West, in 1883, many of the men were away fishing on the east coast of England, and the celebration of the festival was put off until their return, when it took place with more than usual rejoicings. The afternoon was given up to aquatic sports, and in the evening, in addition to the usual bonfires and tar-barrels, squibs, hand and sky-rockets were let off. The young people finished the day with an open-air dance, which ended before twelve. In this village effigies of objectionable characters, after they have been carried through the streets, are sometimes burnt in the St. Peter's bonfire. I have often in Cornwall heard red-haired people described "as looking as if they were born on bonfire night." At Wendron, and many other small inland mining villages, the boys at St. Peter's-tide fire off miniature rock batteries called "plugs."

I must now again quote from Mr. T. Q. Couch, and give his account of how this day is observed at Polperro.

"The patron saint of Polperro is St. Peter, to whom the church, built on the seaward hill (still called chapel hill) was dedicated. His festival is kept on the 10th of July (old style). At Peter's-tide is our annual feast or fair. Though a feeble and insignificant matter, it is still with the young the great event of the year. On the eve of the fair is the prefatory ceremony of a bonfire. The young fishermen go from house to house and beg money to defray the expenses. At nightfall a large pile of faggots and tar-barrels is built on the beach, and, amid the cheers of a congregated crowd of men, women, and children (for it is a favour never denied to children to stay up and see the bonfire), the pile is lighted. The fire blazes up, and men and boys dance merrily round it, and keep up the sport till the fire burns low enough, when they venturously leap through the flames. It is a most animated scene, the whole valley lit up by the bright red glow, bringing into strong relief front and gable of picturesque old houses, each window crowded with eager and delighted faces, while around the fire is a crowd of ruddy lookers-on, shutting in a circle of impish figures leaping like salamanders through the flames.

"The next day the fair begins, a trivial matter, except to the children, who are dressed in their Sunday clothes, and to the village girls in their best gowns and gaudiest ribbons. Stalls, or 'standings,' laden with fairings, sweetmeats, and toys, line the lower part of Lansallos Street, near the strand. There are, besides, strolling

Thespians; fellows who draw unwary youths into games of hazard, where the risk is mainly on one side; ballad-singers; *penny-peep* men, who show and describe to wondering boys the most horrid scenes of the latest murder; jugglers and tumblers also display their skill. In the neighbouring inn the fiddler plays his liveliest tunes at twopence a reel, which the swains gallantly pay. The first day of the fair is merely introductory, for the excitement is rarely allayed under three. The second day is much livelier than the first, and has for its great event the wrestling-match on the strand, or perhaps a boat-race. On the third day we have the mayor-choosing, never a valid ceremony, but a broad burlesque. The person who is chosen to this post of mimic dignity is generally some half-witted or drunken fellow, who, tricked out in tinsel finery, elects his staff of constables, and these, armed with staves, accompany his chariot (some jowster's huckster's cart, dressed with green boughs) through the town, stopping at each inn, where he makes a speech full of large promises to his listeners, of full work, better wages, and a liberal allowance of beer during his year of mayoralty. He then demands a quart of the landlord's ale, which is gauged with mock ceremony, and if adjudged short of measure is, after being emptied, broken on the wheel of the car. Having completed the perambulation of the town, his attendants often make some facetious end of the pageant by wheeling the mayor in his chariot with some impetus into the tide."—*Polperro*, 1871, pp. 156—159.

The ceremony of choosing a mock mayor was also observed at Penryn (near Falmouth), but it took place in the autumn, on a day in September or October, when hazel-nuts were ripe, and "nutting day" was kept by the children and poor people. The journeymen tailors went from Penryn and Falmouth to Mylor parish, on the opposite side of the river Fal. There they made choice of the wittiest among them to fill that office. His title was the " Mayor of Mylor." When chosen, he was borne in a chair upon the shoulders of four strong men from his " goode towne of Mylor" to his " anciente borough of Penryn." He was preceded by torch-bearers and two town-sergeants, in gowns and cocked hats, with cabbages instead of maces, and surrounded by a guard armed with staves. Just outside Penryn he was met with a band of music, which played him into the town. The procession halted at the town-hall, where the mayor made a burlesque speech, often a clever imitation of the phrases and manners of their then sitting parliamentary representative. This speech was repeated with variations before the different inns, the landlords of which were expected to provide the mayor and his numerous attendants liberally with beer. The day's proceedings finished with a dinner at one of the public-houses in Penryn. Bonfires, &c., were lighted, and fireworks let off soon after dusk. It was popularly believed that this choosing of a mock mayor was permitted by a clause in the town charter.

A festival, supposed to have been instituted in honour of Thomas-à-Beckett, called "Bodmin-Riding," was (although shorn of its former importance) until very recently held there on the first Monday and Tuesday after the 7th of July.

In the beginning of this century all the tradespeople of the town, preceded by music and carrying emblems of their trades, walked in procession to the Priory. They were headed by two men, one with a garland and the other with a pole, which they presented and received back again from the master of the house as the then representative of the Prior. Mr. T. Q. Couch had the following description of this ceremony from those who took part in its latest celebration :—

"A puncheon of beer having been brewed in the previous October, and duly bottled in anticipation of the time, two or more young men, who were entrusted with the chief management of the affair, and who represented 'the Wardens' of Carew's Church-ales, went round the town (Bodmin) attended by a band of drummers and fifers, or other instruments. The crier saluted each house with— 'To the people of this house, a prosperous morning, long life, health, and a merry riding.' The musicians then struck up the riding-tune, a quick and inspiriting measure, said by some to be as old as the feast itself. The householder was solicited to taste the riding-ale, which was carried round in baskets. A bottle was usually taken in, and it was acknowledged by such a sum as the means or humour of the townsmen permitted, to be spent on the public festivities of the season. Next morning a procession was formed (all who could afford to ride mounted on horse or ass, smacking long-lashed whips), first to the Priory to receive two large garlands of flowers fixed on staves, and then in due order to the principal streets to the town-end, where the games were formerly opened. The sports, which lasted two days, were of the ordinary sort— wrestling, foot-racing, jumping in sacks, &c. It is worthy of remark that a second or inferior brewing from the same wort was drunk at a minor merry-making at Whitsuntide."—(Popular Antiquities, *Journal Royal Institute of Cornwall,* 1864.)

In former days the proceedings ended in a servants'-ball, at which dancing was kept up until the next morning's breakfast-hour.

A very curious carnival was originally held under a Lord of Misrule, in July, on Halgaver Moor, near Bodmin, thus quaintly described by Carew :—

"The youthlyer sort of Bodmin townsmen vse to sport themselves by playing the box with strangers whom they summon to Halgauer. The name signifieth the Goat's Moore, and such a place it is, lying a little without the towne, and very full of quauemires. When these mates meet with any rawe seruing-man or other young master, who may serue and deserue to make pastime, they cause him to be solemnely arrested, for his appearance before the Maior of Halgauer, where he is charged with wearing one spurre, or going vntrussed, or wanting a girdle, or some such felony. After he had been arraygned and tryed, with all requisite circumstances, iudgement is given in formal terms, and executed in some one vngracious pranke or other, more to the skorne than hurt of the party condemned. Hence is sprung the prouerb when we see one slouenly appareled to say he shall be presented at Halgauer Court (or take him before the Maior of Halgauer).

" But now and then they extend this merriment with the largest, to preiudice of ouer-credulous people, persuading them to fight with a dragon lurking in Halgauer, or to see some strange matter there, which concludeth at least with a trayning them into the mire."—*(Survey of Cornwall.)*

Heath says in his *Description of Cornwall,* "These sports and pastimes were so liked by King Charles II., when he touched at Bodmin on his way to Scilly, that he became a brother of the jovial society."

"Taking-day."—"An old custom, about which history tells us nothing, is still duly observed at Crowan, in West Cornwall. Annually, on the Sunday evening previous to Praze-an-beeble fair (July 16th) large numbers of the young folk repair to the parish church, and at the conclusion of the service they hasten to Clowance Park, where still large crowds assemble, collected chiefly from the neighbouring villages of Leeds-town, Carnhell-green, Nancegollan, Blackrock, and Praze. Here the sterner sex select their partners for the forthcoming fair, and, as it not unfrequently happens that the generous proposals are not accepted, a tussle ensues, to the intense merriment of passing spectators. Many a happy wedding has resulted from the opportunity afforded for selection on 'Taking-day' in Clowance Park."—(*Cornishman,* July, 1882.)

At St. Ives, on the 25th July, St. James's-day, they hold a quiennial celebration of the "Knillian-games." These have been fully described by the late J. S. Courtney in his *Guide to Penzance,* as follows:—

"Near St. Ives a pyramid on the summit of a hill attracts attention. This pyramid was erected in the year 1782, as a place of sepulture for himself, by John Knill, Esq., some time collector of the Customs at St. Ives, and afterwards a resident in Gray's Inn, London, where he died in 1811. The building is commonly called 'Knill's Mausoleum'; but Mr. Knill's body was not there deposited, for, having died in London, he was, according to his own directions, interred in St. Andrew's church, Holborn. The pyramid bears on its three sides respectively the following inscriptions, in relief, on the granite of which it is built: 'Johannes Knill, 1782.' 'I know that my Redeemer liveth.' 'Resurgam.' On one side there is also Mr. Knill's coat-of-arms, with his motto, 'Nil desperandum.'

"In the year 1797, Mr. Knill, by a deed of trust, settled upon the mayor and capital burgesses of the borough of St. Ives, and their successors for ever, an annuity of ten pounds, as a rent-charge, to be paid out of the manor of Glivian, in the parish of Mawgan, in this county, to the said mayor and burgesses in the town-hall of the said borough, at twelve o'clock at noon, on the feast of the Nativity of St. John (Midsummer-day) in every year; and, in default, to be levied by the said mayor and burgesses by distress on the said manor. The ten pounds then received are to be immediately paid by the mayor and burgesses to the mayor, the collector of customs, and the clergyman of the parish for the time being, to be by them deposited in a chest secured by three locks, of which each is to have a key; and the box is left in the custody of the mayor.

" Of this annuity a portion is directed to be applied to the repair and support of the mausoleum; another sum for the establishment of various ceremonies to be observed once every five years; and the remainder 'to the effectuating and establishing of certain charitable purposes.'"

The whole affair has, however, been generally treated with ridicule. In order, therefore, to show that Mr. Knill intended a considerable portion of his bequest to be applied to really useful purposes, we annex a copy of his regulations for the disposal of the money:

" First. That, at the end of every five years, on the feast-day of St. James the Apostle, *Twenty*-five pounds shall be expended as follows, viz. *Ten* pounds in a dinner for the Mayor, Collector of Customs, and Clergyman, and two persons to be invited by each of them, making a party of nine persons, to dine at some tavern at the borough. *Five* pounds to be equally divided among ten girls, natives of the borough, and daughters of seamen, fishermen, or tinners, each of them not exceeding ten years of age, who shall between ten and twelve o'clock in the forenoon of that day dance, for a quarter of hour at least, on the ground adjoining the Mausoleum, and after the dance sing the 100th Psalm of the Old Version, 'to the fine old tune' to which the same was then sung in St. Ives church.

" *One* pound to the fiddler who shall play to the girls while dancing and singing at the Mausoleum, and also before them on their return home therefrom.

H

"*Two* pounds to two widows of seamen, fishermen, or tinners of the borough, being 64 years old or upwards, who shall attend the dancing and singing of the girls, and walk before them immediately after the fiddler, and certify to the Mayor, Collector, and Clergyman that the ceremonies have been duly performed.

"*One* pound to be laid out in white ribbons for breast-knots for the girls and widows, and a cockade for the fiddler, to be worn by them respectively on that day and the Sunday following. *One* pound to purchase account-books from time to time and pay the Clerk of the Customs for keeping the accounts. The remaining *Five* pounds to be paid to a man and wife, widower, or widow, 60 years of age or upwards, the man being an inhabitant of St. Ives, and a seaman, fisherman, tinner, or labourer, who shall have bred up to the age of ten years and upwards, the greatest number of legitimate children by his or her own labour, care, and industry, without parochial assistance, or having become entitled to any property in any other manner.

"Secondly. When a certain sum of money shall have accumulated in the chest, over and above what may have been required for repairs of the Mausoleum and the above payments, it is directed that on one of the fore-mentioned days of the festival '*Fifty*' pounds shall be distributed in addition to the '*Twenty-five*' pounds spent quiennially in the following manner; that is *Ten* pounds to be given as a marriage-portion to the woman between 26 and 36 years old, being a native of St. Ives, who shall have been married to a seaman, fisherman, tinner, or labourer, residing in the borough, between the 31st of December previously, and that day following the said feast-day, that shall appear to the Mayor, Collector, and Clergyman, the most worthy, 'regard being had to her duty and kindness to her parents, or to her friends who have brought her up.'

"*Five* pounds to any woman, single or married, being an inhabitant of St. Ives, who in the opinion of the aforesaid gentlemen shall be the best knitter of fishing-nets.

"*Five* pounds to be paid to the woman, married or single, inhabitant of St. Ives, or otherwise, who shall, by the same authorities, be deemed to be the best curer and packer of pilchards for exportation.

"*Five* pounds to be given between such two follower-boys as shall by the same gentlemen be judged to have best conducted themselves of all the follower-boys in the several concerns, in the preceding fishing-season. (A follower is a boat that carries a tuck-net in pilchard-fishing.)

"And *Twenty-five* pounds, the remainder of the said *Fifty*, to be divided among all the Friendly Societies in the borough, instituted for the support of the Members in sickness or other calamity, in equal shares. If there be no such Society, the same to be distribu-ted among ten poor persons, five men and five women, inhabitants of the borough, of the age of 64 years or upwards, and who have never received parochial relief."

The first celebration of the Knillian games, which drew a large concourse of people, took place in Knill's lifetime on July 25th, 1801.

The chorus then sung by the 10 virgins was as follows :—

> ' Quit the bustle of the bay,
> Hasten, virgins, come away :
> Hasten to the mountain's brow,
> Leave, oh! leave, St. Ives below.
> Haste to breathe a purer air,
> Virgins fair, and pure as fair.
> Quit St. Ives and all her treasures,
> Fly her soft voluptuous pleasures,
> Fly her sons and all the wiles
> Lurking in their wanton smiles ;
> Fly her splendid midnight halls,
> Fly the revels of her balls,
> Fly, oh ! fly, the chosen seat
> Where vanity and fashion meet !
> Thither hasten : form the ring,
> Round the tomb in chorus sing.'

These games have been repeated every five years up to the present time.

Morvah feast, which is on the nearest Sunday to the 1st August, is said to have been instituted in memory of a wrestling-match, throwing of quoits, &c., which took place there one Sunday, " when there were giants in the land." On the following Monday there was formerly a large fair, and although Morvah is a very small village without any attractions, the farmers flocked to it in great numbers to drink and feast, sitting on the hedges of the small fields common in West Cornwall. " Three on one horse, like going to Morvah Fair," is an old proverb.

On August 5th a large cattle-fair is held in the village of Gold-sithney, in the parish of Perran-Uthnoe. Lysons, in 1814, says :— " There is a tradition that this fair was originally held in Sithney, near Helston, and that some persons ran off with the glove, by the suspension of which to a pole the charter was held, and carried it off to this village, where, it is said, the glove was hung out for many years at the time of the fair. As some confirmation of the tradition of its removal it should be mentioned that the lord of the manor, a proprietor of the fair, used to pay an acknowledgment of one shilling per annum to the churchwardens of Sithney." The same author makes the statement that Truro fair, on November 19th, belongs to the proprietors of Truro Manor, as high lords of the town, and that a glove is hung out at this fair as at Chester; he also says that these same lords claim a tax called smoke-money from most of the houses in the borough.

In Cornwall the last sheaf of corn cut at harvest-time is " the neck." This in the West is always cut by the oldest reaper, who shouts out, " I hav'et! I hav'et! I hav'et!" The others answer, " What hav'ee? What hav'ee? What hav'ee?" He replies, " A neck! A neck! A neck!" Then altogether they give three loud hurrahs. The neck is afterwards made into a miniature sheaf, gaily decorated with ribbons and flowers; it is carried home in triumph, and hung up to a beam in the kitchen, where it is left until the next harvest. Mr. Robert Hunt says that "after the neck has been cried three times they (the reapers) change their cry to ' we yen! we yen!' which they sound in the same prolonged and slow manner as before, with singular harmony and effect three times." After this they all burst out into a kind of loud, joyous laugh, fling-ing up their hats and caps into the air, capering about, and perhaps kissing the girls. One of them gets the " neck," and runs as hard as he can to the farm-house, where the dairy-maid or one of the young female domestics stands at the door prepared with a pail of water. If he who holds the "neck" can manage to get into the house in any way unseen, or openly by any other way than the door by which the girl stands with the pail of water, then he may lawfully kiss her; but if otherwise he is regularly soused with the contents of the bucket.

The object of crying the "neck" is to give notice to the surrounding country of the end of the harvest, and the meaning of " we yen " is *we have ended.*

The last sheaf of the barley-harvest (there is now but little grown) was the "crow-sheaf," and when cut the same ceremony was gone through; but instead of "a neck," the words "a crow" were substituted.

When "the neck" is cut at the house of a squire, the reapers sometimes assemble at the front of the mansion and cry "the neck," with the addition of these words, "and for our pains we do deserve a glass of brandy, strong beer, and a bun."—(John Hills, Penryn, *W. Antiquary*, October, 1882.)

In East Cornwall "the neck," which is made into a slightly different shape, is carried to the mowhay (pronounced mo-ey) before it is cried (a mowhay is an inclosure for ricks of corn and hay). One of the men then retires to a distance from the others and shouts the same formula. It is hung up in the kitchen until Christmas-day, when it is given to the best ox in the stalls.

The harvest-home feast in the neighbourhood of Penzance goes by the name of "gool-dize," or "gool-an-dize." In Scilly it is known as the "nickly thize." Farmers there at that season of the year formerly killed a sheep, and as long as any portion of it was left the feast went on.

Ricks of corn in Cornwall are often made, and left to stand in the "arish-fields" (stubble-fields) where they were cut. These are all called "arish-mows," but from their different shapes they have also the names of "brummal-mows" and "pedrack-mows."

Probus and Grace fair is held on the 17th of September, through a charter granted by Charles II. after his restoration, to a Mr. Williams of that neighbourhood, with whom he had lived for some time during the Civil Wars.

Probus is in East Cornwall, and its church is famed for its beautiful tower. Tradition has it that this church was built by Saint Probus, but for want of funds he could not add the tower, and in his need asked St. Grace to help him. She consented, but when the church was consecrated Probus praised himself, but made no mention of her. Then a mysterious voice was heard, repeating the following distich:—

> " St. Probus and Grace,
> Not the first but the la-ast."

This town, consequently, has two patron saints.

I know of no other feasten ceremonies in this month; but here, as elsewhere, the children of the poor make up parties " to go a blackberrying." This fruit, by old people, was said not to be good after Michaelmas, kept by them 10th October (old style); after that date they told you the devil spat on them, and birds fouled them.

I knew an old lady whose birthday falling on that day she religiously kept it by eating for the last time that year blackberry-tart with clotted cream.

This brings me round to the month from which I started. Many of the feasts are of course omitted, as no local customs are now connected with them. There must be one for nearly every Sunday in the year, and a mere record of their names would be most wearisome. I cannot do better, therefore, than finish this portion of my work with two quotations. The first, from " Parochialia," by Mr. T. Q. Couch, *Journal Royal Institute of Cornwall, 1865,* runs thus:—

" The patron saint of Lanivet feast is not known; it is marked by no particular customs, but is a time for general visiting and merry-making, with an occasional wrestling-match. A local verse says:—

> " On the nearest Sunday to the last Sunday in A-prel,
> Lanivet men fare well.
> On the first Sunday after the first Tuesday in May,
> Lanivrey men fare as well as they."

In some parishes the fatted oxen intended to be eaten at these feasts were, the day before they were killed, led through the streets, garlanded with flowers and preceded by music.

Quotation number two is what Carew wrote in 1569:—

"The saints' feast is kept upon dedication-day by every house-holder of the parish within his own doors, each entertayning such forrayne acquaintance as will not fayle when their like time cometh about to requite him with the like kindness."

These remarks, and the jingling couplets, could be equally well applied to all the unmentioned feasts.

LEGENDS OF PARISHES, ETC.

ORNISH people possess in a marked degree all the characteristics of the Celts. They are imaginative, good speakers and story-tellers, describing persons and things in a style racy and idiomatical, often with appropriate gestures. Their proverbs are quaint and forcible, they are never at a lack for an excuse, and are withal very superstitious. Well-educated people are still to be met with in Cornwall who are firm believers in apparitions, pixies (fairies, called by the peasantry pisgies), omens, and other supernatural agencies. Almost every parish has a legend in connection with its patron saint, and haunted houses abound; but of the ghosts who inhabit them, unless they differ from those seen elsewhere, I shall say but little.

This county was once the fabled home of a race of giants, who in their playful or angry moments were wont to hurl immense rocks at each other, which are shown by the guides at this day as proofs of their great strength. To illustrate how in the course of time truth and fiction get strangely mingled, I will mention the fact that old John of Gaunt is said to have been the last of these giants, and to have lived in a castle on the top of Carn Brea (a high hill near Redruth). He could stride from thence to another neighbouring town, a distance of four miles. I do not know if he is supposed to be the one that lies buried under this mighty carn, and whose large protruding hand and bony fingers time has turned to stone. Here, too, in the dark ages, a terrific combat took place between Lucifer and a heavenly

host, which ended in the former's overthrow. A small monument
has been erected on Carn Brea, to the memory of Lord de Dunstanville ; and I once heard an old woman, after cleaning a room, say,
"It was fine enough for Lord de Dunstanville." Every child has
heard of Jack the Giant Killer, who, amongst his other exploits,
killed by stratagem the one who dwelt at St. Michael's Mount:

> "I am the valiant Cornishman
> Who slew the giant Cormoran."

He did not however confine himself to this neighbourhood, for of
an ancient earth-work near Looe, known as the "Giant's Hedge," it
is said :—

> "Jack the giant had nothing to do,
> So he made a hedge from Lerrin to Looe."

But the sayings and doings of these mighty men have been told
far better than I could tell them in Mr. Halliwell Phillipps' book,
Rambles in West Cornwall by the Footsteps of the Giants; Mr. Robert
Hunt's *Drolls, Traditions, and Superstitions of West Cornwall;* Mr.
Bottrell's *Hearthside Stories of West Cornwall;* and by many other
writers.

Tourists visit West Cornwall to see the Land's End and its fine
coast scenery, and express themselves disappointed that none of the
country people in that district know anything of King Arthur. They
forget that Uther's* heir was washed up to Merlin's feet by a wave
at the base of "Tintagel Castle by the Cornish sea," which is in the
eastern part of the county. This castle was built on one of the
grandest headlands in Cornwall (slate formation).

The ruins of King Arthur's Castle are most striking. They are
situated partly on the mainland and partly on a peninsula, separated
by a ravine, once said to have been spanned by a drawbridge con-
necting the two.

The ascent of this promontory, owing to the slippery nature of the
path cut in the friable slate, is far from pleasant ; and, as there was
a stiff breeze blowing when I mounted it, I thought old Norden was

* Uther is still used as a Christian name in Cornwall.

I

right when he said: "Those should have eyes who would scale Tintagel." You are, however, amply repaid for your trouble when you get to the top.

In addition to telling you of the grandeur of the castle in good King Arthur's days, the guides show you some rock basins to which they have given the absurd names of "King Arthur's cups and saucers."

Tradition assigns to this king another Cornish castle as a hunting-seat, viz.—the old earth-round of Castle-an-dinas, near St. Columb, from whence it is said he chased the wild deer on Tregoss Downs.

A dreary drive through slate-quarries takes you from Tintagel to Camelford. Near that town is Slaughter Bridge, the scene of a great battle between King Arthur and his nephew Modred, whom by some writers he is said to have killed on the spot; others have it that Arthur died here of a wound from a poisoned arrow shot by Modred, and that, after receiving his death wound at Camelford, he was conveyed to Tintagel Castle, where, surrounded by his knights, he died. All the time he lay a-dying supernatural noises were heard in the castle, the sea and winds moaned, and their lamentations never ceased until our hero was buried at Glastonbury. Then, in the pauses of the solemn tolling of the funeral bells, sweet voices came from fairy-land welcoming him there, from whence one day he will return and again be king of Cornwall. No luck follows a man who kills a Cornish chough (a red legged crow), as, after his death, King Arthur was changed into one.

"In the parish of St. Mabyn, in East Cornwall, and on the high road from Bodmin to Camelford, is a group of houses (one of them yet a smith's shop), known by the name of Longstone. The legend which follows gives the reason of the name:

" In lack of records I may say: 'In the days of King Arthur there lived in Cornwall a smith. This smith was a keen fellow, who made and mended the ploughs and harrows, shod the horses of his neighbours, and was generally serviceable. He had great skill in farriery, and in the general management of sick cattle. He could also extract the stubbornest tooth, even if the jaw resisted, and some gyrations around the anvil were required.

"'There seems ever to have been ill blood between devil and smith, and so it was between the fiend and the smith-farrier-dentist of St. Mabyn. At night there were many and fierce disputes between them in the smithy. The smith, as the rustics tell, always got the advantage of his adversary, and gave him better than he brought. This success, however, only fretted Old Nick, and spurred him on to further encounters. What the exact matter of controversy on this particular occasion was is not remembered, but it was agreed to settle it by some wager, some trial of strength and skill. A two-acred field was near; and the smith challenged the devil to the reaping of each his acre in the shortest time. The match came off, and the devil was beaten, for the smith had beforehand stealthily stuck here and there over his opponent's acre some harrow-tines or teeth.

"'The two started well, but soon the strong swing of the fiend's scythe was brought up frequently by some obstruction, and as frequently he required the whetstone. The dexterous and agile smith went on smoothly with his acre, and was soon unmistakeably gaining. The devil, enraged at his certain discomfiture, hurled his whetstone at his rival, and flew off. The whetstone, thrown with great violence, after sundry whirls in the air, fell upright into the soil at a great depth, and there remained a witness against the Evil One for ages. The devil avoided the neighbourhood whilst it stood, but in an evil hour the farmer at Treblethick, near, threw it down. That night the enemy returned, and has haunted the neighbourhood ever since.

"'This monolith was of granite, and consequently brought hither from a distance, for the local stone is a friable slate. It yielded four large gate-posts, gave spans to a small bridge, and left much granite remaining.'"—T. Q. Couch, *Notes and Queries*, April, 1883.

Upon St. Austell Down is an upright block of granite, called "the giant's staff, or longstone," to which this legend is attached:—
"A giant, travelling one night over these hills, was overtaken by a storm, which blew off his hat. He immediately pursued it; but, being impeded by a staff which he carried in his hand, he thrust this into the ground until his hat could be secured. After

wandering, however, for some time in the dark, without being able to find his hat, he gave over the pursuit and returned for the staff; but this also he was unable to discover, and both were irrevocably lost. In the morning, when the giant was gone, his hat and staff were both found by the country people about a mile asunder. The hat was found on White-horse Down, and bore some resemblance to a mill-stone, and continued in its place until 1798, when, some soldiers having encamped around it, they fancied, it is said, as it was a wet season, this giant's hat was the cause of the rain, and therefore rolled it over the cliff. The staff, or long-stone, was discovered in the position in which it remains; it is about twelve feet high, and tapering toward the top, and is said to have been so fashioned by the giant that he might grasp it with ease."—*Murray's Guide.*

There is another longstone in the parish of St. Cleer,* about two miles north of Liskeard, which bears an inscription to Doniert (Dungerth), a traditional king of Cornwall, who was drowned in 872. In fact, these "menhirs," supposed to be sepulchral monuments, are to be found scattered all over the county.

The following curious bit of folk-lore appeared in the *Daily News* of March 8th, 1883, communicated by the Rev. J. Hoskyns Abrahall, Coombe Vicarage, near Woodstock :—"A friend of mine, who is vicar of St. Cleer, in East Cornwall, has told me that at least one housemaid of his—I think his servants in general—very anxiously avoided killing a spider, because Parson Jupp, my friend's predecessor (whom he succeeded in 1844), was, it was believed, somewhere in the vicarage in some spider—no one knew in which of the vicarage spiders." Spiders are often not destroyed because of the tradition that one spun a web over Christ in the manger, and hid him from Herod.

There are other superstitions current in Cornwall somewhat similar to the above. Maidens who die of broken hearts, after they have been deceived by unfaithful lovers, are said to haunt their betrayers as white hares. The souls of old sea-captains never

* The Cornish manner of pronouncing the name of St. Clare.

sleep; they are turned into gulls and albatrosses. The knockers (a tribe of little people), who live underground in the tin-mines, are the spirits of the Jews who crucified our Saviour, and are for that sin compelled on Christmas morning to sing carols in his honour. "Jew" is a name also given to a black field-beetle (why, I know not). It exudes a reddish froth: country children hold it on their hands and say, "Jew! Jew! spit blood!" "A ghost at Pengelly, in the parish of Wendron, was compelled by a parson of that village after various changes of form to seek refuge in a pigeon-hole, where it is confined to this day."—Through Rev. S. Rundle.

After this digression I will return to St. Cleer, and, beginning with its holy well, briefly notice a few others. It is situated not far from the church, and was once celebrated as a "boussening," or ducking-well for the cure of mad people. Considerable remains of the baptistery, which formerly enclosed it, are still standing, and outside, close by, is an old stone cross. Carew says,—"There were many bowssening places in Cornwall for curing mad people, and amongst the rest one at Alter Nunne, in the hundred of Trigges, called S. Nunne's well, and because the manner of this bowssening is not so vnpleasing to heare as it was vneasie to feele, I wil (if you please) deliuer you the practise, as I receyued it from the beholders. The water running from S. Nunne's well fell into a square and close-walled plot, which might be filled at what depth they listed. Vpon this wall was the franticke person set to stand, his backe toward the poole, and from thence with a sudden blow in the brest, tumbled headlong into the pond, where a strong fellowe, provided for the nonce, tooke him and tossed him vp and downe, alongst and athwart the water, vntill the patient by foregoing his strength had somewhat forgot his fury. Then was hee conueyed to the church and certain Masses sung ouer him; vpon which handling if his wits returned S. Nunne had the thanks: but if there appeared small amendment, he was bowssened againe and againe, while there remayned in him any hope of life for recouery." The same writer says of Scarlet's "well neare vnto Bodmin, howbeit the water should seem to be healthfull, if not helpfull: for it retaineth this extraordinary quality, that the same is waightier than the ordinary of his kind, and will continue the best part of a yeere without alteration or sent or taste, only you shall see it represent many colours, like the Rain-bowe which (in my conceite) argueth a running throu some minerall veine and therewithall a possessing of some vertue." I must give one more quotation from Carew before I finish with him, about a well at Saltash :—" I had almost forgotten to tell you that there is a well in this towne whose water will not boyle peason to a seasonable softnes."

The holy wells in Cornwall are very numerous ; the greater part were in olden times enclosed in small baptisteries. Luckily the poor people believe that to remove any of the stones of the ruins of these chapels would be fatal to them and to their children, and for that reason a great number yet remain. It is considered unlucky, too, to cart away any of the druidical monuments ("pieces of ancientcy"), and many are the stories told of the great misfortunes that have fallen on men who have so done. The innocent oxen or horses who drag them away are always sure to die, and their master never prosper. Persistent ill-luck also follows any one defiling these wells ; and a tradition is current in one of the "West Country" parishes, of a gentleman, who, after he had washed his dogs, afflicted with the mange, in its holy well, fell into such poverty that his sons were obliged to work as day labourers. Mr. T. Q. Couch, in *Notes and Queries*, vol. x., gives this legend in connection with St. Nunn's well in Pelynt :—"An old farmer once set his eyes upon the granite basin and coveted it ; for it was not wrong in his eyes to convert the holy font to the base uses of the pig's stye ; and accordingly he drove his oxen and wain to the gateway above for the purpose of removing it. Taking his beasts to the entrance of the well, he essayed to drag the trough from its ancient bed. For a long time it resisted the efforts of the oxen, but at length they succeeded in starting it, and dragged it slowly up the hill-side to where the wain was standing. Here, however, it burst away from the chains which held it, and, rolling back again to the well, made a sharp turn and regained its old position, where it has remained ever since. Nor will any one again attempt its removal, seeing that the farmer, who was previously well-to-do in the world, never prospered from that day forward. Some people say, indeed, that retribution overtook him on the spot, the oxen falling dead, and the owner being struck lame and speechless."

This St. Nunn's well is not the "boussening" well formerly mentioned, but another dedicated to the same saint, and is resorted to as a divining and wishing well; it is commonly called by the people of that district the "Piskies' well." Pins are thrown into it, not only to see by the bubbles which rise on the water whether the wisher will get what he desires, but also to propitiate the piskies and to bring the thrower good luck. This county has many other divining wells which were visited at certain seasons of the year by those anxious to know what the future would bring them. Amongst them the Lady of Nant's well, in the parish of Colan, was formerly much frequented on Palm Sunday, when those who wished to foretell their fate threw into the water crosses made of palms. There was once in Gulval parish, near Penzance, a well which was reported to have had great repute as a divining well. People repaired to it to ask if their friends at a distance were well or ill, living or dead. They looked into the water and repeated the words:

> " Water, water, tell me truly,
> Is the man that I love duly
> On the earth, or under the sod,
> Sick or well? in the name of God."

Should the water bubble up quite clear, the one asked for was in good health; if it became puddled, ill; and should it remain still, dead. Of the wells of St. Roche, St. Maddern (now Madron), and St. Uny, I have spoken in the first part of this work.

The waters from several wells are used for baptismal rites (one near Laneast is called the "Jordan"), and the children baptized with water from the wells of St. Euny (at the foot of Carn Brea, Redruth) and of Ludgvan (Penzance), &c., it was asserted could never be hanged with a hempen rope; but this prophecy has unfortunately been proved to be false. The water from the latter was famed too as an eye-wash, until an evil spirit, banished for his misdeeds by St. Ludgvan, to the Red Sea, spat into it from malice as he passed. The Red Sea is the favourite traditional spot here for the banishment of wicked spirits, and I have been told stories of wicked men whose souls, immediately after their death, were carried off to well-known volcanoes.

Almost all these holy wells were once noted for the curing of diseases, but the water from St. Jesus' well, in Miniver, was especially famed for curing whooping-cough. St. Martin's well, in the centre of Liskeard at the back of the market, known as "Pipe Well," from the four iron pipes through which four springs run into it, was formerly not only visited for the healing qualities of its chief spring, but for a lucky stone that stood in it. By standing on this stone and drinking of the well's water, engaged couples would be happy and successful in their married life. It also conferred magical powers on any person who touched it. The stone is still there, but has now been covered over and has lost its virtue.

The saints sometimes lived by the side of the holy wells named after them, notably St. Agnes (pronounced St. Ann), who dyed the pavement of her chapel with her own blood. St. Neot in whose pool were always three fish on which he fed, and whose numbers never grew less.* St. Piran, the titular saint of tin-miners, who lived 200 years and then died in perfect health. Of these three saints many miraculous deeds are related; but they would be out of place in this work, and I will end my account of the wells by a description of St. Keyne's, more widely known outside Cornwall through Southey's ballad than any of the others. It is situated in a small valley in the parish of St. Neot, and was in the days of Carew and Norden arched over by four trees, which grew so closely together that they seemed but one trunk. Both writers say the trees were withy, oak, elm, and ash (by withy I suppose willow was meant). They were all blown down by a storm, and about 150 years ago, Mr. Rashleigh, of Menabilly, replaced them with two oaks, two elms, and one ash. I do not know if they are living, but Mr. J. T. Blight in 1858, in his book on *Cornish Crosses*, speaks of one of the oaks being at that time so decayed that it had to be propped. The reputed virtue of the water of St. Keyne's well is,

---

* Supposed to have been shads, vulgarly here called "Chuck-cheldern," from the number of bones in them.

(as almost all know), that after marriage "whether husband or wife come first to drink thereof they get the mastery thereby."—Fuller.

> " In name, in shape, in quality,
> This well is very quaint ;
> The name, to lot of ' Kayne ' befell,
> No ouer—holy saint.
>
> " The shape, four trees of diuers kinde,
> Withy, oke, elme, and ash,
> Make with their roots an arched roofe,
> Whose floore this spring doth wash.
>
> " The quality, that man or wife,
> Whose chance or choice attaines,
> First of this sacred streame to dr' ike,
> Thereby the mastry gaines."—*Carew*.

Southey makes a discomfited husband tell the story, who ends thus :

> " I hasten'd as soon as the wedding was done,
> And left my wife in the porch ;
> But i'faith she had been wiser than me,
> For she took a bottle to church."

St. Keyne not only thus endowed her well, but during her stay at St. Michael's Mount she gave the same virtue to St. Michael's chair. This chair is the remains of an old lantern on the south-west angle of the tower, at a height of upwards of 250 feet from low water. It is fabled to have been a favourite seat of St. Michael's. Whittaker, in his supplement to Polwhele's *History of Cornwall*, says, " It was for such pilgrims as had stronger heads and bolder spirits to complete their devotions at the Mount by sitting in this St. Michael's chair and *showing themselves as pilgrims to the country round;*" but it most probably served as a beacon for ships at sea. To get into it you must climb on to the parapet, and you sit with your feet dangling over a sheer descent of at least seventy feet; but to get out of it is much more difficult, as the sitter is obliged to turn round in the seat. Notwithstanding this, and the danger of a fall through giddiness, which, of course, would be certain death, for there is not the slightest protection, I have seen ladies perform the feat. Curiously enough Southey has also written a ballad on St.

Michael's chair, but it is not as popular as the one before quoted; it is about "Richard Penlake and Rebecca his wife," "a terrible shrew was she." In pursuance of a vow made when Richard "fell sick," they went on a pilgrimage to the Mount, and whilst he was in the chapel,

> "She left him to pray, and stole away
> To sit in St. Michael's chair.

> "Up the tower Rebecca ran,
> Round and round and round ;
> 'Twas a giddy sight to stand atop
> And look upon the ground.

> "'A curse on the ringers for rocking
> The tower !' Rebecca cried,
> As over the church battlements
> She strode with a long stride.

> "'A blessing on St. Michael's chair !'
> She said as she sat down :
> Merrily, merrily rung the bells,
> And out Rebecca was thrown.

> "Tidings to Richard Penlake were brought
> That his good wife was dead ;
> 'Now shall we toll for her poor soul
> The great church bell ?' they said.

> "'Toll at her burying,' quoth Richard Penlake,
> 'Toll at her burying,' quoth he ;
> 'But don't disturb the ringers now
> In compliment to me.'"

Old writers give the name of "Caraclowse in clowse" to St. Michael's Mount, which means the Hoar Rock in the Wood ; and that it was at one time surrounded by trees is almost certain, as at very low tides in Mount's Bay a "submarine forest," with roots of large trees, may still be clearly seen. At these seasons branches of trees, with leaves, nuts, and beetles, have been picked up.

Old folks often compared an old-fashioned child to St. Michael's Mount, and quaintly said, "she's a regular little Mount, St. Michael's Mount will never be washed away while she's alive."

Folk-lore speaks of a time when Scilly was joined to the mainland, which does not seem very improbable when we remember that within the last twenty-five years a high road and a field have been washed away by the sea between Newlyn and Penzance. An old lady, whose memory went back to the beginning of the present century, told me that she had often seen boys playing at cricket in some fields seaward of Newlyn, of which no vestige in my time remained.

But the Lyonnesse, as this tract of land (containing 140 parish churches) between the Land's End and Scilly was called, and where, according to the Poet Laureate, King Arthur met his death-wound,

> " So all day long the noise of battle roll'd
> Among the mountains by the winter sea,
> Until King Arthur's Table, man by man,
> Had fallen in Lyonnesse about their lord,
> King Arthur . . . . . "

is reputed to have been suddenly overwhelmed by a great flood. Only one man of all the dwellers on it is said to have escaped death, an ancestor of the Trevilians (now Trevelyan). He was carried on shore by his horse into a cove at Perran. Alarmed by the daily inroad of the sea, he had previously removed his wife and family. Old fishermen of a past generation used to declare that on clear days and moonlight nights they had often seen under the water the roofs of churches, houses, &c., of this submerged district.

Whether the memory of this flood is perpetuated by the old proverb, "As ancient as the floods of Dava," once commonly current in West Cornwall, but which I have not heard for years, I know not, as I have never met with any one who could tell me to what floods it referred.

Tradition also speaks of a wealthy city in the north of Cornwall, called Langarrow, which for its wickedness was buried in sand, driven in by a mighty storm. All that coast as far west as St. Ives is sand, known as " Towans," and the sand is always encroaching.

There is a little church now near Padstow, dedicated to St. Enodock, which is often almost covered by the shifting drifts. It is in a solitary situation, and service is only held there once a year, when a path to it has to be cut through the sand. It is said that the clergyman, in order to keep his emoluments and fees, has been sometimes obliged to get into it through a window or hole in the roof.

About eight miles from Truro is the lost church of Perran-zabuloe, which for centuries was supposed to have been a myth, but the shifting of the sand disclosed it in 1835.

In Hayle Towans is buried the castle of Tendar, the Pagan chief who persecuted the Christians, and in the neighbouring parish of Lelant that of King Theodrick, who, after beheading, in Ireland, many saints, crossed over to Cornwall on a millstone.

Many of the Cornish saints are reputed to have come into Cornwall in the same way as this king; but St. Ia, the patron saint of St. Ives, chose a frailer vessel. She crossed from Ireland on a leaf.

The afore-mentioned lost city was most likely a very small place, as I asked an old woman three or four years ago, who lived not far from the little village of Gwithian, where I could get something I wanted, and she told me, " In the city."

The bay between this place and St. Ives (St. Ives Bay) has the reputation of being haunted at stormy times before a shipwreck by a lady in white, who carries a lantern.

At Nancledra, a village near St. Ives, was formerly a logan rock, which could only be moved at midnight; and children were cured of rickets by being placed on it at that hour. It refused to rock for those who were illegitimate.

Not far from here is Towednack, and there is a legend to the effect that the devil would never allow the tower of its church to be completed, pulling down at night what had been built up in the day. When a person makes an incredible statement he is in West Cornwall told " To go to Towednack quay-head where they christen calves." (No part of this parish touches the sea.)

Mr. Robert Hunt records a curious test of innocency which, not long since, was practised in this parish. " A farmer in Towednack having been robbed of some property of no great value was resolved, nevertheless, to employ a test which he had heard the ' old people' resorted to for the purpose of catching the thief. He invited all his neighbours into his cottage, and, when they were assembled, he placed a cock under the ' brandice' (an iron vessel, formerly much employed by the peasantry in baking when this process was carried out on the hearth, the fuel being furze and ferns). Every one was directed to touch the brandice with his, or her, third finger, and say: 'In the name of the Father, Son, and Holy Ghost, speak.' Every one did as they were directed, and no sound came from beneath the brandice. The last person was a woman, who occasionally laboured for the farmer in his fields. She hung back, hoping to pass unobserved amongst the crowd. But her very anxiety made her a suspected person. She was forced forward, and most unwillingly she touched the brandice, when, before she could utter the words prescribed, the cock crew. The woman fell faint on the floor, and when she recovered, she confessed herself to be the thief, restored the stolen property, and became, it is said, 'a changed character from that day.' "

The following was told me by a friend. It took place in a school of one of our western parishes about sixty years ago:—" It was in the days of quill pens, and the master had lost his penknife. Every boy pleaded not guilty. At twelve the master said no boy should leave the school for half-an-hour, when he would return and see if they had found his knife. The door was locked, and at the appointed time he came back with a small, round table, on which he had inverted a 'half-strike' (4 gallons) measure. The table was placed in the middle of the gangway; the master stood by the side of it, and asked if they had found his knife. All said 'No!' 'Well then,' answered he, 'come out slowly one at a time and let each touch this measure with the right forefinger, and the bantam-cock under it will crow at the thief.' The boys went out boldly, as they passed touching the tub, but the master missed one whom from the first he had suspected. He again locked the door, searched the rooms, and there, under a desk, not in his own place, he found the boy hiding. He began to cry, confessed the theft, and gave up the knife."

Another test of innocency, practised in bygone days, was to kindle a fire on one of the table-mên (large flat stones), so common in villages in West Cornwall. A stick lit at this was handed to the accused, who had to put out the fire by spitting on it. It is well-known that fear dries up saliva. It is still supposed in remote districts that no one can bear witness to a misdemeanour, seen through glass.

I will describe another rough ordeal before I go on to the legends of the Land's End district. It is called "Riding the hatch," or "heps" (a half-door often seen at small country shops). Any man formerly accused of immorality was brought before a select number of his fellow parishioners, and by them put to sit astride the "heps," which was shaken violently backwards and forwards: if he fell into the house he was judged innocent; but out on the road, guilty. When any one has been brought before his superiors and remanded he is still figuratively said "to have been made to ride the 'heps.'" Hands are washed, as by Pontius Pilate, to clear a person from crime, and to call any one "dirty-fingered" is to brand him as a thief.

On a bench-end in Zennor church there is a very singular carving of a mermaid. To account for it Zennor folks say that hundreds of years ago a beautifully-attired lady, who came and went mysteriously, used occasionally to attend their church and sing so divinely that she enchanted all who heard her. She came year after year, but never aged nor lost her good looks. At last one Sunday, by her charms, she enticed a young man, the best singer in the parish, to follow her: he never returned, and was heard of no more. A long time after, a vessel lying in Pendower cove, into which she sailed one Sunday, cast her anchor, and in some way barred the access to a mermaid's dwelling. She rose up from the sea, and politely asked the captain to remove it. He landed at Zennor, and related his adventure, and those who heard it agreed that this must have been the lady who decoyed away the poor young man.

Not far from St. Just is the solitary, dreary cairn, known as Cairn Kenidzhek (pronounced Kenidjack), which means the "hooting cairn," so called from the unearthly noises which proceed from it on dark nights. It enjoys a bad reputation as the haunt of witches. Close under it lies a barren stretch of moorland, the "Gump," over it the devil hunts at night poor lost souls; he rides on the half-starved horses turned out here to graze, and is sure to overtake them at a particular stile. It is often the scene of demon fights, when one holds the lanthorn to give the others light, and is also a great resort of the pixies. Woe to the unhappy person who may be there after night-fall : they will lead him round and round, and he may be hours before he manages to get out of the place away from his tormentors. Here more than once fortunate persons have seen "the small people" too, at their revels, and their eyes have been dazzled by the sight of their wonderful jewels; but if they have ever managed to secrete a few, behold next morning they were nothing but withered leaves, or perhaps snail-shells.

"Sennen Cove was much frequented by mermaids. This place was also resorted to by a remarkable spirit called the Hooper—from the hooping, or hooting sounds it was accustomed to make. In old times, according to tradition, a compact cloud of mist often came in from over the sea, when the weather was by no means foggy, and rested on the rocks called Cowloc, thence it spread itself like a curtain of cloud quite across Sennen Cove. By night a dull light was mostly seen amidst the vapour, with sparks ascending as if a fire burned within it : at the same time hooping sounds were heard proceeding therefrom. People believed the misty cloud shrouded a spirit, which came to forewarn them of approaching storms, and that those who attempted to put to sea found an invisible force—seemingly in the mist—to resist them. A reckless fisherman and his son, however, disregarding the token, launched their boat and beat through the fog with a "threshal" (flail); they passed the cloud of mist which followed them, and neither the men nor the hooper were ever more seen in Sennen Cove. This is the only place in the county where any tradition of such a guardian spirit is preserved."
—Bottrell.

The same author tells a story of a reputed astrologer called Dionysius Williams, who lived in Mayon, in Sennen, a century ago. He found his furze-rick was diminishing faster than it ought, and discovered by his art that some women in Sennen Cove were in the habit of taking it away at night. The very next night, when all honest folks should be in bed, an old woman from the Cove came as was her wont to his rick for a "burn"* of furze. She made one of

* Burn, a load, a burden.

no more than the usual size but could not lift it, neither could she after she had lightened her "burn" by half. Frightened, she tried to take out the rope and run away, but she could neither draw it out nor move herself. Of course Mr. Williams had put a spell upon her, and there she had to remain in the cold all night. He came out in the morning and released her, giving her, as she was poor, the furze. Neither she nor the other women ever troubled him again.

Before proceeding any further, to make an allusion in the next legend intelligible, I must say something about Tregeagle (pronounced Tregaygle), the Cornish Bluebeard, who was popularly supposed to have sold his soul to the devil, that his wishes might be granted for a certain number of years; and who, in addition to several other crimes, is accused of marrying and murdering many rich heiresses to obtain ther money. One day, just before his death, he was present when one man lent a large sum to another without receiving receipt or security for it (the money was borrowed for Tregeagle). Soon after Tregeagle's death the borrower denied that he had ever had it, and the case was brought into Bodmin Court to be tried, when the defendant said, " If Tregeagle ever saw it I wish to God that Tregeagle may come into court and declare it." No sooner were the words spoken than Tregeagle appeared, and gave his witness in favour of the plaintiff, declaring "that he could not speak falsely; but he who had found it so easy to raise him would find it difficult to lay him." The money was paid, but the wretched man was followed night and day by the spirit, and great labour had the parsons and wise men before they could finally rid him of his tormentor. There are many versions of this transaction. Tregeagle himself is said in another to have received the money for an estate of which he was steward, and not to have entered it in his books. His ghost was doomed to do many impossible things, such as to empty Dosmery pool, near Bodmin Moor, with a limpet shell that had a hole in the bottom. This pool had the reputation, too, of being bottomless; but it has lately been cut into and drained by the workers of the granite quarries. Strange tales are told in that neighbourhood of his appearing to people, and of his dismal howls at not being able to fulfil his tasks. Mothers all over Cornwall when their children are loudly crying may be often heard to declare "that they are roaring worse than Tregeagle." "A tradition of the neighbourhood says that on the shores of this lonely mere (Dosmery pool) the ghosts of bad men are ever employed in binding the sand in bundles with 'beams' (bands) of the same. These ghosts, or some of them, were driven out (they say horsewhipped out) by the parson from Launceston."—H. G. T. *Notes and Queries*, December, 1850.

Tregeagle had also to remove the sand from one cove to another, where the sea always returned it. It was on one of these expeditions that either by accident or design he dropped a sackful at the mouth of Loe-pool, near Helston. (When in wet seasons the waters of this pool rise to such a height as to obstruct the working of the mills on its banks, and heavy seas have silted up the sand at its mouth, the Mayor of Helston presents by ancient custom two leather purses containing three halfpence each as his dues to the lord of Penrose who owns Loe-pool, and asks for permission to cut a passage through the bar to the sea). Another of Tregeagle's tasks is to make and carry away a truss of sand bound with a rope of sand from Gwenvor (the cove at Whitsand Bay) near the Land's End. But his unquiet spirit finds no rest, for whilst he is trying to do his never-ending work the devil hunts him from place to place, until he hides for refuge in a hermit's ruined chapel on St. Roche's rocks (East Cornwall).

When the sea roars before a storm, people in the Land's End district say "Tregeagle is calling," and often, too, his voice may be heard lamenting around Loe-pool.*

The substance of the following I had from a Penzance man (H. R. C.), to whom I must own I am indebted for much information about Cornish folk-lore. All his life he has in his business mingled with the peasantry of West Cornwall, and, unlike myself, he comes from a long line of Cornishmen.

"You know Gwenvor Sands, in Whitsand Bay, at the Land's

---

* A fuller account of Tregeagle and his wonderful doings may be found in Bottrell's *Traditions, West Cornwall.*

End, and have heard of the unresting spirit of Tregeagle, by whom that spot is haunted. He foretells storms, and calls before the wind reaches home. I have often heard him howling before a westerly hurricane in the still of midnight at my house in Penzance, a distance of ten miles."

Tradition tells that on these sands, many centuries ago, some foreigners landed, and fought a great battle with the inhabitants, under King Arthur, on Vellan-drucher Moor. "Where Madron, Gulval, and Zennor meet, there is a flat stone where Prince Arthur and four British kings dined, and the four kings collected the native Cornish who fought under them at the battle of Vellan-drucher."—(Bottrell.) This was long before the Spaniards (pronounced Spanyers) in 1595 came ashore at the same place from a galley "high by day" (in broad daylight), and burnt Vellan-dreath, a mill close by.

These foreigners are popularly supposed to be red-haired Danes, and they stayed so long "that the birds built in the rigging of their ships." In all the western parishes of Cornwall there has existed time out of mind a great antipathy to certain red-haired families, who are said to be their descendants, and, much to their disgust, they are often hailed as Danes (pronounced Deanes). Indeed this dislike was carried so far that few would allow any members of their families to intermarry with them. In addition to the usual country gossip in the beginning of this century amongst the women of this district whilst knitting at their doors (for the Cornish are famous "knitsters"), or sitting round "breeding" (netting) fishing-nets, they had one never-failing topic of conversation in their fears that the foreigners would land once more on Gwenvor Sands, or at Priest's Cove,* in Pendeen, near St. Just. Who these strangers were to be they were not at all sure, but they knew that the red-haired Danes were to come again, when Vellan-drucher (a water mill-wheel) would once more be worked with blood, and the kings for the last time would dine around the Garrick Zans (Table Mên); and the end of the world would come soon after: for had not Merlin so prophesied more than a thousand years ago? Garrick Zans is

* A monastery existed there, and in 1883 portions of the building were still standing.

the old name for a large flat stone, the Table Mên (pronounced Mayon), at Sennen, near the Land's End, and seven mythical Saxon kings are said to have dined at it when on a visit to Cornwall, A.D. 600. "Around it old folk went nine times daily, from some notion that is was lucky and good against witchcraft."—(Bottrell.)

Off the Land's End is a very striking rock rising out of the sea. It is known as the Irish Lady, from the fact that an Irish vessel was once wrecked on it, and out of all on board one poor lady alone managed to scramble up to the top ; but no boat could get to her, and, exhausted by fatigue, she fell into the water, and was drowned. Her spirit still haunts the spot. This is most probably a fanciful tale, as the rock bears some resemblance to a human figure.

"During a dreadful thunderstorm and hurricane on the 30th January, 1648, the day on which King Charles was beheaded, a large stone figure of a man, called the ' Armed Knight,' which stood in an upright position at the extremity of the Land's End, forty fathoms above the level of the sea, was thrown down. On the same day a ship riding in St. Ives Bay, having on board the king's wardrobe and other furniture belonging to the royal family, bound for France, broke from her moorings, and ran ashore on the rocks of Godrevy Island, where all on board, about sixty persons, were drowned, except one man and a boy."—G. S. Gilbert's *Cornwall.*

The name of Armed Knight has been transferred to another pile of rocks off the Land's End. The "stone figure" thrown down was most probably a natural formation, as one of the rocks there now bears the fanciful name of Dr. Johnson's Head, from a supposed likeness. Other versions of this legend say "that the Armed Knight was only ninety feet high, with an iron spire on its top."

Porthgwarra in olden times was known as Sweethearts' Cove from the following circumstance : The daughter of a well-to-do farmer loved a sailor, who was once one of her father's serving-men. Her parents, especially her mother, disapproved of the match ; and when the young man returned from sea and came to see his sweetheart, he was forbidden the house. The lovers however met, and vowed to be true to each other, Nancy saying, " That she would never marry any other man," and William, " That, dead or alive, he would one day claim her as his bride." He again went to sea, and for a long time no tidings came, neither from nor of him. Poor Nancy grew melancholy, and spent all her days, and sometimes nights, looking out seaward from a spot on the cliff, called then Nancy's Garden, now Hella Point. She gradually became quite mad; and one night fancied she heard her lover tapping at her bed-room window, and calling her to come out to him, saying: "Sleepest thou, sweetheart? Awaken, and come hither, love. My boat awaits us at the cove. Thou must come this night, or never be my bride." She dressed, went to the cove, and was never seen again. Tradition says that the same night William appeared to his father, told him that he had come for his bride, and bade him farewell; and that next day the news arrived of his having been drowned at sea. Bottrell gives this legend under the title of "The Tragedy of Sweet William and Fair Nancy.'

Not far from the parish of St. Levan is a small piece of ground — "Johanna's Garden," which is fuller of weeds than of flowers. The owner of it was one Sunday morning in her garden gathering greens for her dinner, when she saw St. Levan going by to catch some fish for his. He stopped and greeted her, upon which she reproved him for fishing on a Sunday, and asked him what he thought would be his end if he did so. He tried to convince her that it was not worse than picking greens, but she would not listen to reason. At last St. Levan lost patience, and said, "From this time for ever thou shalt be known, if known at all, as the Foolish Johanna, and thy garden shall ever continue to bear, as now, more hemlocks and nettles than leeks and lentils. Mark this! to make thy remembrance the more accursed for all time to come, if any child of thy name be baptised in the waters of Parchapel-well (close at hand) it shall become a fool, like thyself, and bad luck follow it."—Bottrell.

There is a cleft-stone in St. Levan churchyard called St. Levan's stone; but it is said to have been venerated in the days of King Arthur; and Merlin, who once visited these parts with him, uttered this prophecy concerning it:—

> "When, with panniers astride,
> A pack-horse can ride
> Through St. Levan's stone,
> The world will be done."

Unless some earthquake splits it further the world will last thousands of years longer.

On an almost inaccessible granite peak seaward of the pile of rocks known as Castle Treryn (pronounced Treen), once the haunt and meeting-place of witches, on the summit of which is perched the far-famed Cornish logan-rock, is a sharp peak with a hole in it, large enough to insert a hand. At the bottom lay an egg-shaped stone, traditionally called the key of the castle, which, although easily shifted, had for ages defied all attempts at removal. It was said that should any one ever succeed in getting it out, Castle Treryn— in fact the whole cairn—would immediately disappear. It was unfortunately knocked out by the men who replaced the logan-rock, thrown down by Lieutenant Goldsmith. Its position was often altered by heavy seas, and from it the old folk formerly foretold the weather.

In Buryan parish, named after an Irish saint, a king's daughter, who came into Cornwall with some of her companions in the fifth century, is the famous circle of Dawns Myin, or the Merry Maidens, originally consisting of nineteen upright stones. They are nineteen maidens, who for their sin of dancing on a Sunday were all turned into stone. Two mênhirs in a neighbouring field are the pipers, who at the same time suffered the same fate. Of these and other stone circles an old writer says, "No man when counting them can bring the stones twice the same number."

Not far from Buryan, between Sennen and Penzance, is a very solitary weird spot—a disused Quakers' burial-ground. In its lonely neighbourhood is sometimes seen by a privileged few, "high by day," the spirit of a huntsman, followed by his dogs. He is dressed in the hunting costume of bygone ages; he suddenly appears (for neither his horse's hoofs nor his dogs' feet make any sound), jumps over an adjacent hedge, and is as suddenly lost to view. I do not know if tradition has ever connected this huntsman with Wild Harris of Kenegie,* who was killed when hunting by a fall from his horse —it was frightened by a white hare, the spirit of a deserted maiden, which crossed its path. His ghost, in his hunting-dress, appeared

* A gentleman's seat in the parish of Gulval, near Penzance.

standing at the door of his house the night he was buried—the funeral, according to an old custom, had taken place at midnight. For years after he might be met in the vicinity of his home, and he and his boon companions were often heard carousing at nights in a summer-house on the bowling-green. Few then cared to pass Kenegie after dark, for his was said not to be the only spirit that haunted the place. Wild Harris's ghost was finally laid to rest by a famous ghost-laying parson, and put as a task to count the blades of grass nine times in an enclosure on the top of Castle-an-Dinas, an old earth fortification near where he is said to have met his death.* Ghosts only "walk" (appear) in the parish where their bodies were buried.

On the opposite side of Buryan to the Quakers' burial-ground is the parish of Paul (St. Pol-de-Leon). Its church was burnt by the Spaniards in 1595. They landed on a rock, said to have been named after Merlin—Merlin's car, and marched from Paul to Penzance, which they also fired in several places. I am afraid the inhabitants did not make a very bold stand against them; for Merlin had prophesied centuries before—

"That they should land on the rock of Merlin,
Who would burn Paul, Penzance, and Newlyn."

And this caused them to lose courage, and falsify the old proverb:

"Car and Pen, Pol and Tre,
Would make the devil run away."

Close by the highway, where the Buryan road joins the high-road from Paul to Penzance, is a smoothly-cut, conical granite stone, popularly supposed to have been placed there in memory of some woman who was found murdered at that spot, with nothing on to identify her, and with only a thimble and ring in her pocket. It really marks the place where an ancient gold ring, three inches and a half in diameter, bearing the motto, "In hac spe vivo," was discovered in 1781. In the same parish, a short walk from this place,

* There is a small enclosure near the castle, where several members of the family of Hosking were interred, owing to a quarrel that Mr. Hosking had with the vicar of Ludgvan over some tithes. The last funeral took place in 1823. On one of the stones is inscribed, "It is virtue alone that consecrates this ground," and "Custom is the idol of fools."

are some Druidical remains, which have the curious name of
"Kerris roundago." Some stones taken from it to repair Penzance
pier were fatal to the horses who drew them, although they were
young and healthy.

In the adjacent parish of Newlyn, a fishing village, the favourite
resort of artists, a great deal of gossiping on summer evenings goes
on around the small wells (here called peeths), whilst the women
wait patiently for each in turn to fill her earthen pitchers; some of
the most industrious bring their knitting in their pockets with them.
Opposite one of these wells, towering over St. Peter's church, is a
striking pile of rocks, "Tolcarn." On the summit are some curious
markings in the stones, which, when a child, I was told were the
devil's footprints; but the following legend, which I give on the
authority of the Rev. W. S. Lach-Szyrma, Vicar of St. Peter's, is
quite new to me:—

"The summit of the rock is reticulated with curious veins of
elvan, about which a quaint Cornish legend relates that the Bucca-
boo, or storm-god of the old Cornish, once stole the fishermen's
net. Being pursued by Paul choir, who sang the Creed, he flew to
the top of Paul hill and thence over the Coombe to Tolcarn, where
he turned the nets into stone."

We have now reached the town of Penzance, and through its
streets folks of the last generation often heard rumbling at midnight
an old-fashioned coach drawn by headless horses; or saw a procession of coffins slowly wending its way to the churchyard. It
was unlucky to meet this, as death was sure soon to follow, and
tradition speaks of a woman who accidentally struck against one
and died in the same night. A coach with headless horses and
coachman, also just before Christmas, went through the streets of
Penryn; this coachman had the power of spiriting away people who
met and stared at him, unless they turned their heads and averted
the evil by some mystical signs. In Penzance town were many
haunted houses, but space will only allow of my noticing a few.
One in Chapel Street (formerly Our Lady's Street) was tenanted by
the spirit of Mrs. Baines, an eccentric old lady. At the back of her
house was a very fine orchard well stocked with fruit-trees, which

the boys were too fond of visiting. She determined at last that her gardener should watch for them, armed with an old blunderbuss, charged with peas and small shot. She gave him strict orders should he see any one, to say one, two, three, and then fire. He watched two nights, but the boys were too cunning for him, and still the fruit went. On the third, Mrs. Baines, thinking to catch him napping, went herself into the garden and began to shake the apples down from one of the trees. Some say that the man recognised his mistress, and, vexed at her suspecting him, said one, two, three, as quickly as he could utter the words, and fired; others, that he was sleeping, and awakened by the noise she made, shot her by mistake, exclaiming, "I know-ee, you thief, I do; now I'll sarve-ee out, I will." Terrified after he had done the deed, he ran off into the country and there hid himself for some days. The poor old lady was more frightened than hurt, and all the shot were successfully extracted by her doctor; but very soon after this adventure she died. From this time her house and grounds began to have an evil reputation; Mrs. Baines's ghost, dressed in antiquated garb, a quaint lace cap on her powdered hair, lace ruffles hanging from her sleeves, and a short *mode* mantle over her shoulders, was often seen walking in the gardens or standing under an apple-tree, leaning on the gold-headed cane she always carried. Indoors, too, her high-heeled shoes were plainly heard night after night tapping on the floors as she paced up and down the rooms, which noise was often varied by the whirring of her spinning-wheel. For some time the house was unoccupied, now it is divided into two, and the ghost has been laid to rest. But long after Mrs. Baines ceased to appear her wheel was heard. At last it was discovered that some leather, which had been nailed around a door to keep out draughts, was loose in places, and that the whistling of the wind through this made the peculiar sound. Mr. Bottrell says "that her spirit was laid by a parson, whose name he thinks was Singleton, and he succeeded in getting her away to the Western Green (west of Penzance), which was then spread over many acres of land, where the waves now roll.* Here this powerful

* The Penzance Promenade is built on part of it. In my childhood it was said to be one of the resorts of "Spring-heeled Jack," of whom I then lived in mortal dread.

parson single-handed bound her to spin from the banks, ropes of sand for the term of a thousand years, unless she, before that time, spun a sufficiently long and strong one to reach from St. Michael's Mount to St. Clement's Isle (across the bay)." About a stone's throw from Mrs. Baines's house, on an eminence above Quay street, stood in her days Penzance Chapel of Ease (for Penzance was then in Madron parish), called our Lady's or St. Mary's Chapel. On the same site was built, in 1835, the present parish church of St. Mary's. Here, in the memory of a few who still survive, a gentleman in the early part of this century did penance, and afterwards walked from thence through the streets to his house, wrapped in a sheet, with a lighted taper in his hand. It was usual then, as now, for the Mayor and Corporation of Penzance, with the mace-bearers and constables, to go once a month in state to church. Before the reading of the first lesson the mace-bearers left, and visited the public-houses, in order to see that they were shut during service time. When the sermon began they came back and returned to their seats in order to be in readiness to escort the Mayor home. Quay street was once the most fashionable part of Penzance, but the large houses are now divided into smaller tenements ; in some of them bits of finely-moulded ceilings, &c., still exist. One of the houses reputed to have been haunted was torn down in 1813, when the skeleton of a man was found built into a wall. It was, of course, put down to be the sailor's whose spirit was so often seen there, and who (tradition said) had been murdered in that house for the sake of his money. It was well known that he had brought back great riches from foreign parts. There is a myth that Sir Walter Raleigh landed at Penzance Quay when he returned from Virginia, and on it smoked the first tobacco ever seen in England, but for this statement I believe there is not the slightest foundation. Several western ports, both in Devon and Cornwall, make the same boast.

It is a fact, however, that the news of Nelson's death was first heard here. It was brought into the port by two fishermen, who had it from the crew of a passing vessel. A small company of strolling actors were playing that night at the little theatre then standing over

M

some stables in Chapel street, and the play was stopped for a few moments whilst one of the actors told the audience.

Another haunted house, at the opposite side of Penzance, is cele- brated in a poem called "The Petition of an Old Uninhabited House," written and published in 1811, by the Rev. C. V. Le Grice, who was then Vicar of Madron. He was a friend of Charles Lamb, who mentions him in his "Essay on Christ's Hospital." About this house a lady once told me a strange story, that I will relate. Forty years ago, she, a perfect stranger to the place, never having been in Penzance before, came to it with her husband and her first child, for she was then a young wife. As they meant to settle in the town, they went to this hotel, where they intended staying until they could get a suitable house. On the evening of their arrival, her husband having gone out, she sat alone before the fire nursing her child, when she suddenly saw a little old man, in a very old-fashioned dress, come into the room. He sat down in a chair near her, looked steadfastly into the fire, and, after some time, without saying a word, he rose and left. On her husband's return, she told him of her queer visitor. The next morning they made enquiries about him, and found that the hotel had been built on the site of the old uninhabited house; that nearly the whole of it had been destroyed, but a few of the best rooms remained; and that they were in a haunted chamber. She declared that she could never sleep there another night, and, temporarily, they engaged some furnished lodgings. These old rooms are now pulled down and billiard and other rooms cover the place where they stood.

Outside the boundary-stone, west of Penzance, stands, in its own grounds, a house to which additions have been made by many succeeding generations. Tradition, of course, gave it a ghost. With the other members of my family I lived there for several years, but none of us ever saw it. I am bound, however, to state that we never slept in the haunted chamber. For a short period it was occupied by a groom, who one morning came to me with a very long face, and said he dared not sleep there any more, for some mysterious being came night after night, and pulled all the bed-clothes off him; rather than do so, he would sleep in the harness-room.

Still further west of Penzance is a much larger house, to which, like the former, many additions have been made. And up its avenue, after dark, a carriage may be often heard slowly making its way until it reaches the hall-door, where it stops. In this house, about sixty years ago, lived, in very great style, a gentleman, who was a regular autocrat, and of him one of his old servants related to me this anecdote, which is curious as an illustration of the manners of those times. When in his employ, he gave an answer to some question, which afterwards his master discovered to be an untruth. The next Sunday he made him, as the congregation came out, stand at Madron church door, by a tombstone covered with loaves of bread. Of these, he had to give one to each poor person that passed, and say, in an audible tone, " I, William ——, last week told my master a lie."

Mr. G. B. Millett, in his *Penzance Past and Present*, gives a tale well known in this district, about the drinking habits of our ancestors, which, as I am now on the subject of manners, I will quote.

" A particular gentleman, not far from Penzance, loved good liquor, and one evening had gathered some of his jovial companions together, determined to make a night of it. His wife, having had some experience of such gatherings before, with wise precaution, saw as much wine taken out of the cellar as she thought would be good for her husband and his friends. Then, safely locking the strong oak door, she put the key in her pocket, and announced her intention of spending the evening with some lady friends. The hours were passing pleasantly away, and, with a smile of inward satisfaction, she was congratulating herself upon the success of her forethought, when a heavy stumbling noise was heard upon the stairs, and shortly afterwards two burly footmen staggered into the room, groaning under the weight of a ponderous cellar door, with its posts and lintel, which had been sent by their master for the mistress to unlock."

The manor of Conerton, which at one time nearly included the whole of West Penwith, had many privileges in Penzance. Before the days of county courts the lord held a monthly court here for the trial of small cases not criminal. Its prison, a wretched place (visited by Howard), no longer exists, but people were confined there early in this century—sometimes for long periods. I was once shown a beautiful patchwork quilt made by a poor woman, who had been imprisoned for debt.

Until within the last fifty years every butcher in Penzance market had to pay to the bailiff of this manor at Christmas a marrow-bone or a shilling. The first butcher who refused to pay it also defied one of the bye-laws of the market that compelled them to wear white sleeves over their blue blouses. He was brought before the magistrates, and declared "that he would be incarcerated before he would do it." The following is a favourite story handed down amongst the butchers from father to son. A solicitor in Penzance had a very large dog that was in the habit of coming into their market and stealing joints of meat from the stalls. One day one of them went to the lawyer, and said,—"Please sir, could I sue the owner of a dog for a leg of mutton stolen from my stall ?" "Certainly, my good man." "Then, please sir, the dog is yours, and the price of the mutton is 4s. 6d." The money was paid, and the man was going away in triumph, when he was called back by these words : "Stay a moment, my good man, a lawyer's consultation is 6s. 8d., you owe me the difference:" which sum the discomfited butcher had to pay.

Every stream in Cornwall however small is called a river (pro-nounced revvur). One flows into the sea west of Penzance, between it and Newlyn, known as Laregan, and another at the east in Gulval parish, as Ponsandane river. There is an old rhyme about them that runs thus :

> " When Ponsandane calls to Laregan river,
> There will be fine weather.
> But we may look for rain
> When Laregan calls to Ponsandane."

Years ago there was a marsh between Penzance and Newlyn, now covered by the sea, known to the old people as the " Clodgy ; " when the sea moaned there they said, " Clodgy is calling for rain."

Sometimes at the present day it is "Bucca" is calling, Bucca being the nickname in Penzance for the inhabitants of Newlyn.

> " Penzance boys up in a tree,
> Looking as wisht (weak, downcast) as wisht can be ;
> Newlyn ' Buccas,' strong as oak,
> Knocking them down at every poke."

The weather at Mount's Bay is also foretold by the look of the Lizard land, which lies south :

> " When the Lizard is clear, rain is near."

The marsh on Marazion Green still exists, and not many years ago no one cared to cross it after nightfall, especially on horseback, for at a certain spot close by the marsh a white lady was sure to arise from the ground, jump on the rider's saddle, and, like the "White Lady of Avenel," ride with him pillion-fashion as far as the Red river* that runs into the sea just below the smelting-works at Chyandour, a suburb of Penzance. The last person who saw her was a tailor of this town, who died in 1840. He was commonly called "Buck Billy," from his wearing till the day of his death a pigtail, a buff waistcoat, and a blue coat with yellow buttons.

Marazion, or Market-jew, which latter is a corruption of its old Cornish name, Marghaisewe, meaning a Thursday's market, is a small town exactly opposite St. Michael's Mount. Until its present church was built its mayor sat in a very high seat with his back against a window. This is the origin of the Cornish proverb: "In your own light, like the mayor of Market-jew." This mayor is jokingly said to have three privileges. The first is, "That he may sit in his own light;" the second, "Next to the parson;" and the third, "If he see a pig in a gutter he may turn it out and take its place."†

In the churchyard of the neighbouring parish of St. Hilary is a monument to the Rev. John Penneck, M.A., who, in the early part of the last century, was Chancellor of Exeter Cathedral. His ghost is very eccentric, sometimes getting into a passion, and on these occasions raising a great storm of wind.

---

* A small stream coloured by running through tin mining works.

† Marazion is no longer a Corporate town.

In the parish of Breage, near the sea, about four miles from Marazion, are the ruins of Pengersick Castle, of which only some fragments of walls and a square tower now stand. Some of the upper rooms in the latter have fallen in, and they are all in a state of decay. The lower have oak-panels curiously carved and painted, but time has almost effaced the designs. The most perfect is one representing " Perseverance," under which are the following lines :

> " What thing is harder than the rock ?
> What softer is than water cleere ?
> Yet wyll the same, with often droppe,
> The hard rock perce as doth a spere.
> Even so, nothing so hard to attayne,
> But may be hadde, with labour and payne."

So many are the legends told of the former inhabitants of Pengersick, that it would be almost impossible at this date to decide which is the original. These ruins stand on the site of a much older castle, and in it dwelt, far back in the dark ages, a very wicked man, who, when he was fighting in foreign parts, forgetting his wife at home, courted a king's daughter, who gave him a magic sword, which ensured in every battle the victory to its owner. He deceived and left her ; but she, with her son in her arms, followed him to his home by the Mount. There she met him, and upbraided him with his cruelty, and in a fit of passion he threw them both into the sea. The lady was drowned, and after her death she was changed into a white hare, which continually haunted the old lord ; but her boy was picked up alive by a passing ship. The lord's wife afterwards died, and he married again a woman as bad as himself, reputed to be a witch, who was very cruel to her step-son, who lived with his father at the castle. One night there was a great storm in Mount's Bay, and the young man went down to the shore to see if there were any vessels in distress, and spied on the beach an almost exhausted sailor, who had been washed in by the waves, and whom he bade his servants carry to his home, and put into his own bed. When he revived, all were struck by the marvellous resemblance to the young heir ; and they conceived a great affection for each other. Together they went to Marazion to see if they could find the vessel from whose deck the stranger had fallen into the sea. It was safe in harbour, and the captain, whom the sailor had always thought to be his father, told him then for the first time, "How, when he was an infant, he had rescued him from drowning where last night he had nearly lost his life." Thus they were discovered to be brothers, and a day or two after, when out hunting, guided by the white hare, they accidentally came upon the miraculous sword that had disappeared when his mother was drowned. Then these two brothers sailed away from Cornwall, and dwelt in peace in the land of a strange princess; where the Cornishman studied, under a celebrated master, astrology and all other occult sciences. After some time the old lord of Pengersick met his death in this wise: As he was riding out one fine morning, the white hare suddenly sprang up in front of his horse and startled it, so that it ran madly with its rider into the sea, where both were swallowed up. When this news was brought to him, the Cornishman bade his brother an affectionate farewell, and, with his wife, a learned princess, went back to Pengersick, where they lived happily for several generations, for amongst many other wonderful things, the young lord had discovered an elixir of life which, had they so wished, would have kept them alive to the present day. (*See* Bottrell.)

In addition to being well versed in occult lore, Pengersick's wife was a fine musician; she could with her harp charm and subdue evil spirits, and compel the fish in Mount's Bay, also the mermaids who then dwelt there, to come out of the sea.

Another account of the old lord's death says that he and a party of his friends were dining in his yacht around a silver table when she went down, and all on board perished. This happened off Cudden Point, which juts into the sea just opposite Pengersick. Children living there formerly used to go down to the beach at low water to try and find this silver table. (A ship laden with bullion is reported to have been lost here in the time of Queen Elizabeth.) "The present castle," one tradition says, "was built in the reign of Henry VIII. by a merchant who had acquired immense wealth beyond the seas, and who loaded an ass with gold, and broke its back. He sold the castle to a Mr. Milliton, who, having slain a man, shut himself up in it to escape punishment."

Another legend says that Sir William Milliton built it, and, soon after its completion, married a very rich but extremely ugly and shrewish woman, of whom he tried by various ways to rid himself but in vain. One day, after a desperate quarrel, he begged her forgiveness, and asked her, in proof of having pardoned him, to sup with him that evening in a room overlooking the sea. She agreed; and at the conclusion of the feast they pledged each other in goblets of rich wine. Then Sir William's looks altered, and, in a fierce voice, he said, "Woman, now prepare for death! You have but a short time to live, as the wine that you have just drunk was poisoned." "Then we die together," she answered, "for I had my suspicions, and mixed the contents of the goblets." Up to this time the moon, which was at its full, had been shining brightly through the open windows, for it was a warm summer night, when suddenly a frightful storm of thunder and lightning arose, the winds lashed the waves to fury, and the moon was darkened. The servants, alarmed by this, and the unearthly fiendish yells that came from the banqueting hall, rushed upstairs, and there found the bodies of their master and mistress dead on the floor; and through the open window they saw, by the light of the moon which for a moment shone through a rift in the clouds, their souls borne away on the wings of a demon in the shape of a bird.

The original name of Breage parish was Pembro; but St. Breaca, hearing that the inhabitants were at a loss to raise the money for a peal of bells, offered to extricate them from their difficulty on condition that they should call the parish after her. The condition was accepted, the bells were hung, and the parish henceforth was known as that of St. Breage.—Through Rev. S. Rundle.

St. Germoe (Geronicus) an Irish king, who was converted to Christianity in the fifth century, is said to have been the foster-son of Breaca (or Breage), with whom he crossed over into Cornwall where they settled. Two churches in adjoining parishes are dedicated to them; St. Germoe is reputed to have been the founder of his, and there is a curious structure at the north-east of the churchyard, known as St. Germoe's chair or King Germoe's throne.

"There is more than one story attached to this chair. One is to the effect that the saint sat in the central chair with two assessors, one on either side of him; another legend is that the priests rested in the chair; whilst a third is that pilgrims to the tomb of the saint also rested therein. Be that as it may, however, it is possible that this is a shrine, and that the body of St. Germoe rests underneath it."—Rev. W. A. Osborne, *Transactions Penzance Natural History Society, 1886, 1887.*

At Great Work Mine (Huel Vor) near by, a narrow level (not far down) is still thought to have been made by Christian slaves, when the first church at Germoe was built.

> " Germoe, little Germoe lies under a hill,
>   When I'm in Germoe I count myself well ;
>   True love's in Germoe, in Breage I've got none,
>   When I'm in Germoe I count myself at home."—
>
> Through Rev. S. Rundle.

All Cornishmen at one time were supposed to be "wreckers," and from the peninsular-shape of their county came the proverb, "'Tis a bad wind that blows no good to Cornwall." But the dwellers in Breage and Germoe must in olden times, from the following distich, have been held in worse repute than their neighbours :

> " God keep us from rocks and shelving sands,
>   And save us from Breage and Germoe men's hands."

The most noted and daring Cornish smuggler of the last century, Coppinger, a Dane, lived on the north coast, and of him a legendary catalogue of dreadful tales is told, all to be found in the Rev. R. S. Hawker's book, the *Footprints of Former Men in Far Cornwall.* He lays the scene of his exploits in the neighbourhood of Hartland Bay, my informant near Newquay. He swam ashore here in the prime of life, in the middle of a frightful storm, from a foreign-rigged vessel that was seen in the offing, and of which nothing more was ever heard or known. Wrapped in a cloak, that tradition says he tore from off the shoulders of an old woman who was on the beach, he jumped up behind a farmer's daughter, who had ridden down to see the wreck, and was by her taken to her father's house, where he was fed, clothed, and most hospitably received. He was a fine, handsome, well-built man, and gave himself out to be most highly connected in his own country. He soon won the young woman's affections, and at her father's death, which took place not long after, he easily induced her to marry him; but it was far from a happy union. Luckily they had but one child—a deaf and dumb idiot, who had inherited his father's cruel disposition, and delighted in torturing all living things. It is even said that he cunningly killed one of his young playmates. Coppinger, after his marriage, organized a band of smugglers, and made himself their captain; and quickly through his misdeeds earned the title of cruel Coppinger. One legend relates that he once led a Revenue cutter into a dangerous cove, of which he alone knew the soundings, and that he and his crew came out of it in safety, but the other vessel with all on board perished. Mr. Hawker calls Coppinger's ship the "Black Prince," and says he had it built for himself in Denmark, and that men who had made themselves in any way obnoxious to him on land were carried on board her, and compelled by fearful oaths to enrol themselves in her crew.

In 1835 an old man of the age of ninety-seven related to this writer that when a youth he had been so abducted, and after two years' service he had been ransomed by his friends with a large sum. "And all," said the old man, very simply, "because I happened to see one man kill another, and they thought I should mention it." The same author gives him a wonderfully fleet horse, which no one but Coppinger could master, and says that on its back he made more than one hairbreadth escape. He has also a marvellous account of his end, in which he disappears as he came, in a vessel which he boarded in a storm of thunder, lightning, and hail. As soon as he was in her, "she was out of sight in a moment, like a spectre or a ghost." For this he quotes the following verse :—

> " Will you hear of the cruel Coppinger ?
> He came from a foreign kind ;
> He was brought to us from the salt water,
> He was carried away by the wind."

The one thing certain about him is, that at one time he amassed money enough by smuggling to buy a small freehold estate near the sea, the title-deeds of which, signed with his name, still exist. But in his old age, I have been told, he was reduced to poverty, and subsisted on charity.

That in those bygone days smuggling was thought no sin every one knows. And who has not heard the oft-quoted apocryphal anecdote of the Cornish clergyman, who—when he was in the middle of his sermon and some one opened the church door and shouted in, "A wreck! a wreck!"—begged his parishioners to wait whilst he took off his gown that they might all start fair.

The following is, however, a genuine letter of the last century from a vicar in the eastern part of the county to a noted smuggler of that district :—

> " Martin Rowe, you very well know,
> That Cubert's vicar loves good liquor,
> One bottle's all, upon my soul.
> You'll do right to come to-night ;
> My wife's the banker, she'll pay for the anker."

To the same jovial vicar is credited this grace, given to his hostess' horror at her table after he had dined out several days in succession, and had rabbits offered him, a dish he detested :—

> " Of rabbits young and rabbits old,
> Of rabbits hot and rabbits cold,
> Of rabbits tender, rabbits tough,
> I thank the Lord we've had enough."

Inland from Breage is the small hamlet of Leed's-town (called after the Duke of Leeds, who has property in Cornwall). It is the seat of the following short story :—" The Leed's-town ghost runs up and down stairs in a house during the night, and then sits in a corner of the room weeping and sleeking her hair. It is the ghost of a young woman who was engaged to be married to a man who refused to become her husband until she gave him certain deeds kept in a box in the above room. As soon as the deeds were in his possession, he realised the property and escaped to America, leaving the luckless girl to bemoan her loss. She went mad: night and day she was searching for her deeds; sometimes she would sit and wail in the spot where the box had been. At length she died: her spirit, however, had no rest, and still constantly returns to keep alive the memory of man's perfidy."— Through Rev. S. Rundle.

Close to Leed's-town, at the foot of Godolphin-hill, is the old house, or hall, of Godolphin. The basement-floor of the original house alone remains: it consists of a long façade supported by pillars of white granite, the interior containing many objects of interest well worth a visit. Opposite the inhabited part of the house is the King's room, opening on the King's garden. (The title of King's room was given to it from the legend that Charles II. once slept there.) You could leave it by five ways; as there were three doors, one exit through the floor, and another through the roof. Godolphin is held by a very curious tenure, said to have originated in a bet between the representatives of the Godolphin and St. Aubyn families on a snail race. As the Godolphin snail was being beaten, its owner pricked it with a pin to make it go faster, but it drew in its horns and refused to move, consequently the other won. The following is the ceremony which takes place every Candlemas. Before sunrise a person, appointed as reeve by the Rev. St. Aubyn Molesworth St. Aubyn, the lord of the manor of Lamburn, in the parish of Perranzabuloe (near Truro), knocks at the ancient outer door of the quadrangle, aud repeats this demand thrice:—"Oyez! Oyez! Oyez! Here come I the reeve of the manor of Lamburn, to demand my lord's dues, eight groats and a penny in money, a loaf, a cheese, a collar of brawn, and a jack of the best ale in the house. God save the Queen and the lord of the manor." It is said at the outer door of the quadrangle, at the inner door, and for the third and last time at the table in the kitchen (which is one of the oldest and not the least interesting rooms). The above high lordship is paid by the Duke of Leeds to the St. Aubyn family, to whom should they fail an heir the estate reverts. There is another curious tenure in this part of Cornwall, which as I am on the subject I will, before proceeding further, quote. " The parsonage of St. Grade, with a small portion of land, including an orchard, is held of the manor of Erisey by the following tenure, viz., that on Easter-day, yearly, the parson provide a dinner for the master and mistress of Erisey house, and their man and maid, with a pan of milk for a greyhound bitch."—Lake, *Helston and Lizard*.

The old manor-house of Erisey is in Ruan Major (near the Lizard), and of one of the family the following story is told :— " He was dancing with other ladies and gentlemen at Whitehall before James I., and, through the violent motion and action of his body in the middle of the dance, had his cap slip from his head and fall to the ground ; but he instantly with his foot tossed it on his head again, and proceeded without let or hindrance with his part in that dance, to the admiration of all who saw it, which gave occasion to King James to enquire who that active gentleman was, and being told that his name was Erisey, he forthwith replied, 'I like the gentleman very well, but not his name of Heresey!'" The rector of Ruan Minor by ancient usage and prescription (which is always admitted) claims a right of sending a horse into a certain field in the parish of Landewednack, whenever it is cropped with corn, and taking away as many sheaves as the horse can carry away on its back.

"At Jew's Lane Hill, near Godolphin, a Jew is said to have hung himself on a tree still pointed out, and was buried beneath the road. His ghost appears in the shape of a bull and a fiery chariot. This superstition has been known for generations."— M. H., through Rev. S. Rundle.

CORNWALL STONE.

"I remember this stone a rough cube about three feet in height; it stood by the wayside forty or fifty years ago about a quarter of a mile from the old Godolphin mansion near the coast, where the nobility and gentry of the county were wont periodically to assemble to hear the news from Court. The servants who waited on their masters at the banquet diligently listened to the conversation, and afterwards spread the information thus collected among the crowd assembled for the purpose around Cornwall stone."—G. F. W., *Western Antiquary, 1881.*

An old writer on the Scilly Isles mentions a rock on Bryher, one of the smallest of the islands, where the neighbours were wont to collect to hear and repeat the news. He calls it the News Rock.

Between Helston and the Lizard lies the parish of St. Keverne ; unlike the other parishes of Cornwall it contains no mines. To account for this it is said that St. Keverne cursed it when he lived there, for the want of respect shown him by its inhabitants. Hence the proverb " No metal will run within the sound of St. Keverne's bells."

St. Just, from the Land's End district, once paid a visit to St. Keverne, who entertained him for several days to the best of his power. After his departure his host missed some valuable relics, and determined to go in pursuit of his late guest, and try, if possible, to get them from him. As he was passing over Crousadown, about two miles from St. Keverne church, he pocketed three large stones, each weighing about a quarter of a ton, to use if St. Just should offer any resistance. He overtook him at a short distance from Breage and taxed him with the theft, which was indignantly denied. From words the saints came to blows, and St. Keverne flung his stones with such effect that St. Just ran off, throwing down the relics as he ran. These stones lay for centuries where they fell, about four hundred yards from Pengersick Lane, as when taken away by day, they were in bygone times always brought back at night.

Going along the coast from Breage to the Lizard the solitary church of Gunwalloe is passed, built so close to the sea that the waves wash its graveyard walls. It is said to have been erected as a thank-offering by some man who escaped drowning when shipwrecked. "In the sandbanks near it (or, as others say, at

Kennack cove), the notorious buccaneer Avery is reported to have buried several chests of treasure previously to his leaving England on the voyage from which he never returned. So strongly did this opinion prevail that Mr. John Knill, collector of the Customs at St. Ives, procured about the year 1770 a grant of treasure trove, and expended some money in a fruitless search."—Rev. C. A. Johns, *Week at the Lizard.*

Near by is Mullion parish, of which the celebrated ghost-layer, the Rev. Thomas Flavel, who died in 1682, was the vicar, and the following quaint lines to his memory may still be read in the chancel of his church:—

> " Earth take thine earth, my sin let Satan havet,
> The world my goods, my soul my God who gavet ;
> For from these four, Earth, Satan, World, and God,
> My flesh, my sin, my goods, my soul I had."

Of him the Rev. C. A. Johns writes:—" This Thomas Flavel, during his life, attained great celebrity for his skill in the questionable art of laying ghosts. His fame still lingers in the memories of the more superstitious of the inhabitants through the following ridiculous stories. On one occasion when he had gone to church his servant-girl opened a book in his study, whereupon a host of spirits sprang up all round her. Her master observed this, though then occupied at church, closed his book, and dismissed the congregation. On his return home he took up the book with which his servant had been meddling, and read backwards the passage which she had been reading, at the same time laying about him lustily with his walking-cane, whereupon all the spirits took their departure, but not before they had pinched the servant-girl black and blue. His celebrity, it seems, was not confined to his own parish, for he was once called on to lay a very troublesome ghost in an adjoining parish. As he demanded the large fee of five guineas for his services, two of the persons interested resolved to assure themselves, by the evidence of their own eyes, that the ceremony was duly performed. They accordingly, without apprising one another of their intention, secreted themselves behind two graves in the churchyard a short time before the hour named for the absurd rites. In due time the ghost-layer entered it with a book in one hand and a horsewhip in the other. On the first smack of the whip the watchers raised their heads simultaneously, caught a glimpse of each other, and were both so terrified that they scampered off in opposite directions, leaving the operator to finish his business as he might. So popular are superstitions of this kind, and so long do they linger, that to the present day a spot is pointed out on the downs, named 'Hervan Gutter,' where Thomas Flavel's own ghost was laid by a clergyman, of whom he said before his death, 'When he comes I must go.' In olden days there were several of these ghost-laying clergymen in Cornwall, of whom, before going on with the legends of the parishes, I will mention three known in folk-lore. In the parish of Ladock, on the east side of Truro, dwelt rather more than a century ago the famed ghost-layer, the Rev. Mr. Woods, who, when walking, usually carried an ebony stick with a silver head, on which was engraved a pentacle, and on a broad silver ring below planetary signs and mystical figures. Of him Mr. Bottrell tells many thrilling tales; I will only give the substance of one. Mr. Woods was usually a match for most demons, whom he would change into animals and thrash with his whip; but one more cunning than the rest defied him, by taking the shape of an unknown coal-black bird, and perching on the church tower, from whence during divine service he made all sorts of queer noises, disturbing the congregation, and inciting the irreverent to laughter. He was too high up to be exorcised or reached with the whip. At last the clergyman, at his wit's end, remembered that the Evil One could not endure the sight of innocent children, and he sent his clerk round to all the mothers of his parish who had unchristened children, asking them to bring them to church on the next Sunday to have the rite performed. As he was a great favourite with his people all the mothers, and they were eight, readily agreed to come. But as twelve is the mystical number he invited four other mothers whose children had recently been baptised, to come as well, and bring their children and sponsors with them. The eight children were christened, and the parson walked out of church followed by the twelve mothers with their infants in their arms. The clerk arranged them in lines five deep, the mothers in front, opposite the belfry door. Mr. Woods directed each to pass her child from one to the other of its sponsors, and then hand it to him that he might hold it up for the demon to see; but for some time the cunning bird hid himself behind a pinnacle, and nothing would induce him to look, until one of the children, growing tired, began to cry, and all the others chimed in, screaming in chorus at the top of their voices. Then the demon hopped down from his perch and peered over the parapet to try and find out what could be the matter. The sight of the twelve children had such an effect upon him that he too gave an unearthly yell and flew away never to re-appear. The church bells were soon after put in order, and it is well known that no evil spirit ever ventures within sound of their ringing."

"One of the three Jagos, who were Vicars of Wendron, was much renowned for his powers of necromancy. He was in the habit of taking people to St. Wendron Cross, where a man called Tucker was buried, and asking them whether they had a mind to see Tucker man; he would make him rise from the dead as a mark of delicate attention to them."—*Cornubiana*, Rev. S. Rundle, *Penzance Natural History Society*, 1885-1886.

I will close this list of worthies by a short notice of Parson Dodge, a vicar of Talland, a village on the south coast of Cornwall, and then give an encounter of the famous Nonconformist divine, John Wesley, with some spirits whom he vanquished at St. Agnes on the north. The church of Talland is not in the centre of the parish, but near the sea; a legend accounts for its position thus: It was begun at a spot called Pulpit, but each night a voice was heard saying:

"If you will my wish fulfil,
Build the church on Talland hill;"

and the stones put up by day were removed. (Tales similar to this are told of many Cornish churches. The work of removal is sometimes carried on by the devil; at Altarnon he was accompanied

by a hare and.a deer.) Of this church, about a hundred and fifty
years ago, the Rev. Richard Dodge was vicar.   He had such
command over the spirit-world that he could raise and lay ghosts
at his will, and by a nod of his head banish them to the Red
Sea.   His parishioners looked up to him with great awe, and
were afraid of meeting him at midnight, as he was sure then,
whip in hand, to be pursuing and driving away the demons, that
in all kinds of shapes were to be seen hovering around him.
Amongst his other eccentricities he was fond of frequenting his
churchyard at the dead of night.   Parson Dodge's fame was not
confined to his own immediate district, and one day he received
a letter from a fellow-clergyman, the Rev. Grylls, rector of
Lanreath, asking his assistance in exorcising a man habited in
black, who drove a sable coach, drawn by headless horses, across
Black-a-down (a neighbouring moor), as this apparition, when
they happened to meet it, frightened his people almost out of their
wits.   He acceded to this request, and late at night the two clergymen rode to the spot, where they waited for some time, but seeing
nothing decided to separate and return to their respective homes.
Mr. Dodge, however, had not gone very far when his horse
obstinately refused to proceed a step further in a homeward
direction : this he interpreted to be a sign from heaven which he
must obey, and giving it the rein he allowed it to go as it
willed.   It wheeled round and went back at a great pace to the
moor.   Here through the gloom he saw standing the black coach
with the headless horses: its driver had dismounted, and the
Rev. Grylls lay in a swoon at his feet.   Mr. Dodge was terribly
alarmed, but managed to keep his presence of mind, and began
to recite a prayer: before he could finish it the driver said—
"Dodge is come! I must be gone!" jumped on to his seat and
disappeared for ever. Mr. Grylls' parishioners now arrived in
search of their rector; they knew there must be something amiss,
for his horse, startled by the horrible spectres, had thrown its
rider and galloped off, never stopping until it reached its stable
(his friend's, through fright, had also been, until the apparition
vanished, almost unmanageable). They found him senseless, sup-

ported in Mr. Dodge's arms; but he soon revived, and they took him home, although it was some days before his reason recovered from the shock. A much fuller account of this may be found in the *History of Polperro*, by Mr. T. Q. Couch. It has also been published by Mr. Robert Hunt in his *Popular Romances of the West of England*. The Rev. R. S. Hawker, in his *Footprints of Former Men in Far Cornwall*, gives some very interesting extracts from the "Diurnal" of one Parson Rudall, of Launceston, who in 1665, with the sanction of his Bishop, laid the Botathen ghost—the spirit of a young woman by name Dorothy Dinglet, who could not rest in her grave—"Unquiet because of a certain sin." It is a very well-known fact that the Rev. John Wesley was a firm believer in supernatural agencies; he compiled a book of ghost-stories, that was lent to me when I was about ten years old by a kind but ignorant woman, the reading of which caused me many sleepless nights. "On one occasion Wesley could, when at St. Agnes, find no place to pass the night save a house which had the reputation of being haunted. However, he was not deterred; he entered and went to bed. But he could not rest, for there was a terrible tumult below; the sound of carriages was heard, the noise of feet, and fearful oaths. At length he could bear it no longer; he descended, and then found the large hall filled with guests. They greeted him with loud welcome, and begged him to be seated. He consented, saying, however, that he must say grace first. This remark was hailed with roars of laughter. Nothing daunted he began—"Jesus, the Name high over all." He did not finish; in a moment the lights were extinguished, he was alone, and from that time the house was no more haunted.—Through Rev. S. Rundle.

Clergymen in Cornwall are still supposed to be able to drive out evil spirits. A poor, half-crazed woman, yet living in Madron parish, near Penzance, went about ten years since to the house of a clergyman then residing there, and asked him to walk around her, reading some passages from the Bible, to exorcise the ghost of her dead sister, who had entered into her, she said, and tormented her in the shape of a small fly, which continually buzzed in her ear. Once before the Board of Guardians she talked sensibly for some time, then suddenly stopped and exclaimed, shaking her head: "Be quiet, you brute! don't you see I am talking to the gentlemen ? "

We must now, after this long digression, return to Mullion. Between it and the Lizard is a fine headland, the Rill, and on its summit are a number of loose, rough stones, known as the Apron String, which the country people say were brought here by an evil spirit, who intended to build with them a bridge across to France for the convenience of smugglers. He was hastening along with his load, which he carried in his apron, when one of its strings broke, and in despair he gave up the idea. On the opposite side of the Lizard, at the mouth of Helford river, stands the church of St. Anthony in Meneage; like that of Gunwalloe it is little above the level of the sea, and is, also according to tradition, a votive offering. Some people of high rank, crossing over from Normandy to England, were caught in a storm, and in their peril vowed to St. Anthony that they would build a church in his honour if he would bring them safe into harbour. The saint heard their prayers, and the church was erected on the spot where they landed. Helford river, in Carew's days, was the haunt of pirates, and of it he says: "Falmouth's ower neere neighbour-hood lesseneth his vse and darkeneth his reputation, as quitting it onely to the worst sort of Seafarers, I mean Pirats, whose guilty breasts with an eye in their backs, looke warily how they may goe out, ere they will aduenture to enter, and this at un-fortified Hailford cannot be controlled, in which regard it not vnproperly brooketh his common term of Helford and the nickname of Stealford."

On the subject of pirates a friend writes:—"The popular play of 'The Pirates of Penzance' had not its origin in that town, but in the little fishing village of Penberth, near the Land's End; but that, alas! is in its 'custom port.' The captain of the pirate vessel, and all his ship's crew, were wrestlers. They would go out to the small Spanish, Dutch, and other merchant ships, and would ask for provisions, or tender assistance, and on making sure that the ship was unarmed they would overpower the sailors and plunder it. This was before the time when the Trinity Corporation had begun its work on our Cornish coast.

From Helford we will proceed to Penryn—the scene of Lillo's play, "Fatal Curiosity." The legend on which it is founded is as follows: A gentleman who had rashly squandered his own and his wife's fortune, sent their only son early into the world to seek his. During his absence his parents were reduced to penury; but he prospered, returned home, and sought them out. He did not at first disclose to them who he was, intending to do so later on, but begged to be allowed to rest in their house, and whilst he was sleeping asked his mother to take charge of a casket for him. Her curiosity impelled her to open it, and her avarice was so inflamed at the sight of the rich jewels it contained that she incited her husband by prayers and reproaches to murder the poor young man. After the fatal deed was done, the unhappy pair discovered him to be their son.

It has been said that a party of Spaniards landed at Penryn in 1565, intending to plunder the town, but were alarmed by the sound of a drum beaten by some strolling players, and made a hasty retreat.

Before the year 1600 there were only a few houses where Falmouth now stands, called Pennycomequick, which name tradition declares was given it from the following: A woman, who had been a servant to a Mr. Pendarves, left his employ, and went there to reside, where, I suppose, she kept an ale-house, as the story says that he ordered her to brew a cask of ale, and on a certain day he and some friends would come and drink it. The ale was brewed; but in the meantime a Dutch vessel put into the creek, and she sold it all to the sailors. When her former master and his friends arrived at the appointed time, he was of course very angry. Her excuse was that the "penny comed so quick" that she could not refuse it. The name really means the head of the valley of the creek.

There is a pyramidal monument at the south end of Falmouth erected by one of the Killigrews to the memory of Sir Walter

Raleigh, who had been entertained by an ancestor at their family-seat of Arwenack, when there was only one other house in the place. There is a red stain on it, "A blood-mark," the old people said, "that would not wash out, splashed there from the body of a man employed in making it, who fell from its top and was killed."

On the coast just outside the town is Gyllanvaes, or William's Grave, which is pointed out as the place where King Henry I.'s son, who was drowned on his passage from Normandy to England, was buried.

On the opposite side of Falmouth harbour, where St. Anthony's church now stands, was formerly the priory of St. Mary de Vale, and King Henry VIII. is reported to have landed here in 1537, and told the prior that it would soon be destroyed, and he with all his brethren turned out. It was; but the prior left his curse behind him, and the first holder of the lands lost all his family by untimely deaths, and he himself committed suicide.

Of all the creeks up the Fal from Falmouth to Truro, most marvellous tales of smugglers and their daring deeds are told; and of King Harry's passage, where a ferry-boat crosses the river, this legend: That it is called after bluff King Hal, who forded it with his queen (sometimes Katherine of Arragon) on his back. To have accomplished this feat he must have been taller than the sons of Anak, for in the middle the water is several fathoms deep.

At the head of one of these creeks is Veryan parish. And there is a tradition that should its church clock strike on the Sunday morning during the singing of the hymn before the sermon, or before the Collect against Perils at Evening Prayer (which does not often happen), there will be a death in the parish before the next Sunday.

On a hill near Veryan is a barrow,. in which Gerennius, a mythical king of Cornwall, was said to have been buried many centuries ago, with his crown on his head, lying in his golden boat with silver oars. It was opened in 1855, when nothing but a kistvaen (a rude stone chest) containing his ashes was found.

His palace of Dingerein was in the neighbouring village of Gerrans. A subterranean passage, now known as Mermaid's Hole, one day discovered when ploughing a field, was supposed to have led from it to the sea. Treasures of great value are reputed to be hidden under all the Cornish menhirs and barrows. Carew tells of a gentleman who was persuaded that by digging under a menhir near Fowey he would get great riches. "Wherefore, in a faire moone-shine night, thither with certaine good fellowes hee hyeth to dig it up. A working they fall, their labour shortneth, their hope increaseth, a pot of gold is the least of their expectation. But see the chance. In midst of their toyling the skie gathereth clouds, the moonelight is overcast with darknesse, downe fals a mightie showre, up riseth a blustering tempest, the thunder cracketh, the lightning flasheth. In conclusion, our money-seekers washed instead of loden, or loden with water instead of yellow earth, and more afraid than hurt, are forced to abandon their enterprise and seeke shelter of the next house they could get into."

Malpas (pronounced Mopus) ferry was, nearly a century ago, kept by a woman called "Jenny Mopus," who was quite a character. "Wemmin and pigs" she used to declare were the worst things to ferry across.

The water bounds of the borough of Truro are renewed every six years, and the following curious ceremony takes place: On reaching the limits of their jurisdiction, the mayor, town clerk, members of corporation, &c., go on shore, when a writ for the sum of 999*l.* 19*s.* 11¾*d.* is produced against a person present, selected beforehand. He is arrested by the bailiff of the borough, on which two of the party offer themselves as bail, and the prisoner is liberated. Not far from Perranworthal is one of the most celebrated Cornish Tol-mên, Mên-an-tol, or holed stones. This is an immense egg-shaped mass of granite, perched on a dreary hill nearly 700 feet above the sea, and is thought to weigh 750 tons. It is generally known as the Cornish Pebble, and is supported on the points of two other stones leaving a hollow space beneath. In this it differs from other Mên-an-tol which have the orifice in the centre of the stone (hence their name). There are many in the county. The one at Madron is sometimes called the Crick Stone. It gets this name because in days not very long ago people afflicted with rheumatism, sciatica, &c., in May, and at certain other seasons of the year, crawled on all fours nine times around these Mên-an-tol from east to west, and, if thin enough, squeezed themselves through the aperture. This was then thought such a sovereign remedy for these diseases that parents brought their weak-backed children and carried them around. To work the charm properly there must always be two people, one of each sex, who stand one on each side of the stone. The child, if a male, must first be passed from the woman to the man; if a girl, from the man to the woman, and always from the left of the one to the right of the other. Some sort of divination, too, was formerly practised on these Mên-an-tol by pins laid cross-ways on the top.

In the parish of St. Dennis the church is dedicated to that saint. And when St. Dennis had his head cut off at Paris, blood, a legend says, fell on the stones of this churchyard; a similar occurrence often afterwards foretold other calamities.* The exact centre of the county is reputed to be a hole in a field at Probus, a neighbouring parish.

At Boconnoc, near Lostwithiel, not long ago stood the stump of an old oak, in which, in 1644, when Charles I. made this seat his head-quarters, the royal standard was fixed. It bore variegated leaves. According to tradition, they changed colour when an attempt was made to assassinate the king whilst he was receiving the sacrament under its branches. The ball passed through the tree, and a hole in its trunk was formerly pointed out in confirmation of the story.

Heath, in his *Description of Cornwall*, 1750, speaks of two other trees of the same kind to be seen in this county. "In Lanhadron Park," he says, "there grows an oak that bears leaves speckled with white, as another, called Painter's Oak, grows in the hundred of East. Some are of opinion that divers ancient families of

* Dennis is a very common Cornish surname.

England are preadmonished by oaks bearing strange leaves." A turtle-dove is said to be seen by the Bassetts of Tehidy, in Camborne, before death, and to another Cornish family a white bird appears.

The church of St. Neot, in the parish of St. Neot, is celebrated for its beautifully-painted glass. One of the windows contains many legends of this saint, but they have all been too fully described by other writers to require a lengthy notice from me. St. Neot is the reputed brother of King Alfred, and lived some hundreds of years before the present church dedicated to him was erected. But folk-lore has it that it was built at night entirely by his own hands, and that he drew from a neighbouring quarry, by the help of reindeer, all the stones he used in the building. He is described as a man of short stature, and tradition also says that after the church was finished he found that he was not tall enough to reach the keyhole of the door, and could not therefore unlock it. To remedy this defect he put a stone opposite (still pointed out), from which, when he stood on it, he could throw the key into the lock with unerring precision. About a mile to the west of it, is an elevated spot with a square entrenchment; an ancient granite cross stands at one corner. There is a story attached to it which runs thus:—The crows in this neighbourhood were in his time so numerous that the farmers could not, fearing the mischief they might do in their absence, leave their fields and young crops to attend St. Neot's discourses. He, on hearing of it, determined to put a stop both to the excuse and the thieving habits of the birds, and one day ordered them all to enter this enclosure, from whence they could not stir until he gave the signal; upon which they all immediately flew away and returned no more.

"The church of St. Mawgan, in Kerrier, was formerly at Carminowe, at the end of the parish. It was removed thence to its present site on account of the ghoulish propensities of the giants, who used to dig up the dead from their graves. The inhabitants tried in vain to destroy them by making deep pits, and covering them over with "sprouse" (light hay or grass) so that

P

the unwary giants, walking over them as on firm ground, might fall into them and be killed. As this project failed, they were reluctantly compelled to remove the church to its present place, beyond the reach of their troublesome neighbours."—Rev. S. Rundle, *Penzance Natural History Society*, 1885-1886.

The fine old mansion of Cottrell, situated on the River Tamar, was built in the reign of Henry VII. ; it belongs to the Earl of Mount Edgcumbe, and is full of quaint treasures, many of the rooms and the furniture they contain dating from the time of Queen Elizabeth. But the only part that concerns us is a little chapel in the woods perched on a rock overhanging the river, of which this legend is told. It was erected by Sir Richard Edgcumbe, who was a partizan to Henry, Duke of Richmond, the rival of Richard III. A party of soldiers were sent to take him prisoner, but he managed to elude them and escaped into the woods, where his pursuers were so close upon his heels that he would certainly have been captured had not his cap, as he was climbing down this rock, fallen off his head and floated on the stream. On seeing it the men, thinking that Sir Richard had in despair drowned himself, gave up the chase. He shortly after crossed over to Brittany, where he stayed until the news came of the defeat and death of the king, when he returned home, and, in gratitude for his miraculous escape, caused this chapel to be built.

Dupath Well, not far from Cottrell, was, according to tradition, the scene of a desperate duel between two Saxons, called by one authority Colan and Gotlieb, who were both suitors for the hand of the fair lady Gither; but the Rev. R. S. Hawker, who has written a ballad on part of the legend, gives the name of Siward to the younger and favoured one who killed his rival, but who himself in the combat received a wound from which he soon after died. The same author has also put into verse the well-known story of Bottreaux bells. Bottreaux is the parish church of Boscastle, a corruption of Bottreaux castle, and its tower is, and always has been, silent. When it was built the inhabitants, who had long been jealous of the beautiful peal at Tintagel, a neighbouring village, aided by the Lord of Bottreaux, raised enough money to buy a set for themselves, cast by a famous London founder. But when the ship that brought them was nearly in port the sound of Tintagel bells was in the calm evening borne across the water. The pilot, a native of that parish, hearing them, piously crossed himself, and thanked God that he should soon be safe on shore. On this the captain grew very wroth, and said, "Thank the ship and the canvas at sea, thank God on shore." "No!" meekly replied the pilot, "we should thank God at sea as well as on land." At this the captain grew still more angry, swore and blasphemed, and with an oath exclaimed, "Not so, thank yourself and a fair wind." Upon which a violent storm suddenly arose, the ship became unmanageable, struck on a rock, and went down. All on board, with the exception of the pilot, were drowned. Above the roar of the winds and waves the eager watchers from the shore, who were waiting for the arrival of the vessel with her precious freight, could hear the solemn tolling of their bells. And still before a gale their warning chimes sound from their ocean bed, but woe to the unhappy ship's crew that hears them, for wreck, misfortunes, and deaths are sure to follow. The following proverb would seem to infer that Boscastle, as well as no bells, has no market: "All play and no play, like Boscastle Market, which begins at twelve o'clock and ends at noon." Mevagissey church, on the opposite coast, has neither tower nor bells, and there is a standing joke against its people that they sold their bells to pay the cost of pulling down the tower.

Gorran men, who live in an adjoining parish, seem in former days to have been rivals to the famous "Wise men of Gotham," from the absurd deeds attributed to them, such as "Trying to throw the moon over the cliffs," "Building a hedge to keep in the moonlight," &c. The inhabitants of more than one parish in Cornwall are said "to have built a hedge to keep in the 'guckaw' (cuckoo)." In fact, of nearly all the parishes in the county some joke is current in the neighbouring villages.

Not far from Boscastle is the beautiful waterfall of St. Nighton's Kieve, and close by are the ruins of a cottage, once the habitation of two ladies, who took possession of it at night. They evidently had seen better days, but their names and from whence they came remain a mystery, as from the date of their arrival they held no communication with the outer world. They kept no servant, and from the villagers bought for themselves the necessaries of life, asking but few questions, and not answering any. At first they took long solitary walks in the most secluded spots of the district; when met they were rarely conversing, and never spoke to a stranger. These walks were gradually discontinued, and one day a rumour spread through the village that one of the poor ladies was dead. Tradition says that the neighbours found the other weeping silent tears by the side of the corpse. After the funeral the survivor daily grew more infirm and but rarely left the house, and one morning soon after, no smoke issuing from the chimneys of the cottage, the villagers peeped in through the uncurtained windows and saw her sitting dead in her chair. The friends were buried in one grave, and their secret died with them.

In Wellcombe church, near Morwenstow, against the font in the north wall is a door called the "devil's door," opened at baptisms at the Renunciation, that the devil, which is then supposed to come out of the child, may be able to get away.

Trecarrel, in East Cornwall, formerly belonged to the Trecarrels, the last of whom built Launceston church. A singular story has been handed down from the sixth century of the birth and death of his only son. His father is described as having been very learned in philosophy, astrology, astronomy, and other sciences; and it is said that, having surveyed the planetary orbs just as his child was about to be brought into the world, he perceived that the time was unfavourable to its birth, and foreboded a speedy and accidental death to the child. Overcome with these gloomy ideas he hastened to the house, and requested the midwife to delay the birth (if it were possible) for one hour; but nature, conspiring with fate on the downfall of his house, turned a deaf ear to his entreaties, and a son was born, to the great joy of all present except to him who was the most interested in the event. The child, however, grew up in a very promising way, until a servant-maid, having placed him to stand near a bowl of water in order to wash him, chanced to have forgotten the towel, and having stepped into another room to procure one, on her return found the boy dead, having fallen into the water with his head foremost : and in consequence of this unfortunate event the father spent a large part of his large property in charitable purposes, and in building and repairing churches in the county of Cornwall. —J. C. Gilbert.

A story of a similar nature is related of one of the Arundells, of whom it had been foretold "that he should die in the sands." To prevent this he left his house of Efford, near Stratton, and took up his abode at Trerice, another of his estates, about three-and-a-half miles from Newquay. But the Earl of Oxford, having surprised and taken St. Michael's Mount, Sir John Arundell, who was then sheriff of Cornwall, marched there to besiege and retake it for the king, Edward IV. Here his fate overtook him, for in a skirmish on Marazion sands he lost his life, and was buried in the chapel at the Mount. A funeral procession goes through Stratton before the death of the Bathes of Kilkhampton.

Between Stratton and the village of Marham, about half-a-mile from the former town, in the orchard of Binamy farm-house, is an old quadrangular moat, all that remains to show where stood the castle of the Blanchminsters, an old family now, I believe, extinct in this neighbourhood. Of one of them, who lived in the reign of Edward I. and went with him on a crusade, folk-lore still tells some strange but—through the lapse of time—vague tales. His name was Ranulph de Blanchminster, corrupted by the country people into old Blowmanger, and it is said that after he had been absent for two or three years in the Holy Land, his wife, I suppose thinking that he was dead, married another baron. On his return he shut himself up alone in his castle, with the drawbridge generally raised to keep off intruders. No one was with him when he died; but after his death a will was found leaving the greater part of his property for the benefit of the poor of the parish of Stratton. His effigy may be seen in the church, in the habit of a Crusader, grasping a sword, with his feet resting on the back of a lion. Through his interest Stratton had the charter of its market. His spirit haunts Binamy grounds (avoided after dark by the superstitious) in the form of a hare, which always starts out of the moat and manages to elude the dogs.

Of the doings of the famous Grenvilles of Stow,—Sir Beville, the brave Royalist leader, who lost his life at the battle of Lansdowne in 1643,—Admiral Sir Richard, immortalized by Tennyson in his ballad "The Revenge,"—and of his son, Sir John, who served under Sir Walter Raleigh and died at sea,—I shall say nothing, these noted men belonging more to history than folk-lore.

Under the same head, too, may be classed the Cornish female Whittington, Thomasine Bonaventure, of St. Mary Wike (now Week St. Mary), who lived in the fourteenth century; the daughter of a labourer, she herself was a shepherdess. A London merchant, when travelling in Cornwall, lost himself on our moors, and accidentally met her with her sheep. He asked of her the way, and was so much struck by her good looks and intelligence that he begged her from her parents and took her back with him to be a servant to his wife. In her new situation she conducted herself with so much propriety that on his wife's death he courted and married her. Soon after he himself died, and left her a wealthy widow. Her next marriage was to a much richer man, named Henry Gall. Widowed a second time, and again inheriting her husband's money, she took for her third and last husband Sir John Percival, Lord Mayor of London. Him, too, she outlived, and after his death returned to her native village, where she employed her great riches in works of charity. Amongst her other good deeds she founded and endowed a chantry there, together with a free school, and lodgings for masters, scholars, and officers.

The Rev. R. S. Hawker, in his book before-quoted, has a legend which he calls "The first Cornish Mole. A Morality." I, however, suspect it to be a pure invention of this author; but as it is very pretty, I will give the substance of it. Alice of the Coombe was a very beautiful, but proud and vain, damsel; the only child of her widowed mother, with whom she dwelt at Morwenstow. It chanced one day that they, with all the neighbouring gentry, had been bidden to a grand banquet at Stow; and, as she had set her love on the great and noble Sir Beville Grenville, its owner, Alice, to win his affections, dressed herself in her richest robe—"a woven velvet, glossy and soft"—and put on her fairest jewellery. Her mother, when she saw her thus attired, struck by her exceeding grace and beauty, said, "Often shall I pray to-night that the Grenville heart may yield. Aye, thy victory shall be my prayer." The haughty maiden replied, "With the eyes I now see in that glass, and with this vesture, meet for a queen, I lack no trusting prayer." At this a sudden cry was heard, and the damsel disappeared from their sight for ever. Shortly after, the Coombe gardener discovered in the garden a small, unknown hillock, and on top of it shone a ring, which was recognized as the one the lady wore on the day she vanished. A close examination showed that an old Cornish couplet was now traced on it, which the parish priest interpreted to mean—

> "The earth must hide
> Both eyes with pride."

As he uttered these words a low cry was heard at his feet, and there "They beheld, O wondrous and strange! a small dark creature, clothed in a soft velvet skin, in texture and in hue like the robe of Lady Alice, and they saw as it groped into the earth that it moved along without eyes in everlasting night." "She, herself had become

THE FIRST MOLE
OF THE HILLOCKS OF CORNWALL."

Before finishing this section of my work I must say a few words about the Islands of Scilly and their legends. The Rev. H. J. Whitfield, M.A., in 1852, published a book on this subject, but his legends are for the most part purely fictitious, and its title, *Scilly and its Legends*, a little misleading.

The Scilly Isles, just off the Land's End, are very numerous, but only five are inhabited; some are mere rocks in the sea, and,

counting those, they are said to be a hundred and fifty. The
largest is St. Mary's, and the dwellers on it are apt to look with
contempt on the inhabitants of the other islands (the Off Islands).
The word Scilly is sometimes derived from Sullèh, rocks dedicated
to the sun, and sometimes from Sillyas, a conger. This fish is
very plentiful on these coasts, and a ridiculous rhyme says that
Scilly fare consists of—

> " Scads and 'tates, scads and 'tates,
> Scads, and 'tates, and conger,
> And those who can't eat scads and 'tates—
> Oh, they must die of hunger."

Occasionally the saying runs: " Oh! the Scillonians live on fish
and 'taties every day, and conger-pie for Sundays."

In the beginning of this century, before steam-boats were in-
vented, when communication between Scilly and Penzance (the
mainland) depended upon wind and weather, in winter its people
were often reduced to great straits for want of provisions, which
gave rise to the proverb, "There is always a feast or a fast in
Scilly." This is, however, now far from being the truth, and it
is one of the most prosperous parts of Great Britain ; its inhabitants,
as a rule, are well educated, they are noted for their courteous
manners ; and for its beautiful scenery Scilly is well worth a visit.
The dialect of its poorer people, as also the tones of their voices
(each island has its peculiarity), differ from those of the same
class in West Cornwall. Their pronunciation rather resembles the
Irish. *Thread* with them is *tread*, the *th* at the beginning of words
being rarely sounded, *pint* is *point*, and *point pint*.

Irreverent people declare that when Ireland was made some
little bits of earth fell from the shovel and formed Scilly. Certain
it is that when St. Patrick drove out all venomous reptiles from
the former place he did the same kind service to the latter. The
island of St. Agnes was particularly favoured, for until recently
there was not a rat on it, they were introduced from a wrecked
vessel.

Small as St. Mary's is (about three miles long and nine around)
it boasts of two capitals ; the modern one dates from the time of

Queen Elizabeth, and is called Hugh Town; before that Old Town was the principal village. At the east of Old Town Bay is Tolman Point (a corruption, I suppose, of Tôl Mên, the holed stone). Of it an old legend says when Scilly was under the monks of Tavistock, and Old Town the only port of St. Mary's, that they drew a chain from "Tollman head" across the entrance, and levied a toll from all who embarked and landed there, not excepting the fishermen. It was abolished by Richard Plantagenet, who, coming disguised to the port, was not recognized by the friar in charge, who demanded from him his dues. Upon which Earl Richard, in a fit of passion, struck him dead at his feet. According to Leland, "Inniscan longid to Tavestock, and there was a poor celle of monkes of Tavestock. Sum caulle this Trescau."

There was a settlement of Benedictine monks here long before the Norman Conquest; their cell was dedicated to St. Nicholas. St. Nicholas, as well as St. Peter, is the patron saint of fishermen; the former also takes school-boys under his protection. Fragments of Tresco Abbey which was then founded still exist. It was independent until the reign of Edward I., when it was joined to Tavistock. The same monarch, Edward I., made Ranulph de White Monastery (supposed to be Ranulph de Blankminster, or Randolph de Blancheminster), according to an old archive, constable of these islands, with the castle of Ennor, in Old Town, on his "Paying yearly, at the feast of St. Michael the Archangel, 300 birds, called puffins, or 6s. 8d." Traces of these monastic visitors are to be found in a pile of rocks at St. Mary's, called Carn Friars (a farm near by bears the same name), and one of the most highly cultivated and sheltered spots, where a few trees grow, is known as Holy Vale. Whitfield places a nunnery there, and says Holy Vale takes it name from a miraculous rosebush that grew in it, and that "One of its flowers was deemed to have the power, if worn, to preserve its bearer from mortal sin," but no other authority mentions it.

Giants, of course, frequently played a great part in the history of Scilly. Buzza's Hill, just beyond Hugh Town (St. Mary's), commemorates a giant of the name of Bosow, who made his home on its summit (now crowned by a Spanish windmill), and from whom the family of Bosow were descended. One of the finest promontories on the same island is Giant's Castle—Troutbeck says, built by the Danes. Here, too, is Giant's Chair, where the Arch Druid used in former days to sit and watch the sun rise. Druidical remains are scattered all over the different islands, and the many "barrows" are known as "giants' graves." "In the old abbey gardens at Tresco is a curious stone, about four feet long, two feet wide, and six inches in thickness, in an upright position. Near the top are two holes, one above the other (one being somewhat larger than the other), through which a man might pass his hand. It is supposed to be an old Druidical betrothal or wishing-stone, and used before the monks built the abbey at Tresco. Young people, engaged to be married, would pass their hands through the holes, and, joining them together, would so plight their troth. As a wishing-stone, or to break a spell, a ring would be passed through the holes with some incantations."—J. C. Tonkin's *Guide to the Isles of Scilly.*

The finest headland on St. Mary's is Peninnis, and some of the sheltered nooks under its rocks have rather curious names. One of them is known as Sleep's Abode (or Parlour), and close by is Pitt's Parlour, which commands a lovely view; it is so called after a Mr. Pitt, who, when on a visit to Scilly, spent his summer evenings there with a chosen party of friends. An old lady, a native of Scilly, long since dead, told me that tradition said Mr. Pitt came to Scilly in consequence of a bet he made with a gentleman (I believe the then governor of the islands), who, when in London, spoke in the highest terms of the morality of its women, and offered to lay a heavy wager that not a single courtesan could be found there. Mr. Pitt took up the bet, travelled down to Scilly, and for a long time seemed likely to lose it; but at last, by a large bribe, he overcame the virtue of one very poor woman, and, in gratitude, allowed her a small pension until her death.

At the foot of Peninnis is Piper's Hole (in which there is a pool of fresh water). This is said to be the entrance of a subterranean passage leading to the island of Tresco, where another Piper's Hole is shown as the exit. Old people told marvellous tales of rash people venturing in so far that they never returned, but died in it overcome by fatigue—the passage being too narrow for them to turn. Also of dogs who disappeared in the hole at St. Mary's, and after many days crept out from the one in Tresco, very emaciated, and almost hairless. The Rev. J. W. North, in his *Week in the Isles of Scilly*, has an interesting account of Piper's Hole at Tresco.

Half-way down Giant's Castle, the steep carn before mentioned on St. Mary's, lies a very inaccessible cave known as Tom Butt's Bed, from the fact that a boy of that name hid himself there in Queen Anne's time three days and three nights out of sight of the press-gang.

The wreck of Sir Cloudesley Shovel in 1707, upon Gilston Rock, in Porth Hellick Bay, near Old Town, is of course a matter of history. Very many traditions have, however, gathered around this sad event, related by many authors. I must briefly retell them, as no book of this kind would be complete without them.

The admiral, accompanied by the whole of his fleet, was returning home from Toulon, after the capture of Gibraltar, in his ship the *Association*. When they were off Scilly, on October 22nd, 1707, the weather became thick and dirty, and orders were given "to lie-to." This was in the afternoon. Later on, about six, Sir Cloudesley again made sail, but two hours after his ship showed signals of distress, which were answered from several of the others. In two minutes she struck on the Gilston Rock, sank immediately, and all on board perished. The *Eagle* and the *Romney* with their crews shared the same fate; the *Firebrand* also was lost, but her captain with most of her men were saved. "The other men-of-war with difficulty escaped by having timely notice." In this storm between fifteen hundred and two thousand people were drowned in one night.

A day or two before this took place, one man, a native of

Scilly, is said to have persistently warned the officer of the watch on board the *Association* that unless their ship's course was altered she, with all the fleet, would soon be on the Scilly rocks amongst the breakers. These warnings so exasperated the officer that he repeated them to his admiral, and he, vexed that a common sailor should think that he knew better than his superiors how to navigate a vessel, summarily ordered him to be hanged at the yard-arm for inciting the others to insubordination and mutiny. The man before his execution begged, as a great favour, that the chaplain should be allowed to read him one of the Psalms. His request was granted, and he chose the 109th, repeating after the reader in a loud voice all the curses it contains. And with his last breath he prophesied that the admiral, with those who saw him hanged, would find a watery grave. Up to that time the weather had been fair, but as soon as his body had been committed to the sea it changed, the wind began to blow, and his shipmates were horrified to see the corpse out of its winding-sheet, face up, following in their wake, and even before their vessel struck they gave themselves up for lost men. Some say that Sir Cloudesley's body came ashore on a hatch, on which he had endeavoured to save himself, with his favourite little dog dead by his side. Others, that after the wreck it was cast naked on Porth Hellick beach, where it was discovered by a soldier, who took off his ring which he still wore, and buried him in the sands.

Another account, on the authority of Robert, second Lord Romney, Sir Cloudesley Shovel's grandson, runs thus:—"There is one circumstance relating to Sir Cloudesley Shovel's death that is known to very few persons, namely, he was *not* drowned, having got to shore, where, by the confession of an ancient woman, he was put to death. This, many years after, when on her death-bed, she revealed to the minister of the parish, declaring she could not die in peace until she had made this confession, as she was led to commit this horrid deed for the sake of plunder. She acknowledged having, among other things, an emerald ring in her possession, which she had been afraid to sell lest it should lead to a discovery. This ring, which she delivered to the minister, was by him given to James, Earl of Berkeley, at his particular request, Sir Cloudesley Shovel and himself having lived on the strictest footing of friendship."

In the place and manner of his burial all traditions agree. Where he lay is still pointed out—a bare spot surrounded by green grass. And the Scillonians will tell you that, because he so obstinately refused to hear a warning, and wantonly threw away so many lives, God, to keep alive the memory of this great wickedness, permits nothing to grow on his grave.

Another legend has it that the man who gave the warning escaped death, as the storm suddenly arose whilst the Psalm was being read, before the order for his execution could be carried out, and that he was the only person on board the *Association* who was not drowned.

When Lady Cloudesley Shovel heard of the wreck, she asked that a search might be made for her husband's body. A soldier showed a ring which he had in his possession, which was immediately recognised as Sir Cloudesley Shovel's. The body was dug up and identified by the marks of his wounds. The ring was forwarded to his wife, and she, in gratitude for the soldier's kindness in giving her husband a decent burial, rewarded him with a pension for life. Sir Cloudesley's body was embalmed, first taken to Plymouth by sea, where for some time it lay in state, and finally to London, where it was interred in Westminster Abbey.

The abbey at Tresco, formerly under the jurisdiction of the monks of St. Nicholas* at Tavistock, has been already mentioned. The abbey house, built on its site, is the seat of Mr. Dorrien Smith (the Proprietor, as the Scillonians call him). The gardens that surround it are very beautiful, and famed for the tropical plants that here grow out of doors. There is an anecdote related of one of the inhabitants of Tresco, who, when asked what they did for firewood in a spot where no trees grew, answered, "We kindle

---

* "Old Monk" is a term of contempt in Cornwall, applied to old or young men. "I saw the old monk coming down the garden" (a youth of twenty).

our fires from the loppings of our geranium hedges." Tresco, like St. Levan, at the Land's End, was in bygone days the favourite haunt of witches. A poor man there walking out at nightfall had the misfortune to meet with a party of them taking a moonlight ride on their broomsticks. A relation of his was one of the number, and she warned him, in a stentorian voice, that if he ever mentioned what he had accidentally seen, he should bear the marks of their wrath until his dying day. For a long time the secret weighed heavily upon him, and at last he could not refrain from telling his wife. The witches, in revenge, turned his black hair white in a single night.

The Rev. H. G. Whitfield, in his *Legends of Scilly*, gives some marvellous tales of the family of "Dick the Wicked." They were all hardened wreckers, who generations ago lived on this island, and who also had the gift of second sight. Dick himself, according to this writer, when ill and unrepentant, was, by Satanic agency, taken out of his bed and borne, wrapt in a long loose coat, which he was in the habit of wearing, some considerable distance from his house. Here his friends discovered him on the following morning.

On this island stands Cromwell's castle, built during his Protectorate. Old people thought that he in person visited it. The large china tankard, out of which he was said to have drunk his breakfast-beer, still exists. On a hill above are the ruins of Charles's castle. Scilly always remained loyal and true to the unfortunate monarch, and this verse of a ballad told me by a Scillonian was not written of one of them:

> " In Cromwell's days I was for him,
> But now, my boys, I'm for the king ;
> For I can turn, boys, with the tide,
> And wear my coat on the strongest side."

St. Warna, who presided over wrecks, was the patron saint of St. Agnes, another of the principal islands. She crossed over here from Ireland in a wicker-boat covered with hides, and landed at St. Warna's bay. Like many other saints she had her holy-well; and often the superstitious inhabitants of St. Agnes (five families in all), who enjoyed the reputation of being the most daring and unscrupulous amongst the Scilly wreckers of those days, threw crooked pins into it, and daily invoked and prayed her to send them "a rich wreck." There was no church on it then, and its people rarely visited the other islands. But it chanced one fine morning the entire population started in their boats for the church of Ennor, in St. Mary Old Town, as two of them wished to be married. After the ceremony was over the clergyman in the presence of most of his parishioners, who had assembled to witness it (between whom and the men of St. Agnes there was always a bitter feud), rebuked them for their lawless deeds. They, angry at being put to shame before their enemies, answered with many profane and mocking words, and were with difficulty restrained from coming to blows. So incensed were they that they took no notice of the signs which heralded a coming storm, and hastily got on board their boats to return to their own home, which none of them were ever destined to reach, as it broke with great fury when they were about half-way across. When close to land and the rowers were straining every nerve to get there, one wave larger than the rest broke over them, and every soul found a watery grave. This was of course said to be a judgment on them for their wicked ways. (Leland briefly chronicles it.) From that time St. Warna's well was neglected; there was no one left the day after twelfth-day, as had been the custom, to clean it out and return her thanks for her bounty: it gradually got filled with stones, and at the present day is little more than a hole.

There is a curious labyrinth on this island called "Troy-town," which it is popularly supposed to represent; but all intricate places in Cornwall are so denominated, and I have even heard nurses say to children when they were surrounded by a litter of toys that they looked as if they were in Troy-town.

A peculiar mode of punishment was formerly practised in Scilly. The offenders were placed in a chair called a "ducking chair," and publicly at St. Mary's quay-head "ducked" in the salt water.

⇒ FAIRIES. ⇐

HE fairies of Cornwall may be divided into four classes, the Small People, the Pixies (pronounced Piskies or or Pisgies), the Spriggans, and the Knockers. The first are harmless elfiish little beings known all over England, whose revels on fine summer nights have often been described by those favoured individuals who have accidentally had the privilege of seeing them. As a rule they, however, wish to think themselves invisible, and in this county it is considered unlucky to call them by the name of fairies. The stories told about them by our old folk differed but slightly from those related elsewhere. There was the well-known cow that gave the finest yield of milk, and retained it all the year round when others of the herd ran dry, but always ceased the flow at a certain time, and if efforts were made to draw more from her, kicked over the the milking-pail. The milkmaid discovered that the cow belonged to the small people, by reason of her wearing in her hat a bunch of flowers having in it a four-leaved clover, which rendered them visible, when she saw them climbing up the cow's legs and suck-ing at her teats. The greedy mistress, when the maid told her of this discovery, contrary to advice, washed the poor animal all over with salt water, which fairies particularly dislike (as well as the smell of fish and grease), in order to drive them away. Of course she succeeded in her object, and by so doing brought nothing but ill-luck for ever after on herself and family. When unmolested, fairies bring good fortune to places they frequent; but they are spiteful if interfered with, and delight in vexing and thwarting people who meddle with them. It is well known "that they can't abear those whom they can't abide." Then there were the tales of persons spirited away to fairyland, to wait upon the small people's children and perform various little domestic offices, where the time has passed so pleasantly that they have forgotten all about their homes and relations, until by doing a forbidden thing they have incurred their master's anger. They were then punished by being thrown into a deep sleep, and on awakening found themselves on some moor close to their native villages. These unhappy creatures never, after their return, settled down to work, but roamed about aimlessly doing nothing, hoping and longing one day to be allowed to go back to the place from whence they had been banished. They had first put themselves into the fairies' power by eating or drinking something on the sly, when they had surprised them at one of their moonlight frolics; or by accepting a gift of fruit from the hands of one of these little beings. There are also two or three legends of curious women, who by underhand dealings have got hold of a mysterious box of green ointment belonging to the fairies, which, rubbed on the eyes, gave them the power of seeing them by daylight, when they look old, withered, and grey, and hate to be spied upon by mortals. These women are always interrupted when they have put the ointment on one eye before they have time to anoint both, and by an inadvertent speech they invariably betray their ill-gotten knowledge. They cannot resist making an exclamation when they see a fairy pilfering or up to some mischievous trick. Neither can they keep the secret of the side on which they see, and they are quickly made to pay the penalty of their misdeeds by a well-directed blow from the elf's fist, which deprives them of the sight of that eye for ever. All these old wives' tales are fully related by Mr. Bottrell in his three series of *Traditions, &c., of West Cornwall.*

Fairies haunt the ancient monuments of this county, and are supposed to be the beings who bring ill-luck on the destroyers of

R

them. "Not long ago a woman of Moushal (a village near Penzance) told me that troops of small people, not more than a foot-and-a-half high, used, on moonlight nights, to come out of a hole in the cliff, opening on to the beach, Newlyn side of the village, and but a short distance from it. The little people were always dressed very smart, and if anyone came near them would scamper away into the hole. Mothers often told their children that if they went under cliffs by night the small people would carry them away into 'Dicky Danjy's hole.'"—Bottrell.

These small people are said to have been half-witted people who had committed no mortal sin, but who, when they died, were not good enough to go to Heaven. They are always thought, in some state, to have lived before.

The small people go about in parties, but pisky in his habits, at least in West Cornwall, is a solitary little being. I gather however, from Mr. T. Q. Couch's *History of Polperro* that in the eastern part of the county the name of Pisky is applied indiscriminately to both tribes. He says two only of them are known by name, and quotes the following rhyme:

> "Jack o' the lantern! Joan the wad,
> Who tickled the maid and made her mad ;
> Light me home, the weather's bad."

Here in the west he is a ragged merry little fellow (to laugh like a pisky is a common Cornish simile), interesting himself in human affairs, threshing the farmer's corn at nights, or doing other work, and pinching the maidservants when they leave a house dirty at bed-time. Margery Daw, in our version of the nursery-song, meets with punishment at his hands for her misdoings—

> "See saw, Margery Daw,
> Sold her bed and lay upon straw ;
> Sold her bed and lay upon hay,
> And pisky came and carried her away.
> For wasn't she a dirty slut
> To sell her bed and lie in the dirt?"

Should the happy possessor of one of these industrious, unpaid fairy servants (who never object to taking food left for them by friends) express his thanks aloud, thus showing that he sees him, or try to reward him for his services by giving him a new suit of clothes, he leaves the house never to return, and in the latter case may be heard to say:

> " Pisky fine, pisky gay!
> Pisky now will fly away."

Or in another version :

> " Pisky new coat, and pisky new hood,
> Pisky now will do no more good."—(T.Q.C.)

Mr. Cornish, the Town Clerk of Penzance, mentioned at an antiquarian meeting recently held in that town, "that there was a brownie still existing in it; that a gentleman, whose opinion he would take on many matters, had told him that he had often seen it sitting quietly by the fireside." When mischievously inclined pisky often leads benighted people a sad dance; like Will of the Wisp, he takes them over hedges and ditches, and sometimes round and round the same field, from which they in vain try to find their way home (although they can always see the path close at hand), until they sit down and turn their stockings the wrong side out, as an old lady, born in the last century, whom I well knew, once told me she had done. To turn a pocket inside out has the same effect. But to quote the words of a late witty Cornish doctor, "Pisky led is often whiskey led."

Mr. T. Q. Couch in his before-mentioned book has two or three amusing stories of their merry pranks. One is called "A Voyage with the Piskies." A Polperro lad meeting them one night as he was going on an errand heard them say in chorus, "I'm for Portallow Green" (a place in the neighbourhood). Repeating the cry after them, "quick as thought he found himself there surrounded by a throng of laughing piskies." The next place they visited was Seaton Beach, between Polperro and Plymouth ; the third and last cry was "I'm for the King of France's cellar." Again he decided on joining them, dropped the bundle he was carrying on the sands, and "immediately found himself in a spacious cellar, engaged with his mysterious companions in tasting the richest wines." Afterwards they strolled through the palace, where in a room he saw all the preparations made for a feast, and could not resist the temptation of pocketing one of the rich silver goblets from the table. The signal for their return was soon given, and once more he found himself on Seaton Beach, where he had just time to pick up his bundle before he was whisked home. All these voyages were made in the short space of five minutes. When on his return he told his adventures they were listened to with incredulity until he produced the goblet, which proved the truth of his tale. After having been kept for generations this trophy has disappeared. "These little creatures seem sometimes," Mr. Couch says, "to have delighted in mischief for its own sake. Old Robin Hicks, who formerly lived in a house at 'Quay Head' (Polperro), has more than once, on stormy winter nights, been alarmed at his supper by a voice sharp and shrill—'Robin! Robin! your boat is adrift.' Loud was the laughter and the *tacking* of hands (clapping) when they succeeded in luring Robin as far as the quay, where the boat was lying safely at its moorings."

Another of his legends is about a fisherman of his district, John Taprail, long since dead, who was, on a frosty night, aroused from his sleep by a voice which called to him that his boat was in danger. He went down to the beach to find that some person had played a practical joke on him. As he was returning he saw a group of piskies sitting in a semicircle under a much larger boat belonging to one of his neighbours. They were dividing a heap of money between them by throwing a piece of gold alternately into each of the hats which lay before them. John was covetous, and forgot that piskies hate to be spied upon; so he crept up and pushed his hat slily in with the others. When the pile was getting low he tried to get off with his booty without their detecting the frand. He had got some distance before the cheat was discovered; then they pursued him in such hot haste that he only escaped with his treasure by leaving his coat-tails in their hands. "The pisky's midwife" is common,—a mortal who has been decoyed into fairyland discovers it by accidentally rubbing her eye with a bit of soap whilst washing the baby. Like those who have stolen and applied the green ointment, she loses the sight of it by a blow from an angry pisky's fist. She meets and recognizes the father at a fair where, as usual, he is pilfering, and foolishly asks after the welfare of mother and child. But all these stories in West Cornwall would be told of the "small people," as well as the well-known "Colman Grey" (of course the name varies), which relates how a farmer one day found a poor, half-starved looking bantling, sitting alone in the middle of a field, whom he took home and fed until he grew quite strong and lively. A short time after a shrill voice was suddenly heard calling thrice upon "Colman Grey." Upon which the imp cried "Ho! ho! ho! my daddy is come!" flew through the keyhole, and was never heard of after. Unbaptised children were, in this county at the beginning of the century, said to turn, when they died, into piskies; they gradually went through many transformations at each change, getting smaller until at last they became "Meryons"* (ants) and finally disappeared. Another tradition is that they were Druids, who, because they would not believe in Christ, were for their sins condemned to change first into piskies; gradually getting smaller, they too, as ants, at last are lost. It is on account of these legends considered unlucky to destroy an ant's nest, and a piece of tin put into one could, in bygone days, through pisky power be transmuted into silver, provided that it was inserted at some varying lucky moment about the time of the new moon.

Moths were formerly believed in Cornwall to be departed souls, and are still, in some districts, called piskies.

There is also a green bug which infests bramble-bushes in the late autumn that bears the same name, and one of the reasons assigned for blackberries not being good after Michaelmas is that pisky spoils them then. Pisky is in some places invoked for luck at the swarming of bees.

It was once a common custom in East Cornwall, when houses were built, to leave holes in the walls by which these little beings could enter; to stop them up would drive away good luck. And in

* The word Meryons is also used in Cornwall as a term of endearment, "She's faather's little Meryon."

West Cornwall knobs of lead, known as pisky's paws or pisky feet, were placed at intervals on the roofs of farm-houses to prevent the piskies from dancing on them and turning the milk sour in the dairies.

Country people in East Cornwall sometimes put a prayer book under a child's pillow as a charm to keep away piskies. I am told that a poor woman, near Launceston, was fully persuaded that one of her children was taken away and a pisky substituted, the disaster being caused by the absence of a prayer book on one particular night.—H. G. T., *Notes and Queries*, December, 1850.

Small round stones, known as "Pisky Grinding Stones," are occasionally found in Cornwall; they are most probably parts of old spindles.

If piskies are kind and helpful little beings, spriggans or sprites are spiteful creatures, never doing a good turn for anyone. It is they who carry off poor babies from their mothers, when they have been obliged to leave them for a few hours alone, putting their own ugly, peevish brats in their cradles, who never thrive under the foster-mother's care, in spite of all the trouble they may bestow upon them. Mr. Bottrell tells the story of a spriggan, a married man with a family, who took the place of a poor woman's child one evening when she was at work in the harvest field. For although an innocent baby held in the arms is thought in Cornwall to protect the holder from mischief caused by ghosts and witches, it has no power over these creatures, who are not supposed to have souls. The scene of this legend was under Chapel Carn Brea, on the old road from Penzance to St. Just in Penwith. The mother, Jenny Trayer by name, was first alarmed on her return one night from her work in the harvest field by not finding her child in its cradle, but in a corner of the kitchen where in olden days the wood and furze for the then general open fires were kept. She was however too tired to take much notice, and went to bed, and slept soundly until the morning. From that time forth she had no peace; the child was never satisfied but when eating or drinking, or when she had it dandling in her arms. The poor woman consulted her neighbours in turn as to what she should do with the changeling (as one and all agreed that it was). One recommended her to dip it on the three first Wednesdays in May in Chapel Uny Well,* which advice was twice faithfully carried out in the prescribed manner. The third Wednesday was very wet and windy, but Jenny determined to persevere in this treatment of her ugly bantling, and holding the brat (who seemed to enjoy the storm) firmly on her shoulders, she trudged off. When they got about half-way, a shrill voice from behind some rocks was heard to say,

> "Tredrill! Tredrill!
> Thy wife and children greet thee well."

Not seeing anyone, the woman was of course alarmed, and her fright increased when the imp made answer in a similar voice,

> "What care I for wife or child,
> When I ride on Dowdy's back to the Chapel Well,
> And have got pap my fill?"

After this adventure, she took the advice of another neighbour, who told her the best way to get rid of the spriggan and have her own child returned was "to put the small body upon the ashes' pile, and beat it well with a broom; then lay it naked under a church stile; there leave it and keep out of sight and hearing till the turn of night; when nine times out of ten the thing will be taken away and the stolen child returned." This was finally done; all the women of the village after it had been put upon a convenient pile "belabouring it with their brooms," upon which it naturally set up a frightful roar. After dark it was laid under the stile, and there next morning the woman "found her own 'dear cheeld' sleeping on some dry straw," most beautifully clean and wrapped in a piece of chintz. "Jenny nursed her recovered child with great care, but there was always something queer about it, as there always is about one that has been in the fairies' power— if only for a few days."

There are many other tales of changelings, but they resemble each other so much that they are not worth relating. In the one

---

* See *ante*, "Cornish Feasts and Feasten Customs."

before quoted from Mr. Bottrell he gives a third charm for getting a child restored, as follows: " Make by night a smoky fire, with green ferns and dry. When the chimney and house are full of smoke as one can bear, throw the changeling on the hearthstone; go out of the house, turn three times round; when one enters, the right child will be restored." Spriggans, too, guard the vast treasures that are supposed to be buried beneath our immense carns and in our cliff castles. No matter if the work be carried on by night or by day, they are sure to punish the rash person who ventures to dig in hopes of securing them. When he has got some way down, he finds himself surrounded by hundreds of ugly beings, in some cases almost as tall as he, who scare the unhappy man until he loses all control over himself, throws down his tools, and rushes off as fast as he can possiby go. The fright often makes him so ill that he has to lie for days in bed. Should he ever summon up courage to return to the spot, he will find the pit refilled, and no traces to show that the ground had been disturbed.

Knockers (pronounced knackers) are mine fairies, popularly supposed to be (as related elsewhere) the souls of the Jews who crucified Christ, sent by the Romans to work as slaves in the tin mines. In proof of this, they are said never to have been heard at work on Saturdays, nor other Jewish festivals. They are compelled to sing carols at Christmas time. Small pieces of smelted tin found in old smelting-works are known as " Jews' bowels." These fairies haunt none but the richest tin mines, and many are reputed to have been discovered by their singing and knocking underground; and miners think when they hear them that it is a sign of good luck, because when following their noises they often chance on lodes of good ore. When a miner goes into an "old level" and sees a bright light, it is a sure sign that he will find tin there. Knockers like spriggans are very ugly beings, and, if you do not treat them in a friendly spirit, very vindictive. " As stiff as Barker's knee " is a common saying in Cornwall; he having in some way angered the knockers, either by speaking of them disrespectfully or by not leaving (as was formerly the custom) a bit of his dinner on the ground for them (for good luck), they in revenge threw all their tools in his lap, which lamed him for the rest of his life. Mr. Bottrell tells a similar story of a man named Tom Trevorrow, who when he was working underground heard the knockers just before him, and roughly told them " to be quiet and go." Upon which, a shower of stones fell suddenly around him, and gave him a dreadful fright. He seems however to have quickly got over it, and soon after, when eating his dinner, a number of squeaking voices sang,

> " Tom Trevorrow ! Tom Trevorrow !
> Leave some of thy ' fuggan ' * for bucca,
> Or bad luck to thee to-morrow ! "

But Tom took no notice and ate up every crumb, upon which the knockers changed their song to

> " Tommy Trevorrow ! Tommy Trevorrow !
> We'll send thee bad luck to-morrow ;
> Thou old curmudgeon, to eat all thy fuggan,
> And not leave a ' didjan ' † for bucca"

After this such persistent ill-luck followed him that he was obliged to leave the mine.

Bucca is the name of a spirit that in Cornwall it was once thought necessary to propitiate. Fishermen left a fish on the sands for bucca, and in the harvest a piece of bread at lunch-time was thrown over the left shoulder, and a few drops of beer spilled on the ground for him, to ensure good luck. Bucca, or bucca-boo, was, until very lately (and I expect in some places still is) the terror of children, who were often when crying told "that if they did not stop he would come and carry them off." It was also the name of a ghost ; but now-a-days to call a person a "great bucca" simply implies that you think him a fool. There were two buccas—

> " ' Bucca Gwidden,' the white, or good spirit,
> ' Bucca Dhu,' the black, malevolent one."

---

* Fuggan, a cake made of flour and raisins often eaten by miners for dinner.
† Didjan, a tiny bit.
S

SUPERSTITIONS:

MINERS', SAILORS,' FARMERS.'

LTHOUGH Cornish miners, or "tinners" as they are generally called, are a very intelligent, and since the days of Wesley a religious body of men, many of their old-world beliefs still linger. To this day it is considered unlucky to make the form of a cross on the sides of a mine, and when underground you may on no account whistle for fear of vexing the knockers and bringing ill-luck, but you may sing or even swear* without producing any bad effect. Down one mine-shaft a black goat is often seen to descend, but is never met below; in another mine a white rabbit forebodes an accident.

"The occurrence of a black cat in the lowest depths of a mine will warn the older miners off that level until the cat is exterminated."—Thomas Cornish, *Western Antiquary, October, 1887.*

A hand clasping the ladder and coming down with, or after a miner, foretells misfortune or death. This superstition prevails, also, in the slate quarries of the eastern part of the county.

The miners in the slate quarries of Delabole have a tradition that the right hand of a miner, who committed suicide, is some-times seen following them down the ladders, grasping the rings as they let them go, holding a miner's light between the thumb and finger. It forebodes ill to the seer.—Esmè Stuart. See "Tamsin's Choice," *Longman,* June, 1883.

---

* Some say you must neither whistle nor swear, but you may sing and laugh.

Miners, too, had some superstition in regard to snails, known in Cornwall as "bullhorns;" for if they met one on their way to work they always dropped a bit of their dinner or some grease from their lanthorn before him for good-luck.

Miraculous dreams are related; warnings to some miners, which have prevented on particular days their going down below with their comrades, when serious accidents have happened and several have lost their lives. Rich lodes, too, have been discovered through the dreams of fortunate women, who have been shown in them where their male relatives should dig for the hidden treasure.

" 'Dowsing' (divining with the rod) is of course believed in here as elsewhere, and some men are known as noted 'dowsers.' A forked twig of hazel (also called a 'dowser') is used by our Cornish miners to discover a vein of ore; it is held loosely in the hand, the point towards the 'dowser's' breast, and it is said to turn round when the holder is standing over metal."

Miners still observe some quaint old customs; a horse-shoe is sometimes placed on a convenient part of the machinery, which each, as he goes down to his day's work, touches four times to ensure good-luck. These must be "Tributers" (pronounced tribut-ers), who work on "trib-ut," when a percentage is paid on ores raised; in contradistinction to "Tut-workers," who are paid by the job.

A miner, going underground with shoes on, will drive all the mineral out of the mine.—*Cornubiana*, Rev. S. Rundle.

In 1886, at St. Just in Penwith two men of Wheal Drea had their hats burnt one Monday morning, after the birth of their first children.

Three hundred fathoms below the ground at Cook's Kitchen mine, near Camborne, swarms of flies may be heard buzzing, called by the men, for some unknown reason, "Mother Margarets." From being bred in the dark, they have a great dislike to light.

Swallows in olden times were thought to spend the winter in deep, old disused Cornish tin-works; also in the sheltered nooks of its cliffs and cairns. It is the custom here to jump on seeing the first in spring.

A water-wagtail, in Cornwall a "tinner," perching on a window-
sill, is the sign of a visit from a stranger.

Carew says—"The Cornish tynners hold a strong imagination,
that in the withdrawing of Noah's floud to the sea the same took
his course from east to west, violently breaking vp, and forcibly
carrying with it the earth, trees, and rocks, which lay anything
loosely neere the vpper face of the ground. To confirme the
likelihood of which supposed truth, they doe many times digge
vp whole and huge timber-trees, which they conceiue at that
deluge to haue been ouerturned and whelmed."

Miners frequently in conversation make use of technical proverbs, such as "Capel rides a good horse." Capel is schorl, and
indicates the presence of tin. "It's a wise man that knows tin"
alludes to the various forms it takes. To an old tune they sing
the words—

> "Here's to the devil, with his wooden spade and shovel,
> Digging tin by the bushel, with his tail cocked up."

And on the signboard of a public-house in West Cornwall a few
years ago (and probably still) might be read—

> "Come all good Cornish boys* walk in,
> Here's brandy, rum, and shrub, and gin;
> You can't do less than drink success
> To copper, fish, and tin."

Miners believe that mundic (iron pyrites) being applied to a
wound immediately cures it; of which they are so sure that they
use no other remedy than washing it in the water that runs through
the mundic ore.—*A Complete History of Cornwall, 1730.*

It is an easy transition from mines to fish, the next staple
industry of Cornwall, and to the superstitions of its fishermen and
sailors. Fish is a word in West Cornwall applied more particularly
to pilchards (pelchurs). They frequent our coasts in autumn.

> "When the corn is in the shock,
> Then the fish are on the rock."

And if on a close foggy day in that season you ask the question,—
"Do you think it will rain?" the answer often is—"No! it is

* All men are boys in Cornwall.

only het (heat) and pelchurs," that sort of weather being favourable for catching them.

"A good year for fleas is a good year for fish," the proverb says; and when eating a pilchard the flesh must be always taken off the bone from the tail to the head. To eat them from head to tail is unlucky, and would soon drive the fish from the shore. There are many other wise sayings about pilchards; but I will only give one more couplet, which declares that—

> "They are food, money, and light,
> All in one night." †

Should pilchards when in bulk ‡ make a squeaking noise, they are crying for more, and another shoal will quickly be in the bay.

Fishermen dread going near the spot where vessels have been wrecked, as the voices of the drowned often call to them there, especially before a storm. Sometimes their dead comrades call them by their names, and then they know for certain that they will soon die; and often when drowning the ghosts of their friends appear to them. They are seen by them sometimes taking the form of animals.

Mr. Bottrell speaks of a farmer's wife who was warned of her son's death by the milk in the pans ranged round her dairy being agitated like the sea waves in a storm. There is a legend common to many districts of a wrecker who rushed into the sea and perished, after a voice had been heard to call thrice, "The hour is come, but not the man." He was carried off by the devil in a phantom ship seen in the offing. But ships haunted with seamen's ghosts are rarely lost, as the spirits give the sailors warning of storms and other dangers.

In a churchyard near the Land's End is the grave of a drowned captain, covered by a flat tombstone; proceeding from it formerly the sound of a ghostly bell was often heard to strike four and eight bells. The tale goes that when his vessel struck on some rocks close to the shore, the captain saw all his men safely off

† Train-oil is expressed from them.

‡ To " bulk " pilchards is to place them, after they have been rubbed with salt, in large regular heaps, alternately heads and tails.

in their boat, but refused himself to leave the ship, and went down in her exactly at midnight, as he was striking the time. His body was recovered, and given decent burial, but his poor soul had no rest. An unbelieving sailor once went out of curiosity to try if he could hear this bell; he did, and soon after sailed on a voyage from which he never returned.

Spectre ships are seen before wrecks; they are generally shrouded in mist; but the crew of one was said to consist of two men, a woman, and a dog. These ships vanish at some well-known point. Jack Harry's lights, too, herald a storm; they are so called from the man who first saw them. These appear on a phantom vessel resembling the one that will be lost.

On boarding a derelict, should a live cat or other animal be found, it is thrown into the sea and drowned, under the idea that if any living thing is in her, the finders can claim nothing from the owners. In fact she is not a derelict.

The apparition of a lady carrying a lanthorn always on one part of the Cornish coast* foretells a storm and shipwrecks. She is supposed to be searching for her child who was drowned, whilst she was saved, because she was afraid to trust it out of her arms. For the legends of "The Lady of the Vow" and "The Hooper or Hooter of Sennen Cove," see *ante*, p. 71.† Mermaids are still believed in, and it is very bad to offend them, for by their spite harbours have been filled up with sand. They, however, kindly take idiot children under their protection. The lucky finder of one of their combs or glasses has the power (as long as it remains in his possession) of charming away diseases.

Boats are said to come to a sudden standstill when over the spot where lies the body of a drowned man, for whom search is being made. The body is supposed to rise when drowned, on the seventh, eighth, or ninth day. Sailors regard many things as bad omens, such "as a loaf of bread turned upside-down on a table." (This will bring some ship to distress.) They will not begin a voyage

* St. Ives.
† And " Cornish Feasts and Customs."

on Childermas-day, nor allow a piece of spar-stone (quartz) to be carried on board a vessel: that would ensure her striking on a rock. Of course, they neither whistle when there, nor speak of hares, two most unlucky things; and should they meet one of these animals on their way to the place of embarkation they think it far wiser to turn back home, and put off sailing for a tide. Hares (as already noticed) play a great part in Cornish folk-lore. The following amusing story I had from a friend:—"Jimmy Treglown, a noted poacher living in a village of West Cornwall, became converted at a revival meeting; he was tempted on his way to class-meeting one Sunday morning soon after by the devil in the form of a beautiful hare. Jimmy said, 'There thee art, my dear; but I waaṛ't tooch thee on a Sunday—nor yet on a weeky day, for that matter.' He went briskly on his way for a few paces, and then, like Lot's wife, he was tempted to look behind him. Alas! in Jimmy's own words, 'There she was in her seat, looking lovely. I tooked up a stone, and dabbed at her. Away she runned, and fare-ee well, religion. Mine runned away with her. I went home, and never went to class no more.* You see it was the devil, and 'simmen to me' (seeming) I heard 'un laugh and say, 'Ah! ah! Jimmy, boy, I had thee on the hip then. Thee must confess thee'st had a fair fall.' So I gave in, and never went nigh the 'people' (Wesleyans) no more. Nobody should fire at hares of this sort, except with a silver bullet; they often appear as white, but the devil knowed I couldn't be fooled with a white 'un.'" Nothing is too ridiculous to be told of hares. Another old man from St. Just (still living) once recited this anecdote in our kitchen, and from his grave manner evidently expected it to be believed:—"I was out walking (he said) one Sunday morning, when I saw a hare in a field which I longed to have; so I shied a bit of 'codgy wax' (cobbler's wax), the only thing I had in my pocket, at 'un, when he ran away. What was my surprise on getting over a stile to see two hares in the next field face to face, the 'codgy wax' had stuck to the nose of the first, and he in his fright had runned

* The illiterate Cornish often double their negatives: "I don't know, not I;" "I'll never do it, no, never no more."

against the other, and was holden 'un fast, too. So I quietly broke the necks of both, and carried em home."

"The grapes are sour" is in Cornwall often changed to "Lev-un go! he's dry eaten after all," as the old man said when he couldn't catch the hare.

Sailors and fishermen have naturally many weather proverbs, of which I will give a few :—

"A north wind is a broom for the Channel."

"A Saturday's moon is a sailor's curse."

"A Saturday's and Sunday's moon
Comes once in seven years too soon."

"Between twelve and two you'll see what the day will do."

"A southerly wind with a fog bring an easterly wind in 'snog' (with certainty)."

"Friday's noon is Sunday's doom."

"Friday and the week are never alike."

"There's never a Saturday in the year
But what the sun it doth appear," etc.

"Weather dogs" are pillars of light coloured like the rainbow, which appear on the horizon generally over the sea in unsettled weather, and always foretell storms. The inland dwellers of Cornwall have also their wise sayings on this subject. Rooks darting around a rookery, sparrows twittering, donkeys braying, are signs of rain. Cats running wildly about a house are said to bring storms on their tails. Some of their omens are simply ludicrous, such as "We may look for wet when a cat, in washing its face, puts its paw over its ear," or when "hurlers" (small sparks) play about the bars of a grate. A cock crowing on a stone is a sign of fine weather; on the doorstep, of a stranger. But here it is well known "That fools are weather-wise," and "That those that are weather-wise are rarely otherwise."

In West Cornwall, not very long ago farmers, before they began to break up a grass field or plough for sowing, always turned the faces of the cattle attached to the plough towards the west and solemnly said, "In the name of God let us begin," and then with the sun's course proceeded on their work. Everything in this

county, even down to such a small thing as taking the cream off
the milk-pans set round the dairy, must for luck be done from left
to right. Invalids, on going out for the first time after an illness,
must walk with, not against, the sun, for fear of a relapse.

Farmers here are taught that if they wish to thrive they must
"rise with the craw (crow), go to bed with the yow (ewe)," not
be "like Solomon the wise, who was loth to go to bed and loth
to rise," for does not "the master's eye make the mare fat?"
"A February spring," according to one proverb, "is not worth a
pin," and another says "a dry east wind raises the spring." Sayings
current in other counties, such as "a peck of March dust is worth
a king's ransom," are also quoted, but those I shall not give.
There should be as many frosty mornings in May as in March,
for "a hot May makes a fat church-hay." A wet June makes a
dry September. "Cornwall will stand a shower every day, and two
for Sundays." There is always a black month before Christmas.
The farmer too is told—

> "A rainbow in the morn, put your hook in the corn;
> A rainbow in the eve, put your hook in the sheave."

In Cornwall, as well as in Devon, there is an old prophecy
quoted to the effect, that "in the latter days there will be no
difference between summer and winter, save in the length of the
days and the greenness of the leaf." It is erroneously asserted to
be in the Bible.—*Cornubiana*, Rev. S. Rundle, *Transactions Penzance
Natural History Society, etc.*, 1885-1886.

"Countrymen in Cornwall, if the breeze fail whilst they are
winnowing, whistle to the spriggan, or air spirit, to bring it back."
—*Comparative Folk-lore, Cornhill*, 1876.

A swarm of bees in May is worth a "yow" (ewe) and lamb same
day. It is considered lucky in these parts for a stray swarm to
settle near your house; and if you throw a handkerchief over it
you may claim it as your own. To sell them is unlucky; but you
may have an understanding with a purchaser that he will give you

T

an equivalent for your bees. The inside of hives should be rubbed with "scawnsy buds" (elderflowers) to prevent a new swarm from leaving them. Honey should be always taken from the hive on St. Bartholomew's Day, he being the patron saint of bees. Of course all the principal events happening in the families to whom they belonged, in this as in other counties, were formerly whispered to them, that the bees might not think themselves neglected, and leave the place in anger. At a recent meeting of the Penzance Natural History and Antiquarian Society a gentleman mentioned that when a boy he had seen thirty hives belonging to Mr. Joshua Fox, of Tregedna, tied up in crape (an universal practice) because of a death in the Fox family. Another at the same time said that when, some years since, the landlady of the "First and Last" Inn, at the Land's End, died, the bird-cages and flower-pots were also tied with crape, to prevent the birds and plants from dying. When withering, because this has not been done, if the plants be re-membered in time and crape put on the pots, they may revive. Enquiring a short time ago what had become of a fine maiden-hair fern that we had had for years, I was told "that we had neglected to put it into mourning when a near relative of our's had died, or to tell it of his death ; and therefore it had gradually pined away." After a death, pictures, but especially portraits of the deceased, are also supposed to fade. Snails as well as bees are thought here to bring luck, for "the house is blest where snails do rest." Children on meeting them in their path, for some reason stamp their feet and say,

> "Snail! snail! come out of your hole,
> Or I will beat you black as a coal."

Another Cornish farmers' superstition is that "ducks won't lay until they have drunk 'Lide' (March) water;" and the wife of one in 1880 declared "that if a goose saw a Lent lily (daffodil) before hatching its goslings it would, when they came forth, destroy them." Some witty thieves, many years ago, having stolen twelve geese from a clergyman in the eastern part of the county, tied twelve pennies and this doggerel around the gander's neck—

> " Parson Peard, be not afeard,
> Nor take it much in anger,
> We've bought your geese at a penny a-piece,
> And left the money with the gander."

Hens must never be put to sit on an even number of eggs, eleven or thirteen are lucky numbers; Basilisks are hatched from cock's eggs.

When cocks crow children are told that they say,

> " Cock-a-doodle-doo !
> Grammer's lost her shoe,
> Down by the barley moo (mow),
> And what will grammer do,
> Cock-a-doodle-doo."

Moles in this county are known as "wants," and once in the Land's End district I overtook an old man and asked him what had made so many hillocks in a field through which we were passing. His answer was, "What you rich people never have in your houses, ' wants.' "

To this day in Cornwall, when anything unforeseen happens to our small farmers, or they have the misfortune to lose by sickness some of their stock, they still think that they are " ill-wished," and start off (often on long journeys) to consult a " pellar," or wise man, sometimes called "a white witch" (which term is here used indiscriminately for persons of both sexes). The following I had from a dairy-man I know, who about twelve years ago quarrelled with a domestic servant, a woman living in a neighbouring house. Soon after, from some reason, two or three of his cows died ; he was quite sure, he told me, that she had "overlooked" and " ill-wished " him. To ease his mind he had consulted a " pellar " about the matter, who had described her accurately to him, and, for payment, removed the " spell " (I do not know what rites were used), telling him to look at his watch and note the hour, as he would find, when he returned home, that a cow he had left sick would have begun at that moment to recover (which he says it did).

The "pellar" also added, "The woman who has 'ill-wished' you will be swaddled in fire and lapped in water;" and by a strange coincidence she emigrated soon after, and was lost in the ill-fated *Cospatrick,* that was burnt at sea.

Water from a font is often stolen to sprinkle "ill-wished" persons or things.

The two next examples were communicated to me by a friend: "Some twenty-six years ago a farmer in a neighbouring village (West Cornwall) sustained during one season continual losses from his cows dying of indigestion, known as 'loss of cud,' 'hoven-blown,' etc. After consulting an old farrier called Armstrong he was induced to go to a 'pellar' in Exeter. His orders were to go home, and, on nearing his farm, he would see an old woman in a field hoeing turnips, and that she was the party who had cast the 'evil eye' on him. When he saw her he was to lay hold of her and accuse her of the crime, then tear off some of her dress, take it to his farm, and burn it with some of the hair from the tails of his surviving stock. These directions were fully carried out, and his bad health (caused by worry) improved, and he lost no more cows. A spotted clover that grew luxuriantly that summer was no doubt the cause of the swelling." "Another farmer in the same village eighteen years since lost all his feeding cattle from pleuro-pneumonia; believing them to be 'ill-wished' by a woman, he also consulted the Exeter 'pellar.' He brought home some bottles of elixir, potent against magic, and made an image of dough, pierced it from the nape of the neck downward, in the line of the spine, with a very large blanket-pin. In order to make the agonies of the woman with the 'evil eye' excruciating in the last degree, dough and pin were then burnt in a fire of hazel and ash. The cure failed, as anyone acquainted with the disease might have forecast."

Besides those remedies already mentioned for curing cattle, you may employ these:—"Take some blood from the sick animal by wounding him; let the blood fall on some straw carefully held to the place—not a drop must be lost; burn the straw; when the ill-wisher will be irresistibly drawn to the spot; then by violence you

can compel him to take off the spell." Or, "Bleed one animal
to death to save the whole herd."

A local newspaper, in 1883 *(Cornishman)*, gives the following:—
"Superstitions die hard.—A horse died the other day on a farm
in the neighbourhood of St. Ives. Its carcase was dragged on a
Sunday away up to the granite rock basins and weather-worn bosses
of Trecoben hill, and there burnt, in order to drive away the evil
spell, or ill-wishing, which afflicted the farm where the animal
belonged." I, a few years since, saw a dying cat taken out of a
house on a mat, by two servants, that it might not die inside and
bring ill-luck. "In 1865 a farmer in Portreath sacrificed a calf, by
burning, for the purpose of removing a disease which had long
followed his horses and cows." And in another case a farmer burnt
a living lamb, to save, as he said, "his flock from spells which had
been cast on them."—Robert Hunt.

The *Cornishman*, in another paragraph, says:—"Our Summer-
court (East Cornwall) correspondent witnessed an amusing affair on
Thursday morning (April, 1883). Seeing a crowd in the street, he
asked the reason, and found that a young lady was about to perform
the feat of *throwing a pig's nose over a house for good luck!* This
is how it was done. The lady took the nose of a pig, that was
killed the day before, in her right hand, stood with her back to
the house, and threw the nose over her head, and over the house,
into the back garden. Had she failed in the attempt her luck was
supposed to be bad." "Whet your knife on Sunday, you'll skin on
Monday," is a very old Perranuthnoe and St. Hilary (West Cornwall)
superstition, so that, however blunt your knife may be, you must use
it as it is, lest by sharpening it you bring ill-luck on the farmer,
and he lose a sheep or bullock." Mr. T. Q. Couch, *W. Antiquary*,
1883, says of one, "He is an old-fashioned man, and, amongst his
other 'whiddles' (whims), keeps a goat amongst his cattle for the
sake of keeping his cows from slipping their calves." Branches
of care (mountain ash) were, in the east of the county, hung over
the cattle in their stalls to prevent their being "ill-wished," also
carried in the pocket as a cure and prevention of rheumatism.

"Rheumatism will attack the man who carries a walking stick made of holly."—*Cornubiana*, Rev. S. Rundle.

The belief in witchcraft in West Cornwall is much more general than most people imagine. Several cases have lately come under my own notice; one, that of a man-servant in our employ who broke a blood-vessel, and for a long time was so ill that his life was despaired of. He was most carefully attended by a Penzance physician, who came to see him three times a day. But directly that his strength began to return he asked permission to go to Redruth to consult a "pellar," as he was quite sure that he had been "overlooked" and "ill-wished." An old Penzance man, afflicted with rheumatism, who gained his living by selling fruit in the streets, fancied himself ill-wished. He went to Helston to see a "wiseman" residing there, to whom he paid seven-and-sixpence, with a further promise of five pounds on the removal of the "spell." As he was too poor to pay this himself a brother agreed to do it for him, but somehow failed to perform his contract. Now the poor old man thinks that the pellar's ill-wishes are added to his former pains.

The "pellars" wore formerly magical rings, with a blue stone in them, said to have been formed by snakes breathing on hazel-twigs. Our country-people often searched for these stones.

⇒ CHARMS, ETC. ⇐

MANY are the charms against ill-wishing worn by the ignorant. I will quote some mentioned by Mr. Bottrell: "A strip of parchment inscribed with the following words forming a four-sided acrostic:—

```
S A T O R
A R E P O
T E N E T
O P E R A
R O T A S
```

"At the time of an old lady's decease, a little while ago, on her breast was found a small silk bag containing several charms, among others a piece of parchment, about three inches square, having written on one side of it 'Nalgah' (in capital letters); under this is a pen-and-ink drawing something like a bird with two pairs of wings, a pair extended and another folded beneath them. The creature appears to be hovering and at the same time brooding on a large egg, sustained by one of its legs, whilst it holds a smaller egg at the extremity of its other leg, which is outstretched and long. Its head, round and small, is unlike that of a bird. From the rudeness of the sketch and its faded state it is difficult to trace all the outlines. Under this singular figure is the word 'Tetragrammaton' (in capitals); on the reverse in large letters—

'Jehovah.'
'Jah, Eloim.'
'Shadday.'
'Adonay.'
'Have mercy on a poor woman.'

"A pellar of great repute in the neighbourhood tells me that this is inscribed with two charms, that Nalgah is the figure only. The Abracadabra is also supplied, the letters arranged in the usual way. Another potent spell is the rude draft of the planetary signs for the Sun, Jupiter, and Venus, followed by a cross, pentagram, and a figure formed by a perpendicular line and a divergent one at each side of it united at the bottom. Under them is written, 'Whosoever beareth these tokens will be fortunate, and need fear no evil.' The charms are folded in a paper on which is usually written, 'By the help of the Lord these will do thee good,' and inclosed in a little bag to be worn on the breast."

People in good health visited these pellars every spring to get their charms renewed, and bed-ridden people who kept theirs under their "pillow-beres" were then visited by the pellar for the same purpose. "Of amulets mention must be made of certain small crystal balls called 'kinning stones,' held in high esteem for cure of ailments of the eye. I examined one of these 'kinning stones' recently, which had been lent to a person with a bad eye, who on recovering from his ailment had returned it to the owner. It proved to be a translucent, blueish-white globular crystal, about one-and-a-quarter inch in diameter; in texture, horny rather than vitreous; apparently not made of glass, but perhaps of rock crystal; pierced by a hole containing a boot lace for suspension; having striæ running through the substance of the crystal perpendicular to the hole. It had been for many generations in possession of the family of the owner, who valued it very highly, "but was willing to lend it to anyone to do good." This kind of amulet is worn around the neck, the bad eye being struck with the crystal every morning. There are other 'kinning stones'

within reach, but examples are not common; their virtues are
familiar to the people, and instances are to be met with among
the country folk, whose recovery from a 'kinning' in the eye
('kennel,' West Cornwall) is attributed solely to the use of these
charms."—*Notes on the Neighbourhood of Brown Willy* (North Cornwall), Rev. A. H. Malan, M.A.

In every small Cornish village in olden times (and the race is not
yet extinct) lived a charmer or "white witch." Their powers were
not quite as great as those of a pellar, but they were thoroughly
believed in, and consulted on every occasion for every complaint.
They were not only able to cure diseases, but they could, when
offended, "overlook" and ill-wish the offender, bringing ill-luck
on him, and also on his family and farm-stock. The seventh
son of the seventh son, or seventh daughter of the seventh
daughter, were born with this gift of charming, and made the
most noted pellars; but anyone might become a witch who
touched a Logan rock nine times at midnight. These Logan
rocks are mentioned elsewhere as being in Cornwall their favourite
resorts, and to them they went, it is said, riding on ragwort stems,
instead of the traditional broomsticks.

Or, he might, says another authority, use the following charm:
"Go to the chancel of a church to sacrament, hide away the bread
from the hands of the priest, at midnight carry it around the church
from south to north, crossing east three times. The third time a
big toad, open-mouthed, will be met, put the bread in it; as soon
as swallowed he will breathe three times upon the man, and from
that time he will become a witch. Known by five black spots
diagonally placed under the tongue." There is also a strange
glare in the eye of a person who can "overlook," and the eyelids
are always red.

Witches could in this country change themselves into toads, as
well as hares. Mr. Robert Hunt relates the story of one who met
her death in that form, and Mr. T. Q. Couch tells the tale of a
sailor who was a "witch," who received several injuries whilst
in the shape of that animal. When a very small child, having a
"kennel" (an ulcer) on my eye, I was unknown to my parents taken

U

by an old servant to a Penzance "charmer," who then made a great deal of money by her profession. All I can remember about it is, that she breathed on it, made some curious passes with her hands and muttered some incantation.

About twelve years ago, a woman who lived in the "west country" (Land's End district) as well as being a " white witch was a famous knitster," and we amongst others frequently gave her work. When she brought it back she was treated by our maids, who lived in great fear of her " ill-wishing " them, to the best our kitchen could afford ; and many were the marvellous stories she told me of her power to staunch blood, etc., when doctors failed. It was not necessary for her to see the person ; she could cure them sitting by her fireside if they were miles away. Witches are also consulted about the recovery of stolen property, which, by casting their spells over the thief, it is still supposed they can compel him to return.

A part of Launceston Castle is locally known as Witch's Tower, from the tradition that one was burnt at its foot ; no grass grows on the spot. Another is said to have met with the same fate on a flat stone close to St. Austell market-house.

"Charms are still in use by the simple-minded for thrush, warts, and various complaints ; also for the cure of cattle, when some evil disposed person has 'turned a figure upon (*i.e.* bewitched) them ;' and white witches—those who avert the evil eye—have not yet ceased out of the land."—*Notes on the Neighbourhood of Brown Willy* (North Cornwall), Rev. A. H. Malan, M.A.

I will give some of their charms culled from various sources, and remedies for diseases still used in Cornwall :—Take three burning sticks from the hearth of the " overlooker," make the patient cross over them three times and then extinguish with water. Place nine bramble-leaves in a basin of " Holy Well's water, pass each leaf over and from the diseased part, repeating three times to each leaf. Three virgins came from the east, one brought fire, the others brought frost. Out fire ! In frost ! In the name of the Father, Son, and Holy Ghost." Or take a stick of burning furze from the hearth, pass over and above the diseased part, repeating the above nine times. If you can succeed by any means in drawing blood from the "ill-wisher" you are certain to break and remove the spell. Stick pins into an apple or potatoe, carry it in your pocket, and as it shrivels the "ill-wisher" will feel an ache from every pin, but this I fancy does not do the person "overlooked" any good. Another authority says, "Stick pins into a bullock's heart, when the 'ill-wisher' will feel a stab for every one put in, and in self-defence take off the curse."

A friend writes, "An old man called Uncle Will Jelbart, who had been with the Duke of Kent in America, and also a very long time in the Peninsular, about forty years ago lived in West Cornwall; he had a small pension, and in addition made a good income by charming warts, wildfire (erysipelas), cataracts, etc. He used to spit three times and breathe three times on the part affected, muttering, 'In the name of the Father, Son, and Holy Ghost I bid thee begone.' For cataract he pricked the small white 'dew-snail' (slug), found about four a.m., with a hawthorn spine, and let a drop fall into the eye; and in the case of skin diseases occasionally supplemented the charm with an ointment made of the juice extracted from house-leeks and 'raw-cream;' he sometimes changed the words and repeated those which with slight variations are known all over Cornwall—'Three virgins,' etc.

"The crowfoot locally known as the 'kenning herb' is in some districts used in incantations for curing 'kennings' or 'kennels' (ulcers in the eye).

'Three ladies (or virgins) come from the east :
One with fire and two with frost ;
Out with thee, fire, and in with thee, frost :
In the name of the Father, Son, and Holy Ghost.'

This is often said nine times over a scald. In prose it begins thus: 'As I passed over the river Jordan, I met with Christ. He said, What aileth thee? Oh Lord, my flesh doth burn. The Lord said unto me, Two angels,'" etc.

A lady once told me that about forty years ago she was taken to a "charmer," who stood in a Cornish market-place on fixed days, to have her warts cured. The remedies for this childish complaint are very numerous. I once had my forehead rubbed with a piece of stolen beef, which was then buried in a garden, to send them away, the idea being that as the beef decayed the warts would fall off or dwindle gradually. There are two or three other ways of getting rid of them of a similar kind. Touch each wart with a new pin, enclose them in a bottle, either bury them in a newly-made grave of the opposite sex, or at four cross-roads; as the pins rust, the warts will disappear. Or, touch them with a knot made in a piece of string (there should be as many knots as there are warts), bury it; when the rope decays so will the warts. The two next are selfish remedies. Touch each wart with a pebble, put the stones in a bag, throw them away, and the finder will get them and they will leave you. Or, in coming out of church, wish them on some part of another person's body (or on a tree); they will go from you and appear on him, or on the spot named. One method employed by professional "charmers" is to take two pieces of charred stick from a fire, form them into a cross and place them on the warts, and repeat one of the formulæ above quoted. Yet another is to wash the hands in the moon's rays focussed in a dry metal basin, saying,

> "I wash my hands in this thy dish,
> Oh man in the moon, do grant my wish,
> And come and take away this."

The moon too is invoked for the curing of corns. "Corns down here! No corns up there!" is repeated nine times. The fore-finger pointing first to the ground and then to the sky.

When pricked by a thorn, use one of the following charms :—

> "Christ was of a virgin born :
> And he was pricked by a thorn,
> And it did never ' bell ' (fester),
> And I trust in Jesus this never will."

Or,

> "Christ was crowned with thorns,
> The thorns did bleed but did not rot,
> No more shall thy—(mentioning the part affected) :
> In the name of the Father, Son, and Holy Ghost."

In prose: "When Christ was upon the middle earth the Jews pricked him, his blood sprung up into heaven, his flesh never rotted nor 'fustered,' no more I hope will not thine. In the name," etc.— From Mr. T. Q. Couch, who gives two others very similar.

FOR TETTERS.

" Tetter, tetter, thou hast nine sisters,
 God bless thee, flesh, and preserve thee, bone ;
 Perish thou, tetter, and be thou gone :
 In the name," etc.

"Tetter, tetter, thou hast eight sisters," etc.

This charm is thus continued until it comes to the last, which is,—

"Tetter, tetter, thou hast no sister," etc.—Bottrell.

TOOTHACHE.

In prose and verse slightly varied, common in all parts of the county,—

" Christ passed by his brother's door,
 Saw Peter his brother lying on the floor ;
 What aileth thee, brother ?—
 Pain in thy teeth ?
 Thy teeth shall pain thee no more :
 In the name of," etc.

This is to be worn in a bag around the neck. Mr. T. Q. Couch gives this charm in prose. It begins thus: "Peter sat at the gate of the Temple, and Christ said unto him, What aileth thee ?" etc. Another remedy against toothache is, always in the morning to begin dressing by putting the stocking on the left foot.—Through Rev. S. Rundle.

A knuckle-bone is often carried in the pocket as a cure and preventive of cramp. I once saw an old woman turn out her pocket; amongst its contents, as well as the knuckle-bone, was the tip of an ox-tongue kept for good luck.

Slippers on going to bed are, when taken off, for the same complaint often placed under the bed with the soles upwards, or on their heels against the post of the bed with their toes up. The following is from Mr. T. Q. Couch: "The cramp is keenless, Mary was sinless when she bore Jesus: let the cramp go away in the name of Jesus." All the charms published by the above-named author in his *History of Polperro* were taken from a manuscript book, which belonged to a white witch.

When a foot has "gone to sleep" I have often seen people wet their forefingers in their mouths, stoop and draw the form of a cross on it. This is said to be an infallible remedy. Mr. Robert Hunt has a rather similar cure for hiccough: "Wet the forefinger of the right hand with spittle, and cross the front of the left shoe (or boot) three times, repeating the Lord's Prayer backwards." The most popular cure with children is a heaping spoonful of moist sugar. A sovereign remedy for hiccough and almost every complaint is a small piece of a stale Good Friday bun grated into a glass of cold water. This bun is hung up in the kitchen from one year to the other. Bread baked on this day never gets mouldy.

For a Strain.

"Christ rode over the bridge,
Christ rode under the bridge;
Vein to vein, strain to strain,
I hope God will take it back again."

For Ague.

When our Saviour saw the cross, whereon he was to be crucified, his body did shake. The Jews said, "Hast thou an ague?" Our Saviour said, "He that keepeth this in mind, thought, or writing, shall neither be troubled with ague or fever."

For Wildfire (Erysipelas).

"Christ, he walketh over the land,
Carried the wildfire in his hand,
He rebuked the fire, and bid it stand;
Stand, wildfire, stand (three times repeated):
In the name of," etc.—T. Q. Couch.

Mr. Robert Hunt gives in his book on *Old Cornwall* a Latin charm for the staunching of blood. I find, however, on making inquiries that it is not the one generally used, which is as follows:

"Christ was born in Bethlehem,
Baptised in the river Jordan ;
There he digged a well,
And turned the water against the hill,
So shall thy blood stand still :
In the name," etc.

There are other versions all much alike. A prose one runs thus : "Baptised in the river Jordan when the water was wild, the water was good, the water stood, so shall thy blood. In the name," etc. —T. Q. C.

The Rev. S. Rundle says a charmer once told him the charm for staunching blood consisted in saying a verse from the Psalms ; but she could not read, and he was inclined to believe the form was, "Jesus came to the river Jordan, and said, 'Stand,' and it stood ; and so I bid thee, blood, stand. In the name," etc. For bleeding at the nose, a door-key is often placed against the back. Cuts are plugged with cobwebs, flue from a man's hat, tobacco leaves, and occasionally filled with salt.

Club-moss is considered good for eye diseases. On the third day of the moon, when the thin crescent is seen for the first time, show it the knife with which the moss for the charm is to be cut, and repeat,

"As Christ healed the issue of blood,
So I bid thee begone :
In the name of," etc.

Mr. Robert Hunt says,

"Do thou cut what thou cuttest for good !"

"At sun-down, having carefully washed the hands, the club-moss is to be cut kneeling. It is to be carefully wrapped in a white cloth, and subsequently boiled in water taken from the spring nearest its place of growth. This may be used as a fomentation. Or the club-moss made into an ointment with butter made from the milk of a new cow."

A "stye" on the eye is often stroked nine times with a cat's tail ; with a wedding ring taken from a dead woman's, or a silver one from a drowned man's, hand. The belief in the efficacy of a dead hand in curing diseases in Cornwall is marvellous. I, in a short paper read at an Antiquarian meeting, gave this instance, related to me by a medical man about ten years ago (now dead). A day or two after, a number of other cases in proof of my statement appeared, to my surprise, in our local papers, which, as well as my own, I will transcribe. "Once I attended a poor woman's child for an obstinate case of sore eyes. One day when leaving the house the mother said to me, 'Is there nothing more, doctor, I can do for my little girl?' I jokingly answered, 'Nothing, unless you care to stroke them with a dead man's hand.' About a week after I met the woman in the streets, who stopped me, and said, 'My child's eyes are getting better at last, doctor.' I expressed myself pleased that the ointment I had given her was doing good. To my astonishment, she replied, 'Oh, it is not that, we never used it; we took your advice about the dead man's hand.' Until she recalled it to my memory, I had quite forgotten my foolish speech." "I am one of those who can bear testimony to the fact of a cure having been effected by the means above-named. I was born with a disfigurement on my upper lip. My mother felt a great anxiety about this, so my nurse proposed that a dead man's hand should be passed seven times over my lip. I was taken to the house of one Robin Gendall, Causewayhead, Penzance, who at that time was lying dead, and his hand was passed over my lip in the manner named. By slow degrees my friends had the satisfaction of seeing that the charm had taken effect."—*Octogenarian.*

"I may add my testimony to Miss Courtney's remarks as to the belief in Cornwall in the virtue of the touch of a diseased part by a dead man's hand. A case came under my knowledge at Penzance of a child who had from birth a peculiar tuberous formation at the junction of the nose with the forehead, which the medical men would not cut for fear of severing veins. The child was taken by her mother to a friend's house, in which were lying the remains of a young man who had just died from consumption. The deceased's hand was passed over the malformation seven times, and it soon began to grow smaller and smaller." "I have myself seen the child since Miss Courtney read her paper (November, 1881), and, though the mark is still apparent, I am assured it is surely, if slowly, disappearing. A relation of mine also tells me that, like Miss Courtney, she was taken to the Penzance witch for the purpose of having a 'stye' removed from one of her eyes by charming."—Tramp.

I was told of many other cases—one by another surgeon; but it would be useless to repeat them. I will end with one I have taken from *Notes and Queries*, December, 1859:—

" A lady, who was staying lately at Penzance, attended a funeral, and noticed that whilst the clergyman was reading the burial service a woman forced her way through the pall-bearers to the edge of the grave. When he came to the passage, 'Earth to earth, ashes to ashes, dust to dust,' she dropped a white cloth upon the coffin, closed her eyes, and apparently said a prayer. On making inquiries as to the cause of this proceeding, this lady found that a superstition exists amongst the peasantry in that part, that if a person with a sore be taken secretly to a corpse, the dead hand passed over the sore place, and the bandage afterwards be dropped upon the coffin during the reading of the burial service, a perfect cure will be the result. This woman had a child with a bad leg, and she had followed this superstition with a firm belief in its efficacy. The peasants, also, to the present day wear charms, believing they will protect them from sickness and other evils. The wife of the clergyman of the parish was very charitable in attending the sick and dispensing medicines, and one day a woman brought her a child having sore eyes to have them charmed, having more faith in that remedy than in medicines. She was greatly surprised to find that medicines only were given to her."—E. R.

There is no virtue in the dead hand of a near relation. A curious old troth plight was formerly practised in Cornwall: The couple broke a wedding ring taken from the finger of a corpse, and each kept one half. The editor of a local paper *(Cornishman)* once obtained a piece of rope, with which a man was hanged, for a poor woman who had walked fourteen miles to Bodmin in the hopes of getting it, that she might effect the cure of her sore eyes.

V

The Rev. S. Rundle writes that "a Cornish surgeon recommended a charmer as being more efficacious than himself in curing shingles. According to the same authority, a liquid composed of bramble and butter-dock leaves is poured on the place, whilst a light stick is waved over the decoction by the charmer, who repeats an incantation." It is popularly supposed in Cornwall that should shingles meet around your waist, you would die. The cures and charms against epilepsy are also very numerous, and very generally used here. Thirty pence are collected at the church door by the person afflicted, from one of the opposite sex, changed for sacrament money (silver), and made into a ring to be worn day and night. Very lately, at St. Just-in-Penwith, a young woman begged from young men pennies to buy a silver ring, a remedy which she believed would cure her fits. Another charm, which it requires a person of strong nerves to perform, is to walk thrice round a church at midnight, then enter and stand before the altar. In connection with this rite the Rev. S. Rundle relates the following:—"At Crowan (a village in West Cornwall), an epileptic subject entered the church at midnight. As he was groping his way through the pitchy dark, his heart suddenly leaped, and almost stood still. He uttered shriek upon shriek, for his hand had grasped a man's head. He thought it was the head of the famous Sir John St. Aubyn. He was removed in a fainting state, and it was then discovered that he had seized the head of the sexton, who had come in to see that nothing was done to frighten the man. The unfortunate fellow never recovered from the shock, but died in a lunatic asylum." "A middle-aged Camborne man was subject to violent fits until two years ago, when some one told him to kill a toad, put one of its legs in a bag, and wear it suspended by a string around his neck. He did so, and has never had a fit since."—*Cornishman*, December, 1881.

"In Cornwall a black cock is buried on the spot where the person is first attacked by epilepsy" (to avert a similar attack).—*Comparative Folk-Lore, Cornhill*, 1876.

For other charms see Addenda, *A Bundle of Charms*, by the Rev. A. H. Malan, M.A.

Toads are also worn as charms for other diseases in this county:—
"On the 27th July, 1875, I was lodging with a very intelligent
grazier and horse-dealer, at Tintagel, Cornwall, when he was knocked
down by a very serious attack of quinsey, to which he had been
subject for many years. He pulled through the crisis; and on
being sufficiently recovered he betook himself to a 'wise woman'
at Camelford. She prescribed for him as follows:—'Get a live
toad, fasten a string around its throat, and hang it up till the body
drops from the head; then tie the string around your own neck,
and never take it off, night or day, till your fiftieth birthday. You'll
never have quinsey again.' When I left Tintagel, I understood that
my landlord, greatly relieved in mind, had already commenced the
operation."—Augustus Jessop, D.D.

When a kettle won't boil, instead of the old adage, "A watched
pot never boils," Cornish people say, "There is a toad or a frog
in it." It is here considered lucky for a toad to come into the
house.

This charm for yellow jaundice I culled from the *Western
Antiquary.* "I was walking in a village churchyard near the town
of St. Austell (I think in the autumn of 1839), when I saw a
woman approach an open grave. She stood by the side of it
and appeared to be muttering some words. She then drew out
from under her cloak a good-size baked meal-cake, threw it into
the grave and then left the place. Upon inquiry I found the
cake was composed of oatmeal mixed with dog's urine, baked,
and thrown into the grave as a charm for the yellow jaundice.
This cure was at that time commonly believed in by the peasantry
of the neighbourhood."—Joseph Cartwright, March, 1883.

Snakes avoid and dread ash-trees; a branch will keep them
away. Our peasantry believe however much you may try to kill
quickly an adder or snake, it will never die before sunset.
Mr. Robert Hunt says, "When an adder is seen, a circle is
to be rapidly drawn around it and the sign of the cross made
within it, whilst the first two verses of the 68th Psalm are
repeated." This is to destroy it; there are also charms to be
said for curing their bites, when they are apostrophised "under

the ashen leaf." The following old charm is to make them destroy themselves, by twisting themselves up to nothing :—

> "Underneath this 'hazelen mot' *
> There's a 'braggaty' † worm, with a speckled throat,
> Now! nine 'double' ‡ hath he.
> Now from nine double, to eight double,
> From eight double, to seven double,
> From seven double, to six double,
> From six double, to five double,
> From five double, to four double,
> From four double, to three double,
> From three double, to two double,
> From two double, to one double,
> Now! no double hath he."

The words of charms must be muttered (they lose their efficacy if recited aloud), and the charmer must never communicate them to one of the same sex, for that transfers the power of charming to the other person. Of superstitious rites practised for the cure of whooping-cough, etc., I will speak a little further on. Cornishmen in the last century from their cradles to their graves might have been guided in their actions by old women's "widdles" (superstitions), some as already shown are still foolishly followed; but I hope that few people are silly enough at the present day to leave their babies' heads a twelvemonth unwashed, under the mistaken notion that it would be unlucky to do it.

I have often and very recently seen the creases in the palms of children's hands filled with dirt; to clean them before they were a year old would take away riches—they would live and die poor. Their nails, too, for the same period should be bitten, not cut, for that would make them thieves. Hair at no age must be cut at the waning of the moon, that would prevent its growing luxuriantly; locks shorn off must be always burnt, it is unlucky to throw them away; then birds might use them in their nests and weave them in so firmly that there would be a difficulty in your rising at the last day. Children's first teeth are burnt to prevent dog's or

---

* Hazelen mot—root of a hazel tree.
† Braggaty—spotted.
‡ Double—a ring.

"snaggles" irregular teeth coming in their stead. Coral necklaces are worn to ensure easy teething; the beads are said to change their colour when the wearer is ill. "All locks are unlocked to favour easy birth (or death)."—A. H. Bickford, M.D., Camborne, 1883. Cornishmen in the West are said to be born with tails; they drop off when the Tamar is crossed.

"A popular notion amongst old folks is, that when a boy is born on the waning moon the next birth will be a girl, and vice versâ. They also say that when a birth takes place on the growing of the moon, the next child will be of the same sex." A child born in the interval between the old and new moons is fated to die young, and babies with blue veins across their noses do not live to see twenty-one. A cake called a groaning cake is made in some houses in Cornwall after the birth of a child, of which every caller is expected to partake. The mother often carries "a groaning cake" when she is going to be "upraised" (churched); this she gives to the first person she meets on her way.

"Kimbly" is the name of an offering, generally a piece of bread or cake, still given in some rural districts of this county to the first person met when going to a wedding or a christening. It is sometimes presented to anyone who brings the news of a a birth to an interested party. Two young men, I knew about thirty years ago, were taking a walk in West Cornwall; crossing over a bridge they met a procession carrying a baby to the parish church, where the child was to be baptised. Unaware of this curious custom, they were very much surprised at having a piece of cake put into their hands. A magistrate wrote to the *Western Morning News*, in January, 1884, saying, that on his way to his petty sessions he had had one of these christening cakes thrust into his hand, but unluckily he did not state in what parish this happened. This called forth several letters on the subject, parts of which I will quote.

"About thirty years ago at the christening of a brother (in the Meneage district, Helston), and when the family party were ready for the walk to the afternoon service in Cury church, I well recollect seeing the old nurse wrap in a pure white sheet of paper what she called the 'cheeld's fuggan.'* This was a cake with plenty of currants and saffron, about the size of a modern tea-plate. It was to be given to the first person met on returning, after the child was christened. It happened that, as most of the parishioners were at the service, no one was met until near home, almost a mile from the church, when a tipsy village carpenter rambled around a corner, right against our party, and received the cake. Regrets were expressed that the 'cheeld's fuggan' should have fallen to the lot of this notoriously evil liver, and my idea was that it was a bad omen. However as my brother has always been a veritable Rechabite, enjoys good health, a contented mind, and enough of this world's goods to satisfy every moderate want, no evil can thus far be traced to the mischance."—J. C., *Western Morning News*.

" 'Kimbly' in East Cornwall is the name of a thing, commonly a piece of bread, which is given under peculiar circumstances at weddings and christenings. When the parties set out from the house to go to church, or on their business, one person is sent before them with this selected piece of bread in his or her hand (a woman is commonly preferred for this office), and the piece is given to the first individual that is met. I interpret it to have some reference to the idea of the evil eye and its influence, which might fall on the married persons or on the child, which is sought to be averted by this unexpected gift. It is also observed in births, in order that by this gift envy may be turned away from the infant or happy parents. This 'kimbly' is commonly given to the person bringing the first news to those interested in the birth."—T. Q. Couch, *Western Morning News*.

"I witnessed this custom very frequently at Looe, in South-east Cornwall, from fifty to sixty-five years ago. I believe it is correct to say that this gift was there a small cake, made for the occasion, and termed the 'christening-crib,' a crib of bread or cake being a provincialism for a bit of bread," etc.—William Pengelly, *Western Morning News*.

Children, when they leave small bits of meat, etc., on their plates, are in Cornwall often told "to eat up their cribs."

* Fuggan, a flat cake.

"On the afternoons of Good Friday, little girls of Carharrack, in the parish of Gwennap (West Cornwall), take their dolls to a stream at the foot of Carnmarth, and there christen them. Occasionally a young man will take upon himself the office of minister, and will sprinkle and name the dolls."—Charles James, Gwennap.

The Rev. S. Rundle, Vicar of Godolphin, says, "That once he was sent for to baptise a child, around whose neck hung a little bag, which the mother said contained a bit of a donkey's ear, and that this charm had cured the child of a most distressing cough."

"In some parts of Cornwall it is considered a sure sign of being sweethearts if a young man and woman 'stand witness together,' *i.e.* become godfather and godmother of the same child."—T. C. But not in all, for I remember once hearing in Penzance a couple refuse to do so, saying that it was unlucky. "First at the font, never at the altar." When I was young, old nurses often breathed in babies' mouths to cure the thrush, thrice repeating the second verse of the Eighth Psalm, "Out of the mouths of babes and sucklings," etc. "May children and 'chets' (kittens) never thrive," and it is unlucky to "tuck" (short coat) children in that month.

> "Tuck babies in May,
> You'll tuck them away."

It is of course considered an unfortunate month for marriages. Neither should babies "be tucked" on a week day, but on a Sunday, which day should also be chosen for leaving off any article of clothing; as then you will have the prayers of every congregation for you, and are sure not to catch cold. A friend lately sent me the following charm of one year's duration which prevents your feeling or taking a cold. "Eat a large apple at Hallow-een under an apple-tree just before midnight; no other garment than a bed-sheet should be worn. A kill or cure remedy."

An empty cradle should never be rocked unless you wish to have a large family, for—

> "Rock the cradle empty
> You'll rock the babies plenty."

Rev. S. Rundle says, "It is unlucky to rock an empty cradle, as the child will die."—*Cornubiana.*

The jingles which follow are often repeated by Cornish nursemaids with appropriate actions to amuse their little charges. First, touching each part of the face as mentioned with the forefinger,

> "Brow brender,*
> Eye winker,
> Nose dropper,
> Mouth eater,
> Chin chopper,
> Tickle-tickle."

Second—

> "Tap a tap shoe,† that would I do,
> If I had but a little more leather.
> We'll sit in the sun till the leather doth come,
> Then we'll tap them both together."

Here the two little feet are struck lightly one against the other.

Several letters have lately appeared in the *Western Morning News,* giving different versions of the old rhymes—

> "Matthew, Mark, Luke, and John,
> Pray bless the bed that I 'lay' on,
> Four corners to my bed,
> Four angels there are spread,
> Two 'to' foot and two 'to' head,
> And six will carry me when I'm dead."

Although attributed by the correspondents to Cornwall, I have always understood that they were known all over England.

Children with rickets were taken by their parents on the three first Sundays in May to be dipped at sunrise in one of the numerous Cornish holy wells, and then put to sleep in the sun, with sixpence under their heads. Small pieces torn from their clothes were left on the bushes to propitiate the pixies. For the same disease they were passed nine times through a Mên-an-tol (holed stone). A man stood on one side, and a woman on the other, of the stone. The child was passed with the sun from east to west, and from right to left; a boy from the woman to the man, a girl

* Brend, to knit the brows.
† Tap a shoe, to sole.

from the man to the woman. This order is always, in these charms, strictly observed. As lately as 1883, in the village of Sancred, West Cornwall, a little girl, suffering from whooping-cough, was passed from a man to a woman nine times under a donkey's belly; a little boy standing the while at the donkey's head feeding it with "cribs" of wheaten bread. My informant did not know if on this occasion any incantation was repeated. Another family, he tells me, some years back were in the same neighbourhood cured of the whooping-cough by donkey's hair, which was dried on the baking iron of the open hearth, reduced to powder, and administered to them. There are very various ways of doing this, one is between thin slices of bread and butter. Some authorities say the latter ingredients must belong to a couple called John and Joan. Mr. Robert Hunt gives a charm which in a measure combines the two above-mentioned. "The child must be passed naked nine times over the back and under the belly of a female donkey. Three spoonfuls of milk drawn from the teats of the animal, three hairs cut from its back, and three from its belly, are to stand in the milk three hours, and to be given in three doses repeated on three mornings." Mr. Hunt also says, "There were some doggerel lines connected with the ceremony which have escaped my memory, and I have endeavoured in vain to find anyone remembering them. They were to the effect that as Christ placed the cross on the ass's back when he rode into Jerusalem and so rendered the animal holy, if the child touched where Jesus sat it should cough no more." I will quote another of Mr. Hunt's charms. "Gather nine spar-stones (quartz) from a running stream, taking care not to interrupt the free passage of the water in doing so. Then dip a quart of water from the stream, which must be taken in the direction in which the stream runs—by no means must the vessel be dipped against the stream. Then make the nine stones red-hot, and throw them into the quart of water. Bottle the prepared water, and give the afflicted child a wine-glass of this water for nine mornings." Other remedies are to cross the child over running water nine times, or under a bramble bough bent into the ground (this latter and through a cleft ash are also tried for hernia). Some nurses take children, with whooping-

w

cough, out for a walk, in hopes of meeting a man on a white or piebald horse. Should they be fortunate enough to do so, they ask the rider how they can cure the patient: his advice is always implicitly followed.

Children with dirty habits are often told that a "mousey pasty" shall be cooked for their dinners.

Cornish children are warned by their nurses not to grimace, lest, whilst so doing, the wind should change and their faces always remain contorted. There is another form in which this warning is often given: "Don't make mock of a 'magum' (May-game), for you may be struck comical yourself one day." "Magum" in most cases means a facetious person, one who is full of merry pranks; and the expressions, "He's a reg'lar magum," or "He's full of his magums," are often heard. But the idea intended to be conveyed in the first saying is that it is wrong to make fun of a person suffering from an infirmity, which may at any time afflict the jeerer. The puritanical notion of Sunday lingers in the belief in Cornwall that it is unlucky to use a scissors on that day, even to cut your nails; you must

> "Cut them on Monday, before your fast you break,
> And you'll have a present in less than a week."

Children here are pleased to see "gifts" (white spots) on their thumb-nails, as

> "Gifts on the thumb are sure to come,
> But gifts on the finger are sure to linger."

Occasionally white spots on the five fingers are named as follows: "A gift, a friend, a foe, a true lover, a journey to go." Should the little ones, when picking flowers, sting themselves with nettles, they are of course in this locality, as elsewhere in England, taught to rub the spot with dock-leaves, repeating the words, "In dock, out nettle;" but they are often told in addition to wet the place affected with their spittle, and make a cross over it with their thumb-nails, pressed down as heavily as possible. School-boys and school-girls often years ago practised a cruel jest on their more innocent companions. They induced them to pick a nettle by

saying "Nettles won't sting this month." When the children were
stung and complained, the retort was, "I never said they would not
sting you." The blue scabious in Cornwall is never plucked. It is
called the devil's bit, and the superstition is handed down from one
generation of children to another that, should they transgress and
do so, the devil will appear to them in their dreams at night. But
anyone who wishes to dream of the devil should pin four ivy-leaves
to the corners of his pillow. Flowers plucked from churchyards
bring ill-luck, and even visitations from spirits on the plucker.
Wrens and robins are sacred in the eyes of Cornish boys, for

> "Hurt a robin or a wran,
> Never prosper, boy nor man."

A groom who had, when a lad, shot a robin and held it in one of
his hands told me that it shook ever after. But they always chase
and try to kill the first butterfly of the season; and, should they
succeed, they will overcome their enemies—I suppose, in football,
etc.

"To hear the first cuckoo of spring on the right ear is lucky,
on the left unlucky; as many times as it repeats its notes will the
number of years be before the hearer is married. The cuckoo
song—

> 'In April, come he will,
> In May, he sings all day,
> In June, he alters his tune,
> In July, he prepares to fly,
> Come August, go he must'—

is known all over the county, with additions and slight variations,
such as—

> 'In March, he sits upon his perch,
> In Aperel, he tunes his bell.' "
>
> —South-east Cornwall, W. Pengelly.

"A bat in Cornwall is called an 'airy-mouse;' village boys
address it as it flits over their heads in the following rhymes—

> 'Airy-mouse, airy-mouse! fly over my head,
> And you shall have a crust of bread,
> And when I brew, or when I bake,
> You shall have a piece of my wedding cake.' "
>
> —Polperro, T. Q. Couch.

Sometimes in West Cornwall they say—

> "Bit-bat! bit-bat! come under my hat."

Earwigs they hold in detestation, as they believe that, should they get into their ears, they will cause madness. There is a legend popular amongst them which relates that a poor man was once driven frantic by a very queer sensation in his head. At last, not being able to bear it any longer, he went into a meat-market, laid it down upon a block, and asked a butcher to chop it off. Whilst in this recumbent position an earwig crept out of his ear, and the pain instantly ceased. Our school-boys have other fallacies, such as, the pain caused by a "custice," *i.e.* a stroke across the palm of the hand with a cane, may be neutralised by placing two hairs on it crossways. Also that the wound made by a nail can be kept from festering by wrapping the nail in a piece of fat bacon to prevent its rusting.

School-girls' superstitions are more sentimental, and often connected with wishing. If, when talking together, one accidentally makes a rhyme, she wishes; and, should she be asked a question before she speaks again, to which she can answer Yes, she thinks that she is sure to get it. When an eyelash falls out its owner puts it on the tip of her nose, wishes and blows at it; should she blow it off, she will have her wish. Should she by chance hear a dog dreaming, she stands up, puts a foot on each side of it, and then wishes. Years ago one gravely told me that if I wanted to know a dog's dreams I must throw a pocket-handkerchief over it when sleeping and keep it there until it awoke; then, before getting into bed, put it under my pillow, and I should have the same dream. Dreams in Cornwall are always said to go by contraries. "If you dream of the dead you will hear tell of the living," etc. To dream anyone is kissing you is a sign of deceit. "Of fruit out of season, trouble without reason."

> "A Friday's dream on Saturdays told
> Is sure to come true, be it ever so old."

To see if a friend loves her, a Cornish girl pulls out a hair from her friend's head, and then tries to suspend it by the root from the palm of her own hand. If this can be done the test is successful. When a little older there are many ways in which our maidens "try for their sweethearts." A few of the rules prescribed for these rites, which have been handed down from generation to generation, may be worth transcribing. "Draw a bracken fern, cut it at the bottom of the stalk; there you will find your lover's initials." Take an apple-pip between the forefinger and the thumb, flip it into the air, saying, "North, south, east, west, tell me where my love doth rest," and watch the direction in which it falls. Go into the fields at the time of the new moon and pluck a piece of herb yarrow; put it when going to bed under your pillow, saying—

> "Good night, fair yarrow,
> Thrice good night to thee ;
> I hope before to-morrow's dawn
> My true love I shall see."

If you are to be married your sweetheart will appear to you in your dreams.

"Look out of your bed-room window on St. Valentine's morn, note the first man you see, and you will marry the same, or one of the name."

To lose your apron or your garter shows that your lover is thinking of you. Three candles burning at the same time is the sign of a wedding; and the girl who is nearest to the door, the cupboard, and the shortest candle, will be married first. When two people accidentally say the same thing at the same time the one who finishes first will be married first. There are a great number of omens similar to these last, equally stupid, and not worthy of notice.

"Friday is a cross day for marriage," and "If you marry in Lent you'll live to repent." Should you in marrying

> "Change the name, and not the letter,
> You'll change for the worse, and not for the better."

but it is lucky if your initials form a word.

"The young men of a place, when they know that a person is paying attention to a girl or woman, seize hold of him, place him in a wheelbarrow, in which they wheel him up and down until they are tired, when they upset him on the nearest pile or in a pond. This is called riding in the 'one-wheel coach;' and to say that a man has ridden in the 'one-wheel coach' is tantamount to the expression that he has 'gone-a-courting.'"—Rev. S. Rundle, *Transactions Penzance Natural History Society, etc., 1885-1886.*

When a younger sister marries first the elder is said to dance in the "bruss" (short twigs of heath or furze), from an old custom of dancing without shoes on the furze prickles which get detached from the stalk. Only old maids can rear a myrtle, and they will not blossom when trained against houses where there are none. It is considered extremely unlucky here to break or lose your wedding-ring, also for a wedding-cake to crack after baking. A lady told me of one made for a couple she knew, which fell to pieces when taken out of the oven. Before the wedding-day came the bride had sickened of some disorder, was dead, and buried. A hole in a loaf, too, foretells a separation in a family; and to turn one upside down on a table wrecks a vessel. "If a hare cross the path of a wedding party, the bride or bridegroom will die within seven years."—Rev. S. Rundle, *Cornubiana.*

"A young woman who has been three times a bridesmaid will never be a bride." "It was an old custom, religiously observed until lately in Zennor and adjacent parishes on the north coast of Cornwall, to waylay a married couple on their wedding night and flog them to bed with cords, sheep-spans, or anything handy for the purpose, believing that this rough treatment would ensure them happiness and the 'heritage and gift that cometh of the Lord,' of a numerous family. At more modish weddings the guests merely entered the bridal chamber, and threw stockings in which stones or something to make weight were placed, at the bride and bridegroom in bed. The first one hit of the happy pair betokened the sex of their first-born."—Bottrell.

Should there be a great discrepancy between the ages of the bride and bridegroom, or the marriage of a couple in any way be a matter of notoriety, they are in West Cornwall on their wedding night often treated to a "shallal," a serenade on tin-kettles, pans, marrow-bones, &c. Any great noise in this part of the county is described as being "a reg'lar shallal." In olden times (in fact the custom is not quite discontinued at the present day, for I heard a whisper of one having taken place in a small fishing-village two years ago) married people accused of immorality were in Cornwall punished by a "riding." I will give the description of one by Mr. T. Q. Couch.

"A cart was got, donkeys were harnessed in, and a pair personating the guilty or suspected were driven through the streets, attended by a train of men and boys. At Polperro (East Cornwall) the attendants acted as trumpeters; the bullocks' horns used by the fishermen at sea for fog or night signals were always available for the purpose. The mummers were very cautious, by careful disguise in dress or voice, and avoiding of anything directly libellous in their rather ribald dialogue, to keep themselves out of the clutches of the law. I remember one *riding* when an old rusty cannon of the smuggling period was waked up from its long quiet for service for the occasion, and bursting, led to the mutilation of several and the death of one." On the borders of Devon and in that county this ceremony was known as a "mock-hunt."

A lock of hair hanging down over the forehead is in Cornwall called "a widow's lock;" (and children are still here told when it falls down "to shed their hair back out of their eyes.") A foolish warning says,

> "Go thro' a gate when there's a stile hard by,
> You'll be a widow before you die."

The sudden appearance of rats or mice in Cornish houses is said to be a certain forerunner of sickness and death. Many curious tales are told in confirmation of this superstition; one I particularly remember was in connection with a young man who was killed on the West Cornwall Railway. After the accident, they vanished as quickly as they came. It is also considered to be very unlucky for a bird to perch on the window-sill of a sick person's room, farewell then to all chances of recovery; and strange birds coming into a house (especially a robin through the back door) foretell the death of some one in it, or connected with the family. I was once where a little child lay dying, a small brown bird sang on the window-sill, the nurse told me that it was waiting to carry away the child's soul. "But when a flea bites a sick person he is sure not to be dangerously ill, as it is well known that they never bite those who have had their death-stroke." The superstitions that you cannot die easily on pillows stuffed with wild birds' feathers, and that life goes out with the tide, are as current here as in other places. Death in Cornwall is often spoken of as "going round land," and "gone dead" is a common idiom. A threat to kill is occasionally conveyed in the words "I will give you your quietus." In some cases it is supposed that life may be restored after death if when the breath stops the body be violently shaken. When a member of a family dies, his death it is said will bring two others with it,* from the idea that one misfortune never comes alone. A Cornish country vicarage was lately startled by the tolling at an unwonted hour of the church bell. On sending to ascertain the cause of the disturbance an "old inhabitant was found in the belfry, who had been engaged in the absence or illness of the usual sexton to dig the grave. He said in explanation that in his time it was always usual for the gravedigger to toll the bell three times before breaking the consecrated ground." J. H. C., *Notes and Queries*, 5th series, vol. ii., August, 1874.

A corpse should never be carried to church by a new road, and should a hearse stop on its way to the churchyard there will soon be another death in the house. Singing funerals, or as they are called in Cornwall buryings (pronounced "berrins"), were once almost universal (and one may still occasionally be met). The mourners and friends following the coffin sang as they walked through the streets or lanes their favourite hymns, often to most elaborate tunes.

> "To shaw our sperrits lev-us petch†
> The laast new berrin tune."—Tregellas.

---

* A similar superstition prevails about breakages, and a servant who has had the misfortune to break a valuable piece of china will sometimes smash a common basin or tea-cup to arrest the ill-luck.

† "Pitch a tune," to give the keynote.

Few people in old days were buried on the north side of a church. Flowers and shrubs planted in Cornish churchyards are never plucked, from the fear that the spirits of the departed will at night visit the desecrator. Should an urn found in a "barrow" be taken into a house, the person whose ashes it contained will haunt it; it must be broken up and the pieces hidden. Cross-roads, the former burying-place of suicides, are after nightfall avoided, such spots being haunted; but if you have courage to go there at midnight and wish, you will get your wish.

With a few general superstitions I shall bring this part to an end. It is unlucky in Cornwall to see the new moon first over the left shoulder, or through a window, especially if the day should happen to be a Friday. To ensure good luck on your first sight of her, you should curtsey, spit on your money and turn it in your pocket. (A man well paid for any chance job early in the day calls it here "a hansel," and spits on the money for good luck.) If you particularly desire anything, look at the new moon and wish before you speak. You may also wish when you see a falling star, and if you can succeed in framing it before it disappears your wish will be granted. Seeing the new moon in the old moon's arms is a sign of a change in the weather, so is a star passing over it. The change will be for the worse if the moon goes over the star. "Herbs for drying must be gathered at full moon; winter fruit picked and stored at full moon, not to lose its plumpness. Timber should be felled on the bating of the moon, because the sap is then down, and the wood will be more durable."—Bottrell.

Card-table Superstitions:—"Good luck in cards, bad luck in a husband (or wife)." "A shuffling cut is good for the dealer." "1 2 3 4 played in succession kiss the dealer." To cut an honour for the trump card is unlucky, for "When quality opens the door there is poverty behind;" but "Good luck lurks under a black deuce" (it should be touched by the cutter).

Superstitions connected with the body:—A twitching in the eyelid is lucky; but you must not say when it comes nor when it goes.

Right eye itching, a sign of laughter; but left over right, you'll cry before night.

x

Right cheek burning, some one praising you; left one, abusing (a knot tied in the apron-string will cause the slanderer to bite his or her tongue); but left or right are both good at night. "If the cheek burns, someone is talking scandal of you. I have often heard the lines spoken:—

> Right cheek! left cheek! why do you burn?
> Cursed be she that doth me any harm;
> If she be a maid, let her be staid;
> If she be a widow long let her mourn;
> But if it be my own true love—burn, cheek, burn!"—T. Q. Couch.

Nose itching, you will be kissed, cursed, or vexed; or shake hands with a fool.

Right hand itching, someone will pay or give you money; but the left you will be the payer. In regard to the former,

> "If you rub it on wood,
> It will be sure to come good."

> Sneeze on Sunday morning fasting,
> Enjoy your true love for everlasting.

On every other morning it is lucky to sneeze once before breakfast; but not twice.

Fire Superstitions:—A difficulty in kindling the fire in the mornings is a sign of anger; burning only on one side, of a separation in the family (some say of a wedding). A flake of smut on the bar of the grate shows that a stranger is coming to the house. Should the fire be burning brightly, he will bring good news; but if the contrary, bad. If after you poke the fire it burns up brightly, your sweetheart is in a good temper; but should it not improve he is in a bad one. A coal popping out of the fire is either a cradle or coffin, or a purse. It is allowed to cool and then examined to find out the shape; if pronounced to be a purse, it is shaken close to the ear, when should it jingle it is said to contain money. I once saw this done in a school by its mistress. It is unlucky to put a bellows on a table.

"Ladies' trees," small branches of dried seaweed, are sometimes hung up in chimneys to protect houses from fire; or a Passover biscuit suspended by a string from a nail in the wall.

A bright spark on a candle foretells a letter, but if pointed out it never arrives.

There are so many unlucky omens in Cornwall that to believe in them all would make life miserable, and to enumerate them would fill a volume. The major part of them too are silly and not worth transcribing; three or four of them as examples will, I am quite sure, amply suffice. "A work begun on Friday is never ended."

> "If you sing afore bite,
> You'll cry before night."

"It is unlucky to sing carols before Christmas;" or before the first "arish mow*" is made. Also, "To scat† hands before Christmas," *i.e.*, beat them for warmth.

"It is unlucky to pour out water or any other liquor back-handed."

"It is unlucky to lend, or say thank you for a pin." And

> "If you see a pin, and pass it by,
> You'll want a pin before you die."

"It is unlucky to mend your clothes on you, for then you will never grow rich."

It is unlucky to wear a hole in the bottom of a shoe, for

> "A hole in the sole,
> You'll live to spend whole."

Servants who come to their places after noon never stay, etc., etc.

---

* "Arish mow," a rick of corn made in the field where it was cut.
† Scat, to slap.

⇒ CORNISH GAMES. ⇐

ANY old games worth recording are still played by Cornish children, out of doors in summer, indoors in winter, and at their numerous school-treats. To those common elsewhere, other names in Cornwall are often given, and different words sung. Some well known thirty-five years ago, now (1890) live only in the memory of those who were children then, or linger in a very fragmentary state in some remote country districts. Such as

" Here come three dukes a-riding."

To play this the children were divided into two parties. In the first were only the three dukes; in the second the other players, who stood in a long line, linked hand in hand, facing them,— the mother in the middle, with her daughters ranged according to size on each side of her. One duke was chosen as spokesman, and he began the following dialogue, which was sung; the party singing advanced and retreated, whilst the others stood still:—

> "Here 'comes' three dukes a-riding, a-riding—
> Here 'comes' three dukes a-riding, to court your daughter Jane."

> " My daughter Jane is yet too young
> To bear your silly, flattering tongue."

> " Be she young or be she old,
> She for her beauty must and shall be sold."

" So fare thee well, my lady gay,
　　We'll take our horse and ride away,
　　And call again another day."

" Come back ! come back ! you Spanish knight,
　　And clean your spurs, they are not bright."

" My spurs are bright as "rickety rock" (and richly wrought),
　　And in this town they were not bought,
　　And in this town they shan't be sold,
　　Neither for silver, copper, nor gold.
　　　　So fare thee well," etc.

" Come back ! come back ! you Spanish Jack (or coxcomb)."

" Spanish Jack (or coxcomb) is not my name,
　　I'll stamp my foot *(stamps)* and say the same.
　　　　So fare thee well," etc.

" Come back ! come back ! you Spanish knight,
　　And choose the fairest in your sight."

The dukes retired, consulted together, and then selected one, singing—

　　" This is the fairest I can see,
　　　　So pray young damsel walk with me."

When all the daughters had been taken away, they were brought back to their mother in the same order, the dukes chanting :—

　　" We've brought your daughter, safe and sound,
　　　　And in her pocket a thousand pound,
　　　　And on her finger a gay gold ring,
　　　　We hope you won't refuse to take her in."

　　" I'll take her in with all my heart,
　　　　For she and ' me ' were loth to part."

The Rev. S. Rundle, vicar of Godolphin, near Helston, saw some children lately in his neighbourhood playing a portion of this game, when to "Here comes three dukes a-riding" they added—" My rancy, dancy dukes." Mr. Halliwell Phillips, in his *Nursery Rhymes and Tales of England,* has published three versions of it, but the game as played in Cornwall has some additional couplets.

PRAY, PRETTY MISS.

For this—quite, I think, a thing of the past—the children (a boy and girl alternately) formed a ring. One stood in the middle holding a white handkerchief by two of its corners : if a boy he would single out one of the girls, dance backwards and forwards opposite to her, and sing—

> " Pray, pretty Miss, will you come out ?
> Will you come out ? will you come out ?
> Pray, pretty Miss, will you come out,
> To help me in my dancing ? "

If the answer were " No ! " spoken with averted head over the left shoulder, the rhyme ran—

> " Then you are a naughty Miss !
> Then you are a naughty Miss !
> Then you are a naughty Miss !
> Won't help me in my dancing."

Occasionally three or four in turn refused. When the request was granted the words were changed to—

> " Now you are a good Miss !
> Now you are a good Miss !
> Now you are a good Miss !
> To help me in my dancing."

The handkerchief was then carefully spread on the floor; the couple knelt on it and kissed : the child formerly in the middle joined the ring, and the other took his place, or if he preferred it, remained in the centre ; in that case the children clasped hands and sang together—

> " Pray, pretty Miss (or Sir)," etc.

The last to enter the ring had always the privilege of selecting the next partner.

In all these childish games, to prevent disputes, and decide who shall be middleman, hide first, etc., one or other of the following formulæ is always recited by the eldest of the party,

who as he repeats the words points with his forefinger at each
player in succession until he comes to the end of the rhyme.
The person then indicated goes out:—

> " Vizzery, vazzery, vozery-vem,
> Tizzery, tazzery, tozery-tem,
> Hiram, jiram, cockrem, spirem,
> Poplar, rollin, gem."

> " There stands a pretty maid in a black cap,
> If you want a pretty maid in a black cap,
> Please to take 'she.' "—(East Cornwall).

> " Ene, mene, mona, mi,
> Pasca, lara, bona (or bora), bi,
> Elke, belke, boh ! "

> " Eggs, butter, cheese, bread,
> Stick, stack, stone, dead ! "—(West Cornwall).

To this latter there are several nonsensical modern editions.
A game with a jingle somewhat like the first is played by children
at Newlyn West, near Penzance, called—

> " Vesey, vasey, vum."

One child is blindfolded, the others hide something, and shout—

> " Vesey, vasey, vum,
> Buck-a-boo has come!
> Find if you can and take it home,
> Vesey, vasey, vum ! "

A search is then made for the hidden object: when found the
finder in his turn is blindfolded.

After this digression I will give all the other forgotten games
before describing those still played.

" FRISKEE, FRISKEE, I WAS, AND I WAS."

Known elsewhere as "Now we dance looby, looby, looby." To
play it the children formed a ring and danced around, singing—

> " Friskee, friskee, I was, and I was
> A drinking of small beer."

They then stopped suddenly and said, "Right arms in!" (all were extended towards the centre of the circle); "Right arms out!" (all wheeled round with arms outstretched in the contrary direction); "Shake yourselves a little and little and turn yourselves about." The circle was reformed, "Friskee," etc., was repeated, and the game went on until all the different parts of the body had been named.

"Fool, fool, come to School."

All the children in this game, except one who left the room, called themselves by the name of some bird, beast or fish. The child outside was brought in, and one chosen as schoolmaster said—

> "Fool! fool! come to school,
> And find me out the—— : "

giving the assumed name of one of the players. If the fool fixed on the right person, he stayed in and the other went out, which of course involved re-naming; but if he made a mistake they all cried out—

> "Fool! fool! go back to school,
> And learn your letters better."

He retired, pretended to knock his head against the door, and returned, when he was again asked in the same words to name some other player.

Some of the games were much rougher, such as "Pig in the middle and can't get out," and "Solomon had a great dog."

For the first, one of the children stood in the centre, whilst the others danced around him in a circle, saying, "Pig in the middle and can't get out." He replied, "I've lost my key but I will get out," and threw the whole weight of his body suddenly on the clasped hands of a couple to try and unlock them. When he had succeeded he changed the words to, "I've broken your locks, and I have got out."

One of the pair whose hands he had opened took his place, and he joined the ring.

For the second, the players knelt in a line; the one at the head, in a very solemn tone, chanted, "Solomon had a great dog;" the others answered in the same way, "Just so" (this was always the refrain). Then the first speaker made two or three more ridiculous speeches, ending with, "And at last this great dog died, and fell down," giving at the same time a violent lurch against his next neighbour, who, not expecting it, fell against his, and so on to the end of the line.

"Scat" (Cornish for "slap").

A paper-knife, or thin slip of wood, was placed by one player on his open palm. Another took it up quickly, and tried to "scat" his opponent's hand before he could draw it away. Sometimes a feint of taking the paper-knife was made three or four times before it was really done. When the "scat" was given, the "scatter" in his turn rested the knife on his palm.

Hole in the Wall.

A person, who did not know the trick, was blindfolded, another stood in the corner of the room with his mouth open. The forefinger of the blindfolded player was carefully guided around the walls of the room to find the hole, until at last it was put into the open mouth, when it was sharply bitten.

Malaga, Malaga Raisins (a forfeit game).

The players sat in a circle. One acquainted with the trick took a poker in his right hand, made some eccentric movements with it, passed it to his left, and gave it to his next neighbour on that side, saying, "Malaga, Malaga raisins, very good raisins I vow," and told him to do the same. Should he fail to pass it from right to left, when he in his turn gave it to his neighbour, without being told where the mistake lay he was made to pay a forfeit.

Y

She Said, and She Said.

This required a confederate, who left the room. The other in the secret asked a person inside to whisper to him whom she (or he) loved, then called in his companion, and the following dialogue was carried on:—

> " She said, and she said!
> And what did she say ? "
>
> " She said that she loved."
>
> " And whom did she love ?
> Suppose she said she loved——? "
>
> " No! she never said that, whatever she said."

An indefinite number of names were mentioned before the right one. When that came, to the surprise of the whisperer, the answer was—

> " Yes! she said that."

The secret was very simple, the name of a widow or widower was always given before that whispered.

The two next are played everywhere, but the words I believe are peculiar to Cornwall.

Drop the Handkerchief.

This is much too common to require a description. I will therefore only give the doggerel, which is recited by the holder of the handkerchief as he walks around the ring:—

> " I sent a letter to my love,
> I carried water in my glove,
> And by the way I dropped it.
> I did so ! I did so !
> I had a little dog that said 'Bow ! wow !'
> I had a little cat that said 'Meow ! meow !'
> Shan't bite you, shan't bite you,
> Shall bite you."

Throws the handkerchief, and chases the girl.

How Many Miles to Babylon?

To this game, known elsewhere as "Thread the Needle," the following lines are chanted:—

> " How many miles to Babylon?
> Three score and ten.
> Can I get there by candle-light?
> Yes! if your legs are long and straight.
> Then open your gates as high as the sky,
> And let King George and all his troops pass by."

Rules of Contrary.

Four children hold a handkerchief by the four corners, one moves a finger over it saying, as fast as possible—

> " Here I go round the rules of contrary,
> Hopping about like a little canary,
> When I say 'Hold fast' leave go ;
> When I say 'Leave go' hold fast."

Any player making a mistake pays a forfeit.

Lady Queen Anne.

A very pretty version of this old English game is often played at juvenile parties in Cornwall.

One child is chosen to remain in the room, whilst the others go outside and consult together as to whom shall hold the ball (some small thing). They then troop in, with their hands either hidden under the skirts of their dresses, or clasped in such a way that Lady Queen Anne, by looking at them, cannot tell which has it; all repeating—

> " Here come we to Lady Queen Anne,
> With a pair of white gloves to cover our hand ;
> As white as a lily, as fair as the rose,
> But not so fair as you may suppose."

L. Q. A. " Turn, ladies, turn ! "

(Whirl round.) " The more we turn the more we may,
Queen Anne was born on Midsummer day."

L. Q. A. " The king sent me three letters, I never read them all,
So pray, Miss ——, deliver the ball."

Should she have guessed correctly, all the party courtesy, and say—

> " The ball is yours and not ours,
>   You must go to the garden and gather the flowers."

And the child who had the ball takes the queen's seat, whilst she retires with the others; but should she have made a mistake, the same party go out again, saying as they courtesy—

(Repeat)
> " The ball is yours and not ours,
>   We," etc.

Mr. Halliwell Phillips, in his book before quoted, has shorter versions of this, with different rhymes.

Another game which has descended from generation to generation is—

OLD WITCH.

The children chose from their party an old witch (who is supposed to hide herself) and a mother. The other players are the daughters, and are called by the names of the week. The mother says that she is going to market, and will bring home for each the thing that she most wishes for. Upon this they all name something. Then, after telling them upon no account to allow anyone to come into the house, she gives her children in charge of her eldest daughter Sunday, and goes away. In a moment, the witch makes her appearance, and asks to borrow some trifle.

Sunday at first refuses, but, after a short parley, goes into the next room to fetch the required article. In her absence the witch steals the youngest of the children (Saturday), and runs off with her. Sunday, on her return, seeing that the witch has left, thinks there must be something wrong, and counts the children, saying, " Monday, Tuesday," etc., until she comes to Saturday, who is missing. She then pretends to cry, wrings her hands, and sobs out—" Mother will beat me when she comes home."

On the mother's return, she, too, counts the children, and, finding Saturday gone, asks Sunday where she is. Sunday answers, " Oh, mother! an old witch called, and asked to borrow ——, and, whilst I was fetching it, she ran off with Saturday." The mother scolds and beats her, tells her to be more careful in the future, and again sets off for the market. This is repeated until all the children but Sunday have been stolen. Then the mother and Sunday, hand in hand, go off to search for them. They meet the old witch, who has them all crouching down in a line behind her.

Mother. Have you seen my children?

O. W. Yes! I think, by Eastgate.

The mother and Sunday retire, as if to go there, but, not finding them, again return to the witch, who this time sends them to Westgate, then to Southgate and Northgate. At last one of the children pops her head up over the witch's shoulder, and cries out, " Here we are, mother." Then follows this dialogue :—

M. I see my children, may I go in?

O. W. No! your boots are too dirty.

M. I will take them off.

O. W. Your stockings are too dirty.

M. I will take them off.

O. W. Your feet are too dirty.

M. I will cut them off.

O. W. Then the blood will stream over the floor.

The mother at this loses patience, and pushes her way in, the witch trying in vain to keep her out. She, with all her children, then chase the witch until they catch her; when they pretend to bind her hand and foot, put her on a pile, and burn her, the children fanning the imaginary flames with their pinafores. Sometimes the dialogue after " Here we are, mother," is omitted, and the witch is at once chased.

Mr. Halliwell Phillips calls this the " Game of the Gipsy," and gives some rhymes to which it is played, but I have never heard them in this county.

The next, a game quite unknown to me, I took down from the lips of a little girl in West Cornwall, in 1882, who told me it was a great favourite with her and her playmates.

GHOST AT THE WELL.

One of the party is chosen for ghost (if dressed in white so much the better); she hides in a corner; the other children are a mother and daughters. The eldest daughter says:

"Mother, mother, please give me a piece of bread and butter."

M. Let me (or "leave me") look at your hands, child. Why, they are very dirty.

E. D. I will go to the well and wash them.

She goes to the corner, the ghost peeps up, and she rushes back, crying out—

"Mother! mother! I have seen a ghost."

M. Nonsense, child! it was only your father's nightshirt I have washed and hung out to dry. Go again.

The child goes, and the same thing happens. She returns, saying—

"Yes, mother! I have seen a ghost."

M. Nonsense, child! we will take a candle, and all go together to search for it. The mother picks up a twig for a candle, and they set off. When they come near to the ghost, she appears from her hiding-place, mother and children rush away in different directions; the ghost chases them until she has caught one, who in her turn becomes ghost.

MOTHER, MOTHER, MAY I GO OUT TO PLAY?

I thought this game was a thing of the past, but I came on some children playing it in the streets of Penzance, in 1883. It may be played by any number, and, as in the two former games, one is chosen for mother. This is the dialogue:

C. Mother, mother, may I (or we) go out to play?

M. No, child! no, child! not for the day.

C. Why, mother? why, mother? I won't stay long.

M. Make three pretty courtesies, and away! begone!

C. One for mammy, one for daddy, one for Uncle John.

The child, as she mentions the names, spreads out the skirts of her dress and courtesies, after which she retires to a little distance, and then returns.

M. Where, child! where, child! have you been all the day?

C. Up to granny's.

M. What have you been doing there?

The answer to this is often "Washing dolls' clothes," but anything may be mentioned.

M. What did she give you?

The reply is again left to the child's fancy.

M. Where's my share?

C. The cat ate it. What's in that box, mother?

M. Twopence, my child.

C. What for, mother?

M. To buy a stick to beat you, and a rope to hang you, my child.

The child at this tries to snatch at the box, the mother chases her until she has caught her (when there are several children, until she has caught one), she then pretends to beat her, and puts her hands around her neck as if she were going to hang her.

HERE I SIT ON A COLD GREEN BANK.

The children form a ring around one of the party, who sits in the middle, and says:

> "Here I sit on a cold green bank,
> On a cold and frosty morning."

Then those in the circle dance round her, singing:

> "We'll send a young man (or woman) to take you away,
> To take you away, to take you away;
> We'll send a young man to take you away,
> On a cold and frosty morning."

Child. "Pray tell me what his name shall be?"

Or,

> "Pray, whom will you send to take me away?"

Circle. "We'll send Mr. —— to take you away."

This is repeated three times with the refrain, "On a cold," etc. after which the dancing and singing cease, and the child is asked,

" Sugar, sweet, or vinegar, sour?" Her answer is always taken in a contrary sense, and sung, as before, three times, whilst the children circle round. The one in the middle then rises to her feet. The boy (or girl) named advances and kisses her, they change places, and the game begins again.

JOGGLE ALONG.

This is a very favourite open-air game. To play it there must be an uneven number. He (or she) stands in the middle, whilst the others, arm in arm, circle around him singing:—

> " Come all ye young men, with your wicked ways,
> Sow all your wild oats in your youthful days,
> That we may live happy, that we may live happy,
> That we may live happy when we grow old.
> The day is far spent, the night's coming on,
> Give us your arm, and we'll ' joggle along.' "
> That we may live happy, etc., etc.

At the words "joggle along," they all drop the arm of the person they are leading, and try to catch the arm of the player in front of them, whilst the midle man tries at the same time to get a partner. Should he succeed, the player left without one takes his place. (*Repeat.*)

I am indebted to the Rev. S. Rundle, vicar of Godolphin, for another set of words to this game, which he calls—

THE JOLLY MILLER,

And, under this title, a lady, two years since, saw some children playing it at St. Ives, in Cornwall.

> " There was a jolly miller, lived by himself,
> By grinding corn he got his wealth ;
> One hand in the upper, the other in the bag,
> As the wheel went round, they all called ' Grab.' "

In this county " Tom Tiddler's Ground " is known as " Mollish's Land," " Cat and Mouse" as " The Duffan Ring," and " Blind Man's Buff" as " Blind Buck-a-Davy." To this last the following words are repeated, which I have never seen in print. One of the players takes the blind person by the shoulders, and says :

" How many horses has your father got in his stables ? "

A. Three.

" What colour are they ? "

A. Red, white, and grey.

(*Whirling him round.*) " Then turn about, and twist about, and catch whom you may."

To make barley bread (in other districts, " Cockley bread ") this rhyme is used in West Cornwall :—

> " Mother has called, mother has said,
> ' Make haste home, and make barley bread.'
> Up with your heels, down with your head,
> That is the way to make barley bread."

BOBBY BINGO.

Of this, which is a very common game at school-treats in some parts of West Cornwall, I have only lately, through the kindness of the Rev. S. Rundle, succeeded in getting a description. He saw some children, in 1884, playing it in his parish (Godolphin, Helston). A ring is formed, into the middle of which goes a child holding a stick, the others with joined hands run round in a circle, singing—

> " There was a farmer had a dog,
> His name was Bobby Bingo ;
> B. I. N. G. O.,
> His name was Bobby Bingo."

When they have finished singing they cease running, whilst the one in the centre pointing with his stick asks them in turn to spell Bingo. If they all spell it correctly they again move round singing ; but, should either of them make a mistake, he or she has to take the place of the middle man.

WEIGH THE BUTTER, WEIGH THE CHEESE,

is rather dangerous, and now but rarely played. Two children stand back to back with their arms locked. One stoops as low as he can, supporting the other on his back, and says, " Weigh the butter ; " he rises, and the second stoops in his turn with " Weigh

z

the cheese." The first repeats with "Weigh the old woman;" and it ends by the second, with "Down to her knees."

Libbety, libbety, libbety-lat.

A game of a very different character, which pleases young children. The child stands before a hassock, and as if he were going up-stairs puts on it first his right and then his left foot, gradually quickening his steps, keeping time to the words:—

> "Libbety, libbety, libbety-lat,
> Who can do this? and who can do that?
> And who can do anything better than that?"

This ends the games in which children of both sexes join. I must next give those exclusively for boys. I will begin by a very old one:

Ship Sail

is a game usually played with marbles; one boy puts his hand into his trousers pocket and takes out as many marbles as he feels inclined; he closes his fingers over them, and holds out his hand with the palm down to the opposite player, saying, "Ship sail, sail fast. How many men on board?" A guess is made by his opponent; if less, he has to give as many marbles as will make up the true number; if more, as many as he said over. But should the guess be correct he takes them, and then in his turn says "Ship sail," etc.

Buck shee, buck,

is another game of chance, and is generally played by three boys in the following way. One stands with his back to a wall, the second stoops down with his head against the stomach of the first boy, "forming a back," the third jumps on it, and holds up his hand with the fingers distended, saying—

> "Buck shee, buck, shee buck,
> How many fingers do I hold up?"

Should the stooper guess correctly, they all change places and the jumper forms the back. Another and not such a rough way of playing this game is for the guesser to stand with his face towards a wall, keeping his eyes shut.

Leap-frog is known in Cornwall as "Leap the long-mare," and there is a curious variation of it called—

ACCROSHAY.

A cap or small article is placed on the back of the stooping boy by each in turn as he jumps over him. The first as he jumps says "Accroshay," the second "Ashotay," the third "Assheflay," and the last "Lament, lament, Leleeman's (or Leleena's) war." The boy who in jumping knocks off either of the things has to take the place of the stooper.

BUCKEY-HOW.

For this the boys divide into sides; one "stops at home," the other goes off to a certain distance agreed on beforehand and shouts "Buckey-how." The boys "at home" then give chase, and, when they succeed in catching an adversary, they bring him home and there he stays until all on his side are caught, when they in turn become the chasers.

CUTTERS AND TRUCKLERS (SMUGGLERS).

A remembrance of the old smuggling days. The boys divide into two parties; the "trucklers" try to reach some given point before the cutter catches them.

MARBLE PLAYING

is a favourite recreation with the young fishermen in West Cornwall; "Pits" and "Towns" are the common games. Boys who hit their nails are looked on with great contempt, and are said "to fire Kibby." When two are partners and one in playing accidentally hits the other's marble, he cries out "no custance," meaning that he has a right to put back the marble struck; should he fail to do so, it would be considered out of the game. To steal marbles is "to strakey."

To make ducks and drakes with a stone on the water is in Cornwall called "Tic-Tac-Mollard."

COCK-HAW.

This game is, I believe, known in other counties as "Cob-nut," but in Cornwall the boys give the name of "Victor-nut" to the fruit of the common hazel, and play it to the words:

> "Cock-haw! First blaw! Up hat! Down cap! Victor!"

The nut that cracks another is called a "cock battler."

Children under the title of "Cock battler" often in country walks play a variation of Cock-haw with the "Hoary plantain," which they hold by the tough stem about two inches from the head; each in turn tries to knock off the head of his opponent's flower.

WINKY-EYE.

A rural game, played in the spring. An egg taken from a bird's nest is placed on the ground, at some distance off—the number of paces having been previously fixed. Blindfolded, one after the other, the players attempt with a stick to hit and break it.

UPPA, UPPA HOLYE (pronounced oopa, oopa holly).

When the writer was a boy, the following were the words used in the boys' game of fox-hunting. When the hounds (the boys) were "at fault" the leader cried—

> "Uppa, uppa holye,
> If you don't speak
> My dogs shan't folly."
> (East Cornwall. F. W. P. Jago, M.B., Plymouth.)

Boys here, as probably elsewhere, are very fond of hitting each other and then running away, shouting—

> "Last blaw, never graw,
> For seven years to come."

The old Cornish game of "Hurling" I have already described under the head of "Feasten Customs." Cricket, football, and lawn tennis are of course played in Cornwall.

Tom Toddy,

an old drinking game, now I expect known to but few. Each person in succession has to drink a glass of beer or spirits, on the top of which a piece of lighted candle has been put, whilst the others sing—

> " Tom Toddy es come hoam, come hoam,
> Tom Toddy es come hoam,
> Weth es eyes burnt, and his nawse burnt,
> And es eye-lids burnt also.
> Tom Toddy es," etc.
> *Specimens of Cornish Provincial Dialect.*—Uncle Jan Trenoodle.

Of the old dance "Letterpooch," the name only is remembered.

⇥ BALLADS, ETC. ⇤

HERE are a few well-known old Cornish ballads, which have already been printed and reprinted; my apology for again introducing them here, must be, that a work of this kind would not be complete without them. "John Dory," "An old ballad on a Duke of Cornwall's Daughter," "The Stout Cripple of Cornwall," and "The Baarley Mow," may all be found in *Specimens of Cornish Provincial Dialect*, by Uncle Jan Trenoodle (Sandys); "Tweedily, Tweedily, Twee,"—Through Rev. S. Rundle, in *Transactions Penzance Natural History and Antiquarian Society, 1887-88;* "Ye sexes give ear to my fancy," T. Q. Couch, Polperro, Cornwall; and "A fox went forth one moonshining night," Edward Pole, in *Notes and Queries, 1854;* "The Long Hundred," a song of Numbers, W. Pengelly, *Notes and Queries, 1873;* "When shall we be married?" which I heard many years ago in Scilly, and of which I only remember three verses, I have never seen in print.

The Rev. S. Baring Gould, M.A., is now making a collection of the "Traditional Ballads and Songs of the West of England." Part I. has been published; it contains "Sweet Nightingale," said to be a favourite with the miners of Cornwall and Devon; this must be in North Cornwall, as the nightingale is unknown in the western part of the county, scared away, according to the country-folk, "by the sweet singing of its men and women." And "The Hunting of Arscott of Tetcot," of which as it has been recast, I will only transcribe the first four lines.

"In the month of November, in the year fifty-two (1652),
Three jolly fox-hunters, all sons of the blue,
Came o'er from Pencarrow, not fearing a wet coat,
To have some diversion, with Arscott of Tetcot," etc.

"Trelawny" was for many years supposed to be a genuine old
Cornish ballad, and as such was accepted and admired by several
well-known literary men; but it was written by the late Rev. R.
Hawker, Vicar of Morwenstowe; only the lines—

"And shall Trelawny die?
Here's twenty thousand Cornishmen,
Will know the reason why!"—

being ancient.

John Dory.

As it fell on a holy day,
And upon a holytide a:
John Dory brought him an ambling nag,
To Paris for to ride a.

And when John Dory to Paris was come,
A little before the gate a;
John Dory was fitted, the porter was witted,
To let him in thereat a.

The first man that John Dory did meet,
Was good King John of France a;
John Dory could well of his courtesie,
But fell down in a trance a.

A pardon, a pardon, my liege and my king,
For my merry men and for me a:
And all the churls in merry England
I'll bring them bound to thee a.

And Nichol was then a Cornish man
A little beside Bohyde a;
He manned him forth a goodly bark,
With fifty good oars of a side a.

Run up, my boy, into the main top,
    And look what thou can'st spy a;
Who, ho! who, ho! a good ship do I see,
    I trow it be John Dory a.

They hoist their sails both top and top,
    The mizen and all was tried a,
And every man stood to his lot,
    Whatever should betide a.

The roaring cannons then were plied,
    And dub-a-dub went the drum a:
The braying trumpets loud they cried,
    To courage both all and some a.

The grappling hooks were brought at length,
    The brown bill and the sword a;
John Dory at length, for all his strength,
    Was clapt fast under board a.

This song is mentioned by Carew in his *Survey of Cornwall;* in it he says—"the prowesse of one *Nicholas,* sonne to a widdow neere Foy is deskanted upon." (He was one of the "Fowey gallants.")

An Old Ballad,

on a duke of cornwall's daughter;

WHO AFTER HER MARRIAGE TO A KING OF ALBION, WAS DIVORCED FOR THE SAKE OF A FAVOURITE MISTRESS; AND HER EXEMPLARY REVENGE ON THEM BOTH.

When Humber in his wrathful rage
    King Albanact in field had slain,
Whose bloody broils for to assuage,
    King Locrin then applied his pain;
And with a host of Britons stout,
    At length he found king Humber out:

At vantage great he met him then,
   And with his host beset him so,
That he destroyed his warlike men,
   And Humber's power did overthrow;
And Humber, which for fear did fly,
Leapt into a river desp'rately;

And being drowned in the deep,
   He left a lady there alive,
Which sadly did lament and weep,
   For fear they should her life deprive.
But by her face that was so fair,
The king was caught in Cupid's snare:

He took this lady to his love,
   Who secretly did keep it still;
So that the queen did quickly prove,
   The king did bear her most good will:
Which though by wedlock late begun,
He had by her a gallant son.

Queen Guendolin was griev'd in mind,
   To see the king was alter'd so:
At length the cause she chanc'd to find,
   Which brought her to much bitter woe.
For Estrild was his joy (God wot),
By whom a daughter he begot.

The Duke of Cornwall being dead,
   The father of that gallant queen:
The king with lust being overlaid,
   His lawful wife he cast off clean:
Who with her dear and tender son,
For succour did to Cornwall run.

AA

Then Locrin crowned Estrild bright,
  And made of her his lawful wife:
With her which was his heart's delight,
  He sweetly thought to lead his life.
Thus Guendolin, as one forlorn,
Did hold her wretched life in scorn.

But when the Cornish men did know
  The great abuse she did endure,
With her a number great did go,
  Which she by prayer did procure.
In battle then they march'd along,
For to redress this grievous wrong.

And near a river called Store,
  The king with all his host she met;
Where both the armies fought full sore,
  But yet the queen the field did get:
Yet ere they did the conquest gain,
The king was with an arrow slain.

Then Guendolin did take in hand,
  Until her son was come to age,
The government of all the land;
  But first her fury to assuage,
She did command her soldiers wild,
To drown both Estrild and her child.

Incontinent then they did bring
  Fair Estrild to the river-side,
And Sabrine, daughter to a king,
  Whom Guendolin could not abide;
Who being bound together fast,
Into the river they were cast:

And ever since that running stream
   Wherein the ladies drowned were,
Is called Severn through the realm,
   Because that Sabrine died there.
Thus those that did to lewdness bend,
Were brought unto a woful end.

YE SEXES GIVE EAR.

YE sexes give ear to my fancy;
   In the praise of good women I sing.
It is not of Doll, Kate, nor Nancy,
   The mate of a clown nor a king.

Old Adam when he was created,
   Was lord of the universe round ;
But his happiness was not completed,
   Until that a helpmate was found.

He had all things for food that was wanting,
   Which give us content in this life ;
He had horses and foxes for hunting,
   Which many love more than a wife.

He'd a garden so planted by nature,
   As man can't produce in this life ;
But yet the all-wise great Creator
   Saw still that he wanted a wife.

Old Adam was laid in a slumber,
   And there he lost part of his side ;
And when he awoke, in great wonder
   He beheld his most beautiful bride.

With transport he gazed all on her,
   His happiness then was complete ;
And he blessed the bountiful Donor,
   Who on him bestowed a mate.

She was not took out of his head,
    To reign or to triumph o'er man:
She was not took out of his feet,
    By man to be trampled upon.

But she was took out of his side,
    His equal and partner to be:
Though they are united in one,
    Still the man is the top of the tree.

Then let not the fair be despised
    By man, as she's part of himself;
For a woman by Adam was prized
    More than the whole world with its pelf.

Then man without woman's a beggar,
    Tho' of the whole world he's possessed;
And a beggar that has a good woman,
    With more than the world he is blest.

A Fox went forth.

A FOX went forth one moonshining night,
And he prayed to the moon to give him good light,
For he'd many miles to trot that night,
    Before he got home to his den O,
    His den O, his den O.
For he'd many miles to trot that night,
Before he got home to his den O.

And when he came unto a wood,
As on his hinder legs he stood,
A little bit of goose will do me good,
    Before I get home to my den O.
    My den O, my den O.

So off he set to a farmer's yard,
The ducks and the geese were all of them scared;
The best of you all shall grease my beard,
　Before I get home to my den O.

He seized the great goose by the neck
And flung it all across his back,
The young ones cried out, quack, quack, quack,
　And the fox went home to his den O.

Old mother Slipper-slopper jumped out of bed,
She open'd the window and popp'd out her head,—
John! John! John! the great goose is dead,
　And the fox has gone home to his den O.

So John went up unto a hill,
And blew his horn both loud and shrill;
Says the fox This is very pretty music, still
　I'd rather be safe in my den O.

But when he came unto the den,
Where he had young ones, nine and ten,
Crying out, Daddy Fox, you must go there again,
　For we think its a lucky town O.

The fox and his wife they had such a strife,
They never ate a better goose in all their life;
They tore it abroad, without fork or knife,
　And the little ones pick'd the bones O.

TWEEDILY, TWEEDILY, TWEE (North Cornwall).

THERE was an old couple and they were poor;
They lived in a house that had but one door,
　Tweedily, tweedily, twee.

Now this old man went far from home,
And left his old wife to stay at home,
 Tweedily, tweedily, twee.

Now this old man came home at last,
And found his door and windows fast,
 Tweedily, tweedily, twee.

Ah, I've bin sick whilst you've gone,
If you'd bin in the garden you could 've heard me groan.
 Tweedily, tweedily, twee.

An I'm sorry for that, cries he ;
An I'm sorry for that, cries he ;
 Tweedily, tweedily, twee.

Then pluck me an apple from yonder tree,
That will I willingly do, cries he ;
That will I willingly do, cries he ;
 Tweedily, tweedily, twee.

Pop goes the ladder, and down goes he,
An that's cleverly done, cries she ;
An that's cleverly done, cries she ;
 Tweedily, tweedily, twee.

WHEN SHALL WE BE MARRIED ?

WHEN shall we be married, Willy, my pretty lad ?
To-morrow if you think it fit.
Not before to-morrow, Willy, my pretty lad ?
Would you have me be married to-night ?
 I should think the girl was mad.

What shall we have for dinner, Willy, my pretty lad ?
Roast beef and plum pudding if you think it fit.
Shan't we have anything else, Willy, my pretty lad ?
Would you have me to spend all my money ?
 I should think the girl was mad.

Who shall we have to dinner, Willy, my pretty lad?
Father and mother, if you think it fit.
Shan't we have anyone else, Willy, my pretty lad?
Would you have me ask the king and queen?
   I should think the girl was mad.

SWEET NIGHTINGALE.

My sweetheart, come along,
Don't you hear the fond song,
  The sweet notes of the nightingale flow?
Don't you hear the fond tale
Of the sweet nightingale,
  As she sings in the valley below?

Pretty Betty, don't fail,
For I'll carry your pail
  Safe home to your cot as we go;
You shall hear the fond tale
Of a sweet nightingale,
  As she sings in the valley below.

Pray let me alone,
I have hands of my own,
  Along with you, Sir, I'll not go,
To hear the fond tale
Of the sweet nightingale,
  As she sings in the valley below.

Pray sit yourself down
With me on the ground,
  On this bank where the primroses grow;
You shall hear the fond tale
Of the sweet nightingale,
  As she sings in the valley below.

The couple agreed,
And were married with speed,
   And soon to the church did they go;
No more is she afraid
For to walk in the shade,
   Nor sit in those valleys below.

THE STOUT CRIPPLE OF CORNWALL.

WHEREIN IS SHEWED HIS DISSOLUTE LIFE AND DESERVED DEATH.

OF a stout cripple that kept the high-way,
And begg'd for his living all time of the day,
A story I'll tell you that pleasant shall be,
The Cripple of Cornwall surnamed was he.

He crept on his hands and his knees up and down,
In a torn jacket and a ragged torn gown,
For he had never a leg to the knee;
The Cripple of Cornwall surnamed was he.

He was of a stomach courageous and stout,
For he had no cause to complain of the gout;
To go upon stilts most cunning was he,
With a staff on his neck most gallant to see.

Yea, no good fellowship would he forsake,
Were it in secret a horse for to take;
His stool he kept close in a hollow tree,
That stood from the city a mile, two, or three.

Thus all the day long he begg'd for relief,
And all the night long he played the false thief;
For seven years together this custom kept he,
And no man knew him such a person to be.

There were few graziers went on the way,
But unto the Cripple for passage did pay,
And every brave merchant that he did descry,
He emptied their purses ere they did pass by.

The noble Lord Courtney, both gallant and bold,
Rode forth with great plenty of silver and gold,
At Exeter there a purchase to pay,
But that the false Cripple the journey did stay.

For why, the false Cripple heard tidings of late,
As he sat for alms at the nobleman's gate ;
This is, quoth the Cripple, a booty for me,
And I'll follow it closely as closely may be.

Then to his companions the matter he mov'd,
Which their false actions before had prov'd ;
They make themselves ready, and deeply they swear
The money's their own before they come there.

Upon his two stilts the Cripple did mount,
To have the best share it was his full account,
All clothed in canvass down to the ground,
He took up his place his mates with him round.

Then came the Lord Courtney with half-a-score men,
Yet little suspecting these thieves in their den,
And they perceiving them come to their hand,
In a dark evening bid them to stand.

Deliver thy purse, quoth the Cripple, with speed,
We be good fellows and therefore have need,
Not so, quoth Lord Courtney, but this I'll tell ye,
Win it and wear it, else get none of me.
BB

With that the Lord Courtney stood in his defence,
And so did his servants, but, ere they went hence,
Two of the true men were slain in this fight,
And four of the thieves were put to the flight.

And while for their safeguard they run thus away,
The jolly bold Cripple did hold them in play,
And with his pike-staff he wounded them so,
As they were unable to run or to go.

With fighting the Lord Courtney was out of breath,
And most of his servants were wounded to death,
Then came other horsemen riding so fast,
The Cripple was forced to fly at the last.

And over a river that run there beside,
Which was very deep, and eighteen foot wide,
With his long staff and his stilts leaped he,
And shifted himself in an old hollow tree;

Then throughout the city was hue and cry made,
To have these thieves apprehended and staid;
The Cripple he creeps on his hands and his knees,
And in the high-way great passing he sees.

And as they came riding he begging doth say,
O give me one penny, good masters, I pray,
And thus unto Exeter creeps he along,
No man suspecting that he had done wrong.

Anon the Lord Courtney he spies in the street,
He comes unto him and kisses his feet,
God save your honor and keep you from ill,
And from the hands of your enemies still.

Amen, quoth Lord Courtney, and therewith threw down
Unto the poor Cripple an English crown,
Away went the Cripple, and thus he did think,
Five hundred pounds more will make me to drink.

In vain that hue and cry it was made,
They found none of them though the country was laid,
But this grieved the Cripple night and day,
That he so unluckily missed of his play.

Nine hundred pounds this Cripple had got
By begging and thieving, so good was his lot;
A thousand pound he would make it, he said,
And then he would give over his trade.

But as he striv'd his mind to fulfil,
In following his actions so lewd and so ill,
At last he was taken the law to suffice,
Condemned and hanged at Exeter 'size.

Which made all men amazed to see
That such an impudent cripple as he
Should venture himself such actions as they,
To rob in such sort upon the high-way.

THE BAARLEY MOW (a harvest song).

HERE'S a health to the baarley mow, my braave boys,
Here's a health to the baarley mow.
We'll drenk et out of the jolly brown boul,
Here's a health to the baarley mow.

Chorus.

Here's a health to the baarley mow, my braave boys,
Here's a health to the baarley mow.

Ballads, etc.

We'll drenk et out of the nepperkin,* boys,
Here's a health to the baarley mow.
The nepperkin, and the jolly brown boul.

 Chorus.—Here's a health, etc.

We'll drenk et out of the quaarter pint, boys,
Here's a health to the baarley mow.
The quaarter pint, nepperkin, and the jolly brown boul.

 Chorus.—Here's a health, etc.

This goes on through very many verses until all the different parts of liquid measure are exhausted ; the three last verses are—

We'll drenk et out of the well, my braave boys,
Here's a health to the baarley mow.
The well, the hoosghead,† the haalf hoosghead, ainker,‡
 the haalf ainker, gallon, the pottle, the quaart, the
 pint, the haalf a pint, quaarter pint, nepperkin,
 and the jolly brown boul.

 Chorus.—Here's a health, etc.

We'll drenk et out of the rever, my boys,
Here's a health to the baarley mow.
The rever, the well, etc.

 Chorus.—Here's a health, etc.

We'll drenk et out of the ocean, my boys,
Here's a health to the baarley mow.
The ocean, the rever, the well, etc.

 Chorus.—Here's a health, etc.

"At Looe, in East Cornwall, it was usual forty years ago, and probably it is still, for labourers to sing 'The Long Hundred'

---

* A gill.
† Cornish for hogshead.
‡ Anker.

(a song of numbers), when throwing ballast with shovels from a sand barge into a ship. The object was said to be threefold; 'to keep time (*i.e.* work simultaneously), to prevent anyone from shirking his share of work, and to cheer themselves for the labour,' which was by no means light. A shovelful of ballast was delivered by every man with each line of the song, which ran thus:—

THE LONG HUNDRED.

'There goes one.
One there is gone.
Oh, rare one!
And many more to come
To make up the sum
Of the hundred so long.

'There goes,' etc. on to twenty.

"The song, it will be seen, consisted of twenty six-line stanzas; hence when it was completed, each man had thrown on board one hundred and twenty, *i.e.* 'a long hundred,' shovelfuls of ballast. After a pause both the song and the ballasting were resumed, and so on to the end."—W. Pengelly.

There are a great many jingling local rhymes and modern dialect poems not worth recording; I will only quote two of the first:—

ELICOMPANE.

"What is your name?—Elicompane.
Who gave you that name?—My master and dame.
How long will you keep it?—As long as I like it.
How long will that be?—As long as *me* and my master agree."

Polwhele calls a tomtit "Elicompane;" and says "There is a vulgar tradition that it is a bird by day and a toad by night."

UNCLE JAN DORY.

"I'll tell 'ee a story 'bout Uncle Jan Dory,
Who lived by the side of a well,
He went to a 'plomp' (pump), and got himself drunk,
And under the table he fell."

The Cornish peasantry of the last century were very fond of riddles, but most of them will not bear repetition; they are (as well as many of their sayings and rhymes) much too broad for the taste of this generation, and would only be tolerated in the days when "a spade was called a spade." There are two exceptions that I know worth transcribing; one has already appeared with its answer, through the Rev. S. Rundle, in *Transactions Penzance Natural History and Antiquarian Society, 1885-86.*

> "Riddle me! riddle me right!
> Guess where I was to last Saturday night.
> Up in the old ivy tree,
> Two old foxes under me,
> Digging a grave to bury me.
> First I heard the wind blow,
> Then I heard the cock crow,
> Then I saw the chin-champ chawing up his bridle,
> Then I saw the work-man working *hisself* idle."

Answer.—A young woman made an appointment to meet her sweetheart; arriving first at the place, she climbed into an ivy-covered tree to await his coming. He came in company with another man, and not seeing her "the two old foxes" began to dig a grave, in which from her hiding-place she heard that after murdering they intended putting her. The "chin-champ" was the horse on which they rode away, when they failed to discover her. "Working hisself idle," is working in vain.

> "As I went over London bridge
> Upon a cloudy day,
> I met a fellow, clothed in yellow,
> I took him up and sucked his blood,
> And threw his skin away."

What was he? *Answer.*—An orange.

With a nonsensical acrostic on the word *Finis*, well known in the beginning of this century, I must end this (I fear) long, rambling work.

> "F—for Francis,
> I—for Jancis,
> N—for Nich'las Bony;
> I—for John the water-man,
> S—for Sally Stony."

M. A. COURTNEY.

ADDENDA.

HELSTON BOROUGH BOUNDS, *page* 20.—At the close of this ceremony eleven dozen buns are thrown amongst the crowd to be scrambled for. One is always reserved for the Mayor.

WELLS, *page* 65.—Some wells in Cornwall (not holy) were famed for their wonderful virtues : I will mention two. The water of the first, which was west of Penzance, was esteemed a sovereign cure for sore eyes. People from far and near visited it, and even carried away the water in bottles. It was, however, best if possible to walk to the well before breakfast, and there bathe the eyes. The second was at Castle Chûn, between Penzance and St. Just ; its water endowed the drinkers with perpetual youth. Both have dried up within the last fifty years.

GHOSTS, *page* 99.—The following quaint story was told me by a girl whose grandmother was the friend mentioned.

In the last century there lived in Trezelah (a hamlet in the parish of Gulval, near Penzance), a widow who had been deprived of her rights. Walking one day in the fields near her home she saw a strange spotted dog who semed to know her ; she met it a second time, and decided when she next went out to take a friend with her. Again she saw it (her friend did not), and said " In the Name of the Lord, speak to me." It changed into her husband, who told her to be ready at a certain time, when he would fetch her. Soon after, her friend being in the house, the woman, who was giving her children their supper, said " The time is come, I must be gone ; " she then put on her sun-bonnet and went out. She was away about an hour, when she suddenly appeared with a great noise, as if someone had hurled her in through the door. Her story was that her husband had taken her up in his arms and carried her over the tree-tops as far as Ludgvan Church, where he deposited her on the Church-stile, from whence she saw a great many spirits, some good and some bad. The latter wanted her to join them, but her husband bade her remain where she was. What they told her was never known ; but by their aid she got back her rights. Then her husband bore her home again by the way they had come ; but before he parted from her said " I must take something from you ; either your eyesight, or your hearing." She preferred losing the latter, and from that hour could never hear a word. One of her shoes that in her flight through the air had caught on a tree-top, seven years after was placed on her window-sill.

FARMERS' SUPERSTITIONS, *page* 141.—" If you can throw fire over a witch you will break the spell." " Bleeding a white hen on a millstone prevents danger from the mill ; for they say a mill will have blood every seven years."

CHARMS, *page* 144.—" Some were provided with little bags of earth, teeth, or bones taken from a grave." " Most of the very religious folks had a verse of scripture, concluded with the comfortable assurance that by the help of the Lord the white witch hopes to do them good."—Bottrell.

EPILEPSY, *page* 154.—Another authority says that the thirty pence collected by thirty young men at the Church door is deposited for a half-crown, from which the centre is cut. The flat ring left is worn by the epileptic person day and night."—Through Rev. A. H. Malan, M.A.

" The Bundle of Charms," Rev. A. H. Malan, M.A., is unavoidably omitted.

BURNING THE WITCH, *page* 180.—Still played. A pole about five feet long is placed with its ends resting on low stools, or bottles. On this a person sits lengthways with crossed ancles. He (or she) holds in his hand a long stick with a slit at one end, into which the paper effigy of the witch is stuck. This must be burnt at a candle placed on the floor at a short distance from the sitter ; he must not support himself in any way, nor leave his perch.

BEARE AND SON, PRINTERS, PENZANCE.